Venture Management

Mack Hanan

Venture Management

A Game Plan for
Corporate Growth and Diversification

McGraw-Hill Book Company

New York   St. Louis   San Francisco   Auckland   Mexico   São Paulo
Düsseldorf   Montreal   Singapore   Johannesburg   New Delhi   Sydney
Kuala Lumpur   Panama   Tokyo   London   Paris   Toronto

To my father

*for his persistence in reminding me
that the business edge goes to the innovator*

And to my clients

*for their courage in letting me
practice this belief*

Library of Congress Cataloging in Publication Data

Hanan, Mack.
    Venture management.

    Includes index.
    1. New products.   I. Title.
HD69.N4H35   658.8′3   75-42080
ISBN 0-07-037060-5

1234567890   KPKP   785432019876

The editors for this book were W. Hodson Mogan and
Tobia L. Worth, the designer was Elliot Epstein, and
the production supervisor was Teresa F. Leaden. It was
set in Caledonia by Monotype Composition Co., Inc.

Printed and bound by Kingsport Press.

contents

V HOW TO ACHIEVE VENTURE OBJECTIVES

preface

When venture management became the thing to do in the 1960s, there was no game plan. Everyone innovated. Almost everyone failed. Hardly anyone who was there escaped. Two conclusions seemed to be warranted. Corporations were unable to venture because venturing was too difficult. Or corporations were unable to venture because venturing was basically so simple that major companies felt compelled to make it much more difficult than it was.

The truth is that venture management is small-business management of the most chancy type: start-up management. Few large companies understand it. Few corporate managers have experience in it. Once it is realized for what it is, the basic venture game plan is rather simple to learn and apply. This book tells how. What is not simple is how to play the game after it has been planned. This is the entrepreneur's gift. It must become the corporate entrepreneur's—the *corporateur's*—learned skill. Otherwise, just another cost, and probably a sizable one, will be sunk.

The venture game plan in this book comes out of a good deal of close-in observation and partnership-type consultative participation in multimillions of dollars' worth of failed corporate ventures and some notable successes. It is probable, although there is no way to tell for sure, that few other consultants have shared in more of both failures and successes or shared in them more intimately. Sad to say but true, most of the better rules of the road have come from insights into the failures: why they went wrong and how they could have been put right in the first place. The successes have served principally to validate these insights and to prove that they work. The men and women venture managers who are handed the charge to grow a new-business enterprise, probably in the white heat of urgency and within a time frame that allows for zero defects, can therefore use this game plan with comfort and confidence. It has passed through the flame. It is my hope that they will now take it and improve upon it in their own ways, tempering it still further with their own particular genius and beating it into a second-generation plan for the management of new-business ventures in the 1970s and 1980s.

MACK HANAN

introduction

"The only true profit," it has been said, "is innovative profit. The rest is trying to make last year's profit over again this year."

Profit making is never easy. Making innovative profit has proved to be the most difficult task of all. Over the century or so in which the corporate form of business organization has been in existence, managers have been searching for a predictive way to conceive of profitable new business opportunities and to commercialize them at minimal risk. Yet no single overriding answer has been found. True growth businesses are still few and far between.

The fault is often with the innovators themselves. Their imaginative scientific insights are frequently compromised by a weakness in marketing skill or a lack of grasp of basic managerial technique. Every so often, an innovator is victimized by his own technological nostalgia to create what could have been a breakthrough a product generation or so ago but is now a romantic and overpriced vestige. At other times, the innovator has been all right. But he has been absorbed by the slow reactions and clogged communication channels that can accompany corporate bigness and maturity, or he has been detoured by management preference for improving on past success rather than building for the future. Sometimes he has run headlong into a small group of strongheaded men who have simply been wrong about the merits of a new business idea. All these reasons take their toll. But essentially the business innovator fails because neither he nor the corporate managers he seeks as sponsors have an organized method for creating, validating, and prototyping new-business ventures.

Chester Carlson and his "long march" in search of sponsors for the copying machine that was to evolve as Xerox have become symbolized as the epitome of innovative frustration. Only when Joseph Wilson eventually saw the potential of Carlson's copier did the venture become an exceptional growth business. Yet for every Joseph Wilson, there were dozens of other men who, like Thomas Watson at IBM, looked at Chester Carlson's machine and said "No." Nonetheless, it was the same Watson who saw the potential of the computer when Ralph Cordiner of General Electric did not. Cordiner took GE into data processing too late and never got it out of the red. IBM made its fortune on it. But GE nevertheless was able to see a generation of profit in electrical appliances while Westinghouse's Gwilyn Price could not.

The ability to envision ventures, let alone convert them into businesses, has always been unevenly distributed. In 1913, Lee De Forest was being tried on the charge of fraudulently using the United States mails to sell stock in the Radio Telephone Company which commercialized his invention of the audion broadcasting tube. The United States attorney summarized his prosecution by charging that "De Forest has said in many newspapers and over his signature that it would be possible to transmit the human voice across the Atlantic before many years. Based on these absurd and deliberately misleading statements, the misguided public has been persuaded to purchase stock in his company."

David Sarnoff was persuaded more strongly by De Forest than by the United States attorney. He saw a business in radio. He tried to interest Eldridge Johnson in it, since Johnson was already in the business of sound transmission as president of the Victor Talking Machine Company. But the radio was a different sort of talking machine from the Victrola. Although Johnson could hear the radio, he could not see it. Sarnoff decided to go it alone. When he had made enough money from radio, his RCA bought out Victor and now operates it as a division.

Three years before De Forest's trial, in 1910, an innovator named William Durant had collected Buick, Oldsmobile, Cadillac, and seventeen other automobile companies. Seeking funds to continue his agglomeration, he ventured the suggestion to J. P. Morgan that automobiles would soon become an important factor in American life. Morgan, a railroader at the time, was busy protecting his New York, New Haven and Hartford Railroad by buying up potentially competitive trolley lines and steamboat companies at highly inflated prices. As events turned out, his concern was unwarranted. Durant's automobiles were destined to dispose of these competitors anyway in just a few years' time in the same way that they were to supersede the railroad itself. But Morgan's reaction to Durant's "crackpot suggestion" was to have him escorted from the Morgan offices.

Yet it was Henry Ford and not William Durant who saw the true mass potential of the automobile and turned it into a commodity. So transfixed did he become on this mission, however, that he failed to sense his market's growing needs for more than just one model which came in only one color and sold for a single price. Nor could he see the automobile's inevitable effect on the need for consumer credit. By concentrating on the revolution he had wrought, he blinded himself to its evolution. After a run of twenty years, his one-product line of Model T's began a recession while Alfred Sloan at General Motors was appreciating the desirability of offering multiple models in many price ranges, with consumer credit to boot.

Morgan's negative attraction to the automobile and other dissuasions from the innovator's output are not simply amusing relics of an unenlightened past. Their vestiges live on in attempts to perpetuate an existing generation of products or services as an alternative to establishing a venture business, or in buy-outs of declining businesses at oppressive prices. They are replicated daily in the foreshortened visions of many current venturers who take Campbell into unsuccessful soups, General Foods into unsuccessful fast-food businesses, Bristol-Myers into unsuccessful toothpastes, Rheingold into unsuccessful low-calorie beer, Scott into unsuccessful diapers, and Sylvania into unsuccessful TV slide viewers.

Because failure is such an intimate handmaiden of new-business development and because large corporations are a viscous medium for new ideas to move through, the burden is always on the venturer. Not only must management be presented with a live business concept. A strategy for putting it together operationally must be worked out and a process for giving it commercial vitality prepared for implementation.

Over the past few years, a comparatively small number of innovative business managers have accepted the challenge to create a planned approach to business growth. This approach is called "venture management." In it, they have combined a sparseness of organization with an interdisciplinary mix of the technical, financial, and marketing skills that characterized the classical entrepreneurial businesses of the past. They have established as their central principle the injunction to *find the manager:* to locate the venture entrepreneur who can structure a new business entity, get it off the ground quickly, and bring back a superior profit. Without the manager, nothing happens. Then, gathering minimal resources around the venture entrepreneur, they have chartered businesses to serve emerging market needs based on existing corporate capabilities or on logical entensions of them.

Motivated by a quest for premium profits, these business managers have put to work the belief that a company can venture from any one of several bases within its existing business, moving out from its technical base or from its marketing, managerial, or financial bases to buy and manage external venture properties. They have shown how a technically based company can grow into transportation from its expertise in power generation. The company can market its in-house expertise in economic forecasting, educational programs for other technical companies, or consulting services in operations research, or it can run a vocational school

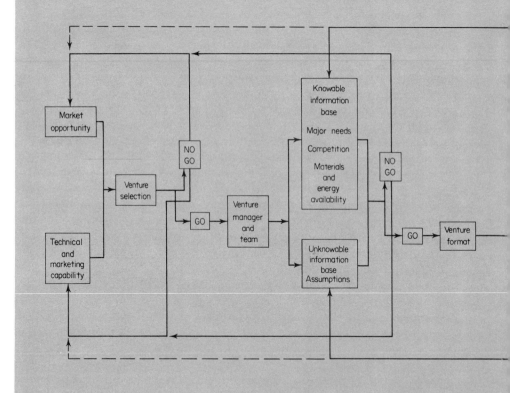

4

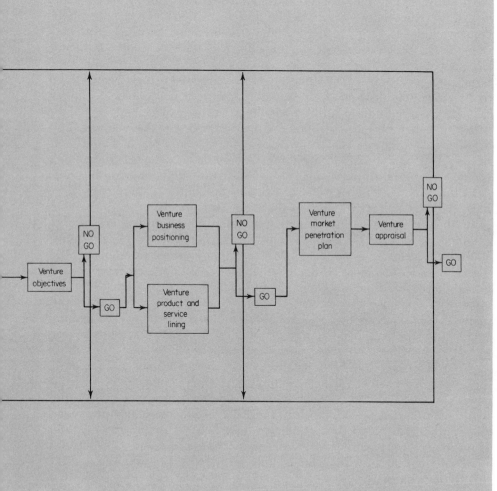

that teaches electronics and set up a venture capital group to invest in new electronics businesses. Chemical-based companies can diversify into agribusinesses, animal breeding, or fish culture. Timber companies can venture from their resource reserves into wood, paper, and packaging products, building materials, and wood-based office supplies. Food processors can grow into the fast-food restaurant business and in-office feeding. Airlines can grow into hotel businesses, food-catering services, and contract cleaning systems.

In the course of their work, these innovative business managers have devised a venture process as the core of their planned approach. Its flow is shown in the accompanying chart. The sequence can be read in this way: First, the venture base must be determined. When a growth extension from this base appears to be found, it is screened through basic selection criteria. Either a venture opportunity will emerge or a NO GO result will show that a venture base does not yet exist or an alleged opportunity is not opportune. If a GO situation prevails for a business proposition that may be able to meet corporate growth and image criteria, a venture manager is appointed to build a development team. The venture team's first task will be to structure an information base for the venture. The knowable base comes first. It will contain an inventory of the market needs which can provide demand for the venture. It will also contain two profiles: a profile of the customer or client groups who are the heaviest potential needers and a profile of existing products and services which meet their needs and which will therefore be competitive with the venture when it comes on-stream. Raw materials availability and energy resource types and allocations, either of which could constrain venture continuity, must be inventoried. When the knowables have been cataloged, assumptions must be made about the remaining factors which can influence venture financing, manufacturing, and marketing but which are unknowable. These unknowable factors represent the venture's chief uncertainties. They include the status and probable effects of the business cycle, governmental legislation, technological innovation, market buying trends, competitive activities, and other imponderables.

If evaluation of the venture information base indicates that a venture business cannot be established or grown, a second NO GO decision point occurs. A new basis for venturing must now be determined. If venture information indicates GO, the venture manager must now use the knowable and unknowable information base to set objectives for the venture. If the objectives cannot satisfy corporate criteria, a third NO GO will occur and another new base for venture growth must be found.

If objectives pass the comparison test with corporate selection bogeys, the venture team can begin to operate as a potential business in order to achieve them. It will style the venture as a business, plan its market penetration by equipping it with financial resources, products and services, a distribution system, promotional strategies, and both manpower and plant facilities. When the market penetration plan is appraised by corporate management, with special attention being paid to its projections of commercial potential for the venture, its market projections, and the assumptions underlying them, the fourth and final NO GO decision point will occur. This is the venture's last evaluation before commitment to market entry, either through test-marketing or a national launch.

Venture management is a prolific growth strategy. Its objectives can be achieved through any one of five basic formats. Two of them, venture business task forces and functional or operational spinouts, are pure forms of *internal development*. Three formats can be used to combine *internal and external development*. Joint ventures with one or two peer companies or by minority investment in smaller growth businesses enable ventures to be developed cooperatively. Ventures can also be accelerated by acquiring foothold businesses based on majority investment or outright ownership.

Each of these venture formats possesses its own assets and liabilities. As a result, it is essential for a company that regards its growth as a prime, continuing consideration to create its own mix of formats to match its needs and opportunities. Venture management's task is to recommend the best growth alternatives for each point in time of its corporate history. A large, long-established company may find functional spinouts to be an organizationally simple but politically complex venture strategy. Foothold acquisition ventures may be expedient methods of coming on-stream swiftly and surely with new-business earnings but may be complicated or even enjoined legally. Joint ventures may present similar legal inhibitions. Or they may simply not be stylistically palatable to a management that prefers to go it alone. A portfolio of new-business task forces and some minority-investment ventures may thus come to represent a major company's optimal mix.

A smaller or new company, on the other hand, may find that organizational and financial considerations eliminate many of these options. A lack of self-contained internal functions can nullify the option of spinout ventures. A lack of internal staff can prevent the spawning of multiple new-business task forces. A lack of investment capital or other equity may rule out foothold acquisitions. A mix of joint ventures and minority-investment ventures may be a small company's best growth portfolio.

Whichever format is chosen, a venture must face up to severe expectations. It must work more profitably than traditional new-product development strategy, which generally innovates only marginally from known successes and yet still sees 7 or 8 or 9 out of every 10 of its outcomes fail. It must work in a far more predictable manner than merger or acquisition, and it must be freer from the restrictions enforced by government on going outside for growth as well as restrictions imposed by inflated costs of capital in the borrowing marketplace. It must promise a genuinely significant return if it is to be worth not only its investment but its risk. And it must be able to bring home the bacon in the condensed time frame which has telescoped the period of expected payback from innovation.

It is worth remembering that there were 1,000 years for the wheel to establish itself. The steam engine had 100 years to come into its own, electrical energy had 50 years, the internal-combustion engine had 25 years, the vacuum tube had 15 years, and the computer had 5 years. Today, the venture manager who plans on enjoying a proprietary life of more than 3 years for a venture is simply being unrealistic. This is the growth challenge: to make it safely back home with the profits in thirty-six months or less.

How to Work Up Your Own Game Plan

Throughout the book, you will find pages labeled "Planning Pages." These are designed for you to use in working up your own game plan based on the book's guidelines. Directions for completing each Planning Page appear in bold type set off in a box from the text. When you have worked up all the Planning Pages in the book, you will have the core of a Market Penetration Plan for your venture.

1

how to consolidate
the venture base

1

the venture commitment

Growth is the single most hazardous management decision.

No other business decision has the power to elevate a company so quickly into significant new profits or to destroy it. In order to grow, a company must marshal its principal strengths, overcome its principal weaknesses, and re-create in spirit and substance much of the genesis of its original enterprise. Most difficult of all, perhaps, it must confront itself with acute intellectual honesty and assay its capabilities with an auditor's eye. All the while, it must continue to operate its current business. If growth is placed before the generation of day-to-day cash flow, it can divert management from its basic task and threaten rather than expand the existing operation. Yet if growth is subjugated to ongoing concerns, it will probably fail. In view of the enormous pressures exerted by even a modest growth effort, rational managers must ask, "Why grow?"

If growth were an option, probably few but the most venturesome managers would adopt it. But growth, for better or worse, is rarely an option. Most successful businesses have growth thrust upon them. Business diversification becomes a mandate as the only strategy to rescue premium profitability. Success breeds the need to grow by squeezing original profit between two relentless constraints. One is competition. It acts to drive branded products and services down into commodity status and deprive them of their ability to command a premium price. A second constraint is the inevitable increase in marketing costs which must be budgeted to support line extension requirements fulfilled by brand-family proliferation from an original product or service.

When these two constraints are aggravated by legislative, consumerism, cyclical, and socioenvironmental constraints, technological obsolescence, and energy or materials shortfalls, the time to grow into new businesses comes for even the most reluctant management.

11

The Venture Option

The strategy of venture management, one of the three options in the corporate growth mix, combines some of the attractions of internal development through research and development and going outside through acquisition. In this sense, venturing itself can be regarded as a strategy of constraint: a constraint on management's inevitable temptation to dilute resources by investing them solely for marginal growth through R&D or by committing them extravagantly in acquiring someone else's growth businesses at unfavorable value/price ratios. Venturing can also be regarded as a strategy of competition. When a company decides to add venture business development to its growth strategies, it increases the ability to generate competitive opportunities for the investment of its capital. Under a venture approach, corporate capital will flow where the promise of return is highest.

In the steel industry, for instance, a dollar invested in more steel produces at most a dollar of annual sales. But the same dollar invested in nonsteel businesses can yield substantially more in sales and profits. If the steel business grows at an annual 2½ percent rate and the real gross national product is growing at 5½ to 6 percent per year, businesses which can promise an 8 percent rate of growth must command consideration. Under this philosophy, steel company management can say, "If a company geologist walks in soaked to the waist in crude oil, we may not turn him around so quickly to go back out to look for iron ore."

Since the 1960s, many companies in just about every field have attempted to grow by developing new-business ventures. In each venturing company, a small interdisciplinary group has been incorporated around a common search-and-find objective. The group members represent the principal disciplines which are required to get a business going: an ability to perceive a market need and qualify it, an ability to quantify the dimensions of the need as well as the willingness of the needers to pay for benefits in the form of product and service systems, and an ability to produce such systems in a technically sophisticated, controlled manner.

These venture groups are expected to provide a value over and above normal growth. Indeed, their performance is evaluated by the size of the increment they are able to achieve beyond the momentum (or lack of momentum) generated by riding the GNP curve. A rule of thumb says that a venture opportunity must promise to return at least double the GNP rate to qualify as an attractive growth option for management. This sets a high standard. Not only does it place a premium on accurate venture selection. It also demands that management consolidate the corporate base for venturing in two ways: first, by committing itself to venturing as the best growth option when compared with new-product growth through R&D or with growth by acquisition; and second, by thoroughly defining the corporate capability base from which ventures will have to take off.

Commitment and Implementation

For virtually all major companies and for many smaller ones as well, venture management can become a normal aspect of their business operations that is budgeted and administered as an ongoing allocation of corporate resources for profit generation. Some companies have taken this approach and been successful with it. Others have not been successful. The critical differences between venture success and failure have been twofold: *commitment* to the venture approach on a long-term, continuing basis and not as a flash-in-the-pan, fast-growth strategy; and *implementation* of the approach along the lines of what can best be described as traditional, conservative small-business principles.

To consolidate a firm venture base, management must make a double commitment. It must make sure that it is committed to the *conceptual base* for venturing. And it must make sure that the *capability base* for venturing is in place so that new-business ventures can grow by means of logical extension from existing resources.

A review of venture success and failure strongly suggests that top management must genuinely want to be in a new business, preferably so badly that it can taste it. Failure to achieve profitable penetration must be regarded as totally unacceptable, not simply as an unfortunate learning experience or an experiment that fizzled. Top management must visibly possess this commitment and transmit it to its venture managers, who must be able to match it with similar vigor.

Management must also possess the capability to implement its commitment. In venturing, being a patient banker is one sign of commitment. But the ability to implement the funds that are allocated—to apply every dollar in the way that will count the most—is the crucial aptitude that separates the men from the boys in venturing. This aptitude enables one company to penetrate an industry while others fail to make a go of it. The proper conclusion to draw from the track record of how major companies venture is not that there are bad growth industries but that there are poor implementers of venture plans to penetrate them. This conclusion makes it difficult to learn what fields to enter or avoid, but it makes it easier to learn the values of commitment and implementation.

The combined importance of commitment and the ability to implement it is difficult to overemphasize. It is reflected in the criteria that are relied on by most venture capitalists before they decide to go ahead with a deal. A popular attitude is expressed this way: "Our main criteria have to do with people. We must be absolutely certain that they are totally committed. If a man has $5,000 in the bank, we want to see $4,000 of it invested in the venture. If it fails, we want it to hurt him more than it will hurt any of the investors."

This exquisite degree of emphasis on commitment cannot be precisely replicated in corporate venturing. Its approximation, however, should be a constant objective.

How Other Options Compare

Companies which choose the option to venture must compare risks and rewards with the potential values, both plus and minus, offered by growth through R&D or acquired growth opportunities. These values include the size and certainty of payback and the effects of legislative and opportunistic factors.

The Venture Option Compared with R&D

In the most common growth strategy a company does what it knows best just a little bit better every year. This places the burden of growth squarely on the ability of R&D to come up with incremental earning opportunities on a predictable, repetitive basis. But R&D growth has largely proved to be a strategy of failure. Up to three-quarters of a company's annual R&D expenditure may be unproductive; that is, it may not yield a profitable product. Failure rates of between 6 and 9 of every 10 new products have consequently become an industrial norm. Such a record suggests that laboratory-based growth produces more scrap than new enterprises. But even companies whose records exceed the norm are rarely able to plan, finance, and execute a sufficient number of development projects to assure the regular production of marketable new products or a periodic penetration of new markets. Once a company finds itself in this kind of fix, R&D finds itself in a classic bind. Should it aim at products which promise early development and quick volume sales as soon as they hit the market but which can be relegated by competition to commodity status just as quickly? Or should it concentrate on the longer-term development of specialty items whose proprietary nature may command a high rate of return over a broader life cycle?

If R&D elects the second option, it may never get a payback under changing market conditions in which need swings are significant or technological innovations are explosive. Under the first option, most R&D investments in new-product development will play around the fringes of innovation. Their creations for the most part will be rather safe, marginal renovations of existing product lines instead of the true innovations which can bring breakthrough profits. The safety factor associated with this sort of marginal renovation may be a delusion. The life cycles of renovated products rarely continue to grow beyond six months after introduction.

Because payback from renovation may not ever recover investments over such a short run, continued renovative success may eventually lead to fiscal failure. As a result, neither option may achieve a profit.

The Venture Option Compared with Acquisition

Because the cost of patience with R&D-sponsored innovation has risen along with the price of failure, many manufacturers have more or less abandoned time-honored dependency on their laboratories in order to rush hither and yon in search of greener pastures in the form of acquisitions. Over the ten-year period from 1960 to 1970, for example, the nine leading ethical drug companies developed only eight new-business diversifications internally. In the same period, they went outside to acquire sixteen new businesses in chemicals, proprietary drugs, cosmetics and toiletries, food and household products, and medical electronics. Many other major industries emulated this strategy. Today, however, and increasingly in the future, there is less and less to buy. What is still available costs more and more, to the point at which the value/price relationship of potential acquisition candidates in a wide range of industries has become prohibitive. At the same time, regulatory standards have become progressively more restrictive against purchases. Conglomerate-type mergers are likely to be ruled out as unduly concentrating economic power. So are market extension mergers involving geographical expansion into similar lines of business or product extension mergers in which related lines are acquired. Any merger of 2 companies that are among the 200 largest corporations is likely to be blocked, as are acquisition attempts by 1 of the 200 of any other company, regardless of its size, which is a leader in its own industry. The heyday of major acquisitions may well have come to an end. But acquisition strategy may nonetheless find a continuing role, and perhaps its most apt positioning, as a foothold step in overall venture operations.

It is an interesting phenomenon of business management that the practices of staking growth on R&D and acquisition have become acceptable as minimal-risk strategies when, in reality, each may invite the maximum risk. Failure, the maximum risk, is not ordinarily a problem for a very large corporation. But any company can be bet in a merger, and a poor acquisition can destroy it in terms of a significant percentage of its assets or even as an institution itself. Far less dramatic than the condensed risk that can be imposed by acquisition is the life-or-death dependency on R&D. Year by year, management may wait for R&D to "come up with something." During that time, the investment required for R&D may dilute earnings and return few or no dividends. At the end of five years or so, management may have no new long-term products and no short-term profits either.

Venture Contributions to Business Development

Venture approaches to new-business development can make three major contributions to corporate management. Venturing can contribute favorably to corporate development costs. It can contribute to the corporate price/earnings ratio. And it can contribute to the reduction of management's fear of prudent risk taking in return for suitable rewards. Companies which can capitalize on these contributions can substantially increase their commitment to venture.

Venture Contribution to Development Costs

Venture development costs can compare favorably with new-product development through R&D. The cost and success record of General Foods provides an example. During a ten-year period spanning the 1960s, the corporation spent more than $76 million to study 600 or so new-product ideas. This sum averages out to about $125,000 per idea. Approximately $30 million went into laboratory work. The remaining $46 million paid for market research and other marketing expenses to test product concepts. About 1 in 6 of these concepts was judged worthy of early development. Further testing eliminated another 31. The investment in these 31 new-product concepts was $11 million. This total was broken down into $5 million for technical research, $5 million for marketing research, and $1 million for capital investments.

After 87 products were test-marketed, 40 survived. After national introduction, 30 remained. These represented a total investment of $243 million. Of this total, $3 million was lost in an attempt to market a single line of gourmet foods. In contrast, the cost of venture development at General Foods has been calculated at less than one-third of new-product development costs.

This is a rather common ratio of venture contribution to development costs. In the rubber industry, to use a significantly different example, it is typical for a company to evaluate 500 new-product concepts a year in the hope of finding 30 which merit enough examination in depth to yield 1 that will ultimately be commercialized at a profit. The cost of this process of elimination may exceed the cost of launching and managing a venture development by as much as 3 or 5 to 1.

In foods, rubber, and practically all other industries, many companies manufacture a product or enter a market just because they command the necessary technical competence. This practice is very often the low road to failure. Nonetheless, a venture that starts with a known process or product, for example, and goes forth to seek a market opportunity may be assigned as much as a 0.90 level of confidence for success. A venture that goes the other way, starting out with an emerging market need and seeking a product and service system to benefit it, may deserve no more than a 0.30 level of confidence. But the market-centered venture may turn out to be the big winner.

It may also be the less costly investment in innovation. In many cases, the cost of true market-oriented venturing which works inward from an external market need may be only 10 to 20 percent of R&D costs for a typical new-product development. A consumer products marketer may require a minimum of $1 million to develop a new product from the concept stage through national introduction planning. This cost may be distributed as follows:

Basic concept research	$ 50,000
Advanced product and market research	100,000
Test marketing	850,000

A venture program to explore new-business potentials in the same market for a wide range of new product and service systems could require an investment of $90,000 to $180,000. This figure and the new-product development cost of $1 million both represent sunk costs. But neither is a complete cost. To a venture's operating investment must be added the usual overhead expenses of venture management compensation, the costs of internal services, and material costs. Large ventures involving the contributions of many prime people and requiring market need–seeking research and basic research in depth may easily be budgeted in the middle six-figure range.

If these costs appear high, it must be remembered that the costs of alternative growth strategies are high, too. An acquisition may sell at 35 times earnings. R&D, because it is such a familiar cost, may seem less expensive than it actually is. Most major corporations estimate that it costs a minimum of $50,000 a year just to field a bench chemist, exclusive of any work he may do. Rules of thumb for budgeting to exploit the bench chemist's work say that for $1 spent on exploratory research, $10 must be allowed for development work and use testing and another $100 to set up prototype manufacturing and test-marketing facilities.

Du Pont has estimated that it spends an average of $70,000 annually to maintain one scientist in its central research department. This figure includes only the salaries of the scientist and his technical aides along with some out-of-pocket costs. It does not include about $90,000 per man in allocated capital investment. Du Pont calculates that it requires the lifetimes of two such research scientists to yield a single commercializable development. In most cases, the time span between the development of a commercial opportunity in idea form and the market entry of a finished product or process is measurable in several years of additional costs incurred by many other specialists.

Companies devoted to R&D have learned to allocate even further

costs to this approach to new profit opportunities. These are intangible
friction costs. Generally, two echelons of researchers divide inventive
labor: the basic, or theoretical, scientists who come up with a breakthrough idea; and the applied scientists and engineers who try to realize
the idea's commercial potential. Their normal interface is friction. The
cost is waste and delay.

Venture Contribution to the Price/Earnings Ratio

Relatively few companies can honestly be classified as true growth companies. The small number for which growth is the name of the game are
generally industry-determined. They operate in an industry whose growth
is greater than average. In other cases, they possess a unique attribute:
patent protection, perhaps, or preemptive marketing or technical skills,
highly innovative research, or the ability to take advantage of price elasticity. The great majority of companies do not possess any of these growth
characteristics. Their price/earnings ratios prove that they do not.

If predictable infusions of new profits can be contributed by venture
development, venturing can help maintain or increase a company's stock
price/earnings ratio: *Consistency of earnings gain is the criterion of a
growth company*. General guidelines set a minimum annual earnings
gain of 10 percent as the threshold of real growth. Earnings rises between
7 and 9 percent a year can be classified as moderate growth. Anything
below 7 or even 8 percent is often downgraded from a growth to an income
stock category.

A track record of dependable venture generation, which permits new
earnings opportunities to come on-stream frequently, can increase the
financial community's willingness to pay a higher multiple for any given
year's earnings in two ways. First, it permits the ability to perceive earnings growth in the future. This enhances current values. Second, it assures
the quality of earnings which are derived legitimately from the application of a company's capabilities to its resources and are not achieved by
fiscal manipulation.

By restricting the corporate dividend rate or accepting new debt,
short-term earnings can often be boosted. But the price/earnings ratio
will not necessarily be affected. The most assured strategy is to expand
the base of reinvested cash flow to subsidize new ventures. This can be
accomplished by a threefold approach:

1. Divest the company of businesses which fail to deliver required profit. If these assets are reinvested in new venture
   businesses, initial venturing may be able to proceed by
   financing from within.

2. Operate "cash cow" commodity businesses for maximum earnings in the mature stages of their life cycle. Apply these earnings to investment-type venture businesses.

3. As ventures progress, be alert to opportunities to market venture by-products. These are fall-out products and services which can be sold for cash or a mix of cash and retained minority investment. Also be alert to market by-product ventures. These are ventures which have failed to meet criteria. Plow back income into new venture businesses.

Venture Contribution to Corporate Risk Reduction

Every corporate management group has its own attitudes on risk and on how much risk is acceptable for how much reward. In venturing by logical extension from an existing business base, risk can be minimized. But it may still exceed the norms established by a tradition of undertaking only low-risk, low-profit product line extensions of a marginally innovative nature.

Norms for developmental success should be complemented by standards of performance, or norms, for venture failure. Venture standards should require that a certain proportion of new-business developments fail. A standard of zero failures may very well predispose management to an overly cautious selection of venture opportunities. This can result in low-reward businesses whose development cost may exceed their return. Or it can entice management to invest a disproportionate amount of resources in faltering ventures in order to save them when a smaller allocation of resources could develop more profitable ventures whose market penetration would be timely rather than late.

Failure need not be courted. But neither should failure avoidance become the objective of the venture process. A comfortable guideline for most companies is: "You are all right as long as your successes gain more than your failures drain."

Vagaries of Venturing

Venture management requires a strong commitment because of two factors. One is that large companies must learn and practice small-business organization and operating methods, since venture businesses are small businesses. A second area of learning is found in the fact that venturing responds to its own set of rules. These are not the same as the rules of the road for running an established business. Two major vagaries of venturing are that growth industries are no guarantors of venture success and that a company can arrive at the right rationale for venturing yet still react wrongly to it.

Adapting Small-Business Management Principles

New-business ventures are small businesses, not large ones in miniature. Large companies generally lack the management capability, the practical experience, and the philosophical climate required to manage small businesses. To venture successfully, a company must commit itself to practice six basic principles of small-business management.

1. Head up each venture with an entrepreneurial manager who is comfortable with high-risk, high-reward opportunities.

2. Burden each venture with minimal costs. Assign small staffs. Avoid venture product overengineering. Imitate the garage genesis of small businesses that grow into large businesses.

3. Organize and operate each venture in a nonestablishment style. Equip ventures with a small, multifunctional capability base. Encourage overlapping role playing and interchangeable responsibilities through buddy-type position descriptions.

4. Concentrate the attention of each venture's staff on three prime functions: marketing, consultative-type selling to heavy-user customers or clients, and stringent cost control.

5. Apply the "razor and blades" approach to product and service lining. Try to combine in each venture's product mix a durable, utilitarian commodity like the razor and a unique, brandable, and high-turnover reusable product like the blades.

6. Apply the "belt and suspenders" approach to profit-centering each venture's sources of income by buttressing venture products with consultative application services and customer educational or information services. Sell the trio as an interrelated system.

Avoiding the Growth Industry Trap

Some industries offer obviously superior growth opportunity. But a growth industry in and of itself cannot assure venture success. The selection of a proper growth strategy is far more important and, in the final analysis, a much better bet to achieve superior new profits. This puts a premium on management decision making, where it belongs, and not on happenstance in a marketplace or in the economy. Two case histories, one of success and the other of failure in the petroleum industry, support this contention.

Universal Oil Products Company is a case of failure to grow. In the early 1960s, UOP's petroleum-based operations were so sizable that management feared they might not be susceptible to growth as fast as that of other industries. The company licensed oil companies to use refining processes developed in its laboratories, sold catalysts and petroleum additives, supplied engineering services, and contracted to build oil refineries. Then it went on an acquisition spree, adding unrelated new businesses like food compounding, hose manufacturing, airplane components, copper mining and fabrication, and forest products, some of which, company officials said, "We really had not expected to get into." Sales rose by almost $400 million in a little over a decade. But earnings peaked out at a little less than $1 for every $25 of sales. At the end of the hoped-for growth decade, UOP reported a net loss of almost $27 million.

Lubrizol Corporation is a case of success in growing without diversification in UOP's original industry. While UOP was diversifying, Lubrizol concentrated essentially on a single business, making chemical additives for petroleum lubricants and fuels. During the 1960s, Lubrizol commanded an average 30 percent of the world's market for lubricant additives. Net profit margins were consistently above 10 percent, the return on equity exceeded 20 percent, and the average annual earnings growth over ten years was 18 percent. Sales grew at a rate of 12 percent. Since 1958, Lubrizol has made only one acquisition, a manufacturer of a rust-proofing chemical. All other candidates have been consistently rejected because none was judged to possess the growth potential and profitability of Lubrizol itself. In the meantime, a number of specialty chemicals have been developed internally in spite of the fact that in the 1950s the company was thought by many observers to have reached maturity in the additive business.

Preventing the Wrong Reaction to the Right Rationale

In some instances, a company can arrive at the right rationale and decide to diversify but make the wrong reaction to its reasoning. General Foods is a case in point. From its origin as the Postum Cereal Company in 1922, General Foods grew by acquisition of the Jello-O Company; Igleheart Bros., the makers of Swans Down cake mixes; the Walter Baker Chocolate Company; Log Cabin Products; the Cheek-Neal Coffee Company, which made Maxwell House; Clarence Birdseye's frozen-food patents; and the patents of Sanka decaffeinated coffee. By the 1950s, the Federal Trade

Commission was acting to inhibit any further acquisitions of leading consumer companies. After a decade of internally developed product failures, General Foods decided to grow by a combination of internal ventures and foothold acquisitions. In 1972, the corporation announced an $83 million loss, largely incurred by one acquisition. By 1973, it had foreclosed all but one of its internal ventures and dismantled its corporate development department.

General Foods' acquisition of the Burger Chef fast-food chain was an initial gross failure. The acquisition was based on two invalid assumptions, that out-of-home eating was a growth industry still at the low point in its eventual life cycle and that roadside convenience feeding was a logical extension of the corporation's expertise in home convenience feeding. The first assumption was shortly disproved by market saturation in many areas with outlets for hamburgers, chicken, and roast beef. The second assumption is more interesting.

Fast feeding is a labor-intensive real estate business. The fact that food is involved is peripheral. The business provided no useful link with General Foods' supermarket retailing experience. In addition, real estate management was an illogical extension of corporate talent. As a result, General Foods made inflated property commitments in many weak marketing areas. The original total of 700 units was expanded to 1,200. Forgetting its hard-won knowledge of concentrating on mass product categories to optimize advertising and sales service, it was engaged in operating the widely and thinly scattered Burger Chef outlets. Controlling labor turnover among unskilled workers, many of them teen-agers, was another area of expertise that could not be extended from the corporate experience. "The fast-food business," General Foods concluded after charging off almost $40 million of its loss to it, "is not like manufacturing a pound of coffee."

Adapting to Market Change

The process of adapting to the accelerating rate of market change has become disproportionately slow and expensive for almost every company. The larger the organization, the slower and more costly the acceptance of change is likely to be. In the markets of the 1970s and 1980s, change will be inevitable in materials, their processing into products, their marketing, and just about every other aspect of business management. As Dr. Eugene Fubini has said:

> The future is not a linear extrapolation of the present. Old technologies will improve but brand new ones will take their place. In anticipating what will happen, we must realize that the creation of new problems, as well as the availability of technologies, shape future events. We live

in a period where, for the first time in history, finding solutions is relatively easy; to anticipate the problem is really difficult.

The only companies which will be able to live successfully in such an environment are those which can consistently anticipate the need for, and innovate to produce, transient product and service systems on a regular basis.

Venture management is well geared to seeking out and serving market needs for benefit systems with a short life style, as well as building the business base for enduring new sources of longer-term income. It can achieve these dual objectives while offering highly personalized and participative work situations for entrepreneurially oriented managers who want deep involvement in the affairs and rewards of their businesses. In this way, venture management's ultimate rationale may lie in its ability to put new-business growth and diversification on a more cost-effective basis that can combine new profits with adaptation to rapid market changes.

2

the venture growth base

If there is a number one rule for venture business development, it is probably "Stay with what you know best." This strongly suggests that diversification should proceed by successive penetration into neighboring business opportunities, each one of which has a straight-line inheritance from a common parental area of strength. Westinghouse has expressed the concept of *businesses related to the same business* in this way: "We only go into new business if we have a strength in the area, something to bring to the party."

To be most cost-effective, venturing should be a process of logical extension from existing corporate capabilities. At the very outset of the commitment to venture, management must answer two questions which will help predict its ventures' formats and business positioning:

1. What is "our game," the venture base of developmental assets we can grow from?

2. What extensions from our base are most logical in terms of their degree of utilization of these assets?

Venturing by means of logical extension from a company's existing business base leads naturally to the development of a congeneric type of company. A congener is a company whose businesses are allied in process origin, technological nature, or market action. In one or more of these allied areas, a congener features a basic commonality that unifies its diversity and gives it logic. Tenneco is an example. When the former Tennessee Gas Transmission Company first sought to break out of pipe-lining, it saw the exploration and production of gas and oil as being only one step removed as an application of its capabilities. Chemicals followed logically from petroleum. The same logic train led to packaging, much of which is made from petroleum-derived plastics.

Unlike a congener, a conglomerate features disparity. Its businesses are not necessarily related to each other or to their parent company's business base. They may serve several widely divergent industries without sharing a common process or technology. As a result, very little operational integration can take place among their decentralized managements, which have access to no central research power and to few, if any, common manufacturing or marketing facilities. It is difficult, if not impossible, for them to generate cross-elasticity of either market demand or business learning experience. The greater the inconsistency among a conglomerate's businesses and the more of a microcosm of the entire economy it attempts to become, the greater the risk and the higher the write-offs.

Defining Our Game

In order to build a logic into diversification, a company must define what its game is in terms of its most important assets. These are the unique values which the company possesses that lie at the heart of its strength. Growing from strength requires that these values be projected outward into new opportunities.

For every business, our game (the things that a business does best) is derived from two major inventories:

1. The millions of *capability units* which have been accumulated in the process of developing, manufacturing, and marketing the company's products and services. Capability units are sometimes expressed as man-hours. Because they represent vested knowledge, they are more accurately defined as mind-hours. They are contributed by the characteristics of a company's industry and by its own areas of expertise.

2. The millions of *acceptance units* which have accrued to the business in the awareness and attitudes of its markets.

A company can draw from either one or both of these inventories as an asset bank which can capitalize growth.

Growing from Capabilities

A business has two types of capabilities to grow from. One type is the industry characteristics with which a business is endowed. The second type is a company's own expert skills.

Basing Ventures on Industry Characteristics

Every industry has its own distinguishing characteristics. Some of these characteristics, like intensive regulation or seasonality, are negative. They inhibit growth and therefore often provide a rationale for venturing. Positive characteristics, which are more conducive to growth, can be built on as foundations for logically extended new businesses.

The airline industry can serve as an example of how positive characteristics can be used as venture bases to counteract the negative characteristics that hinder air travel business development. Exhibit 2-1 shows some of the characteristics which the industry regards as negative and which new businesses should be designed to counteract. An ideal venture for an airline would contain none of these characteristics or certainly as few as possible.

In Exhibit 2-2, venturable characteristics of an airline are shown. Any one of them can be used as a jumping-off place for venturing. Several airlines have already diversified according to some of these characteristics. Eastern Airlines, a company that thinks of itself as being in the distribution industry, formed a new company, National Distribution Services, as a logical extension of its business. National Distribution was set up to help manufacturers lower their inventory cost by reducing the amount of stock that must be kept on hand at any time. It has also been able to help reduce warehouse insurance costs by utilizing its own fireproof warehouses. The company was organized to handle all distribution and transportation requirements for a wide range of manufacturers from the time their products leave the production line to the time they are delivered at retail. Eastern has also invested in Rockresorts, vacation areas to which it distributes many of its passengers.

United Air Lines has extended its data processing and transportation capabilities into its Western International Hotels subsidiary; American Airlines and Braniff International have made similar extensions. United has also formed United Air Lines Food Services to operate the airline's food and beverage service and to expand the sale and distribution of food products to other airlines.

Use Planning Page 1 to work out the negative characteristics of your industry which new venture businesses must be designed to counteract. Then use Planning Page 2 to work out the venturable characteristics of your industry which can serve as a base for new venture businesses.

exhibit 2-1

negative characteristics
of the airline industry

1. Regulated industry

2. Seasonal and cyclical industry

3. Perishable unit of sale

4. Capital-intensive industry

5. Labor-intensive industry

6. Price-controlled industry

7. Highly competitive industry

8. Susceptibility to sudden negative publicity from accidental situations beyond management control

9. Standardized service offering little opportunity for true preemptive marketing

10. Sensitivity to operational problems beyond management control, leading to unplanned costs from delays by downtime or prolonged uptime and a high propensity for customer dissatisfaction

exhibit 2.2

venturable characteristics
of the airline industry

1. Glamour image

2. Young, dynamic, not-yet-mature industry

3. Knowledge of transportation and communication technology

4. Timely distribution of people and goods by air and over the ground

5. Person-to-person contact via multiple media

6. Sale and rental of intangible services dealing with time and place

7. Sale and rental of tangible goods such as food and liquor

8. Provision of entertainment-type information and factual information

9. Knowledge of electronic data processing

10. Experience in obtaining and utilizing credit

NEGATIVE CHARACTERISTICS OF OUR INDUSTRY
WHICH NEW BUSINESSES MUST BE DESIGNED TO COUNTERACT

VENTURABLE CHARACTERISTICS OF OUR INDUSTRY
WHICH CAN SERVE AS A BASE FOR NEW BUSINESS

Basing Ventures on Corporate Capabilities

Every company has its own expert capabilities. Some of them are usually transferable to other businesses of a logically extended nature. The most venturable capabilities, such as the ability to market in mass to consumers, are functional. They may be able to form a basis for venturing into a wide range of new businesses, in this case, businesses in which marketing through supermarket distribution and television advertising are the keystones of management.

In any business three functions form the strongest triad for venturing. They are the market information function and the two other corporate functions which are nourished by it, R&D and sales. Ventures based on strong functions in these categories have the soundest parentage.

In Exhibit 2-3, a food processor's self-assessment of venturable capabilities is shown. Theoretically, any one or, more likely, some combination of two or more capabilities can help the processor jump off logically into a venture. Exhibit 2-4 is the complement of Exhibit 2-3. It shows the processor's evaluation of corporate incapabilities for venturing. Nothing on this list can be used as leverage into extended businesses.

Assaying corporate capabilities that can be used as a venture base is a tricky business. It is difficult to be honest. Truly superior, and therefore venturable, capabilities are few in any company. From understandable corporate pride, however, it is easy to impute superiority to average capabilities. Equally dangerous is the temptation to project what may be genuine superiority in one industry into the same degree of competitive competence in a different or more sophisticated venture category. As General Foods discovered, the food processor who is the best distributor of packaged convenience products through retail supermarkets may prove to be the poorest distributor of fast-food products through freestanding highway outlets. The key capability here is not food distribution but management of a local labor-intensive retail business.

The worst pitfall in the self-evaluation of corporate capabilities is to believe that management capability per se is a venturable base. With few exceptions, management is not infinitely transferable from one business to another. The working tools of management are generally the same, but the ways in which they must be applied are extremely heterogeneous. Financial skill is a common management tool. Yet the specific aspects of financial skill involved in franchising are not necessarily held by all financial officers. Marketing skill is really not a single talent at all. It is a catchall category which includes a variety of disciplines that range from television advertising to mail-order, in-home selling to low-margin pricing. Because a manager has shown a flair for moving products through one marketing channel is no warrant that this skill is transferable across other media or onto other products and services. These critical differences in application more often than not will nullify whatever similarities may exist in a management working tool. For this reason, even the best manager cannot manage everything.

> **Use Planning Page 3 to work out a self-assessment of your corporate capabilities for venturing. Then use Planning Page 4 to work out a self-assessment of your corporate incapabilities for venturing.**

exhibit 2-3

venturable capabilities
of a food processor

1. Manage highly competitive businesses that serve the homemaker and her family

2. Manufacture cost-competitively and in mass volume

3. Market to retail customers and end-user consumers

4. Generate repeat consumption rates that average four times a year, principally through mass supermarket distribution and television advertising

5. Market branded products and services

6. Seek out and evaluate homemaker needs through sophisticated market research

7. Apply economies of standardization to multiple product lines

8. Prolong product life cycles and market franchises beyond industry norms

9. Generate logically extended product families

10. Build in convenience as a major product benefit

11. Support long-term investments to create and sustain long-term earnings

12. Market in mass without causing high-magnitude social or environmental problems

exhibit 2-4

incapabilities
of a food processor

1. Manage high-style businesses dependent on fads, fashion sensitivity, or a managerial flair for the dramatic

2. Manage technologically intensive businesses

3. Manage personal service businesses

4. Manage labor-intensive businesses which must be controlled locally

5. Manage durable goods businesses

6. Manage low-volume, highly customized, or high-markup product lines

SELF–ASSESSMENT OF CORPORATE CAPABILITIES FOR VENTURING

SELF–ASSESSMENT OF CORPORATE INCAPABILITIES
FOR VENTURING

Growing from Acceptance

Market knowledge is a requisite for all venture business growth. For this reason, forming a venture to enter a new market, as contrasted with developing a venture product line to serve an existing market, is the supreme new-business risk.

Many companies have multiple markets into which they can extend businesses. Almost every company has a market of end-user consumers and one or more intermediate markets of customers. For example, a food packager's end-user consumers are homemakers. This is one market in which management may be knowledgeable. There may also be two other markets. One is composed of packing customers such as meat processors. The second is composed of customers' customers, the supermarket chains that sell to homemakers. A glass manufacturer may have four venturable markets: the television tube manufacturers who buy picture tube bulbs, the television set manufacturers who buy the tubes, the retailers who sell the sets, and the householders who buy them. The glass manufacturer will probably be unequally knowledgeable in all four markets. This will be management's major constraint in utilizing marketing capability as a venture base. It will also be the limiting factor in defining a logic for business extension because, in the final analysis, a market will accept a supplier only if the supplier demonstrates knowledge of its needs.

It is a logical extension for the National Steel Corporation, as a steelmaker whose market acceptance includes not just steelmaking but also construction and building consultation, to venture into aluminum fabrication to serve the electronics and aerospace industries, building trades, mobile home builders, highway and bridge builders, packagers, and other traditional steel users. A similar market acceptance enables the Armco Steel Corporation to venture into plastic pipe manufacture for the sewage-disposal-system building market.

For Boise Cascade, as a lumber company whose market accepts it not solely as a supplier of pulp, paper, and wood but also for the broad-based use of the timberlands in which the trees grow, it is a logical extension to venture into many wood-based aspects of the protective shelter business: on-site housing, mobile housing, mobile home parks, and leisure-living communities to shelter people in their residential and recreational life-styles.

It is a logical extension for the Green Giant Company, as a packaged-food processor whose market accepts it not only as a canner of vegetables but also as a producer of outdoor-based health products and services for many "feeding" life-styles, to venture into packaged meats as well as vegetables, fast-food sandwich shops and family restaurants for the direct retailing of prepared foods, and outdoor-living products such as plants and flowers, lawn-feeding fertilizers, and insecticides. The market also accepts another food processor, the Gerber Products Company, as capable of underwriting the healthful life of babies. It is therefore a logical extension for the company to build the Gerber Life Insurance Company as a venture. A further extension along this line could be a mutual fund to enable parents to finance a baby's future education. Still a third food maker, the Quaker Oats Company, can define its business base as serving varied needs of young children–centered families. Its cereal products do this, of course. So could a logically extended venture into entertainment and educational motion pictures for child-centered families.

Miles Laboratories is a vitamin, germicide, and enzyme-based products manufacturer whose market will accept it not simply as a consumer and professional pharmaceuticals maker but also as an expert in household health care. For them it is a logical extension to venture into high-protein nutritional or "functional" foods which are the result of merging drug and food technology with its marketing competencies. Mead Johnson & Company can define its business base as helping medical practitioners in far broader terms than merely manufacturing Metrecal for dietary patients. It is therefore a logical extension for the company to market a computerized disease diagnostic service to physicians, hospitals, and medical schools.

Practicing the Basing Game

Working from its market acceptance, industry characteristics, or corporate capabilities, any business may be able to offer multiple bases of capability for venturing. In the following five examples, various bases are set down for logically extending the businesses of a miller, a packager, a bank, a broadcaster, and an airline.

Venture-Basing a Miller

A milling company like General Mills is a raw materials processor. Physically, in a product-oriented sense, the major outputs of its processes have been variety foods: cereals, baking products, and snacks. If General Mills wants to define its business according to its traditional output, it could say that it was in the business of convenience-food processing. On the basis of this technological capability, the miller could then logically extend its business into new food ventures such as soft drinks, confections, and chewing gum. The convenience-food processing business could therefore become one acceptable business base for venturing.

If the miller looks to its distribution process, the sales force and the supermarkets which act as its primary *physical distribution* channels, along with the television channels which are its primary means of *promotional distribution*, can be seen to be "retailers" of nonfood products as well as foods. On the basis of this distribution capability, a miller could then logically extend its business into new nonfood ventures which are merchandisable through supermarkets and advertisable through television. Home sewing and home decorating items, certain types of apparel and accessories, and crafts, games, toys, and other leisure-time products are examples of this product category. The supermarket-television processing business could therefore become a second business base for venturing.

Finally, the miller can look to its market's life-style processes as a third source of definition for a venture base. The miller's market is composed of mass, middle-majority homemakers and their children in a wide variety of life-style roles. On the basis of the capability to market to these life-styles, a miller could logically extend its business into ventures whose unifying bond is their common ability to add benefit values to young mothers and their families.

Venture-Basing a Packager

A packaging company like the Continental Can Company is a multiple materials processor. The primary physical outputs of its processes are variety packages: metal cans, plastic wraps, and paperboard cartons. If Continental Can wants to define its business according to its products, it could say that it was in the business of convenience-package processing. On the basis of this technological capability, the packager could logically extend its business into new container ventures. The convenience-package processing business could then become its business platform for venturing.

If the packager looks to its distribution process, its sales force and applications engineers can be seen to be "customer consultants" in many aspects of manufacturing and marketing such as precision tooling and machinery construction and operation, film and laminate manufacture, vacuum sealing, pressure containerization, printing and graphics, and market research. On the basis of this personal distribution capability, a packager could then logically extend its business into new consultation-based ventures which could be executed by its sales force and applications technicians.

Finally, the packager can look to its key customers' life-style processes as the third source of a venture base. The packager's customers do business with the packager in their life-style role as profit-conscious businessmen. Their attitude and activity patterns within this role lead them to be concerned with profit improvement through added distribution value. They receive this added value in one of two ways. Their distribution cost can be lowered through the use of more economical packaging material or designs. Or their revenues can be raised by using the packager's convenience openings, reusable lids, self-disposable packages, or new graphic techniques which improve the cosmetic and use value of their products to customers. On the basis of this marketing capability, a packager could define its business capability base as the profit improvement of customer businesses. This could lead logically into multiple-distribution product and service systems which provide the *physical movement* of packaged products and their *promotional movement* into end-user purchase and consumption.

Venture-Basing a Bank

A one-bank holding conpany like the First National City Corporation of New York is a credit processor. The primary physical outputs of its processes have been cash and financial instruments which represent cash. If First National City wants to define its business by these old-line banking outputs, it could call itself a convenience-money processor. Based on this technical capability, the company could then logically extend itself into new money processing ventures that would add value to wealth by investing it in mutual funds, life insurance, real estate, and stocks and bonds as well as demand deposits; in short, by supplying what First National City has called "every useful financial service," which could thereby become an acceptable business definition for venturing.

If the company looks to its distribution process, it can see how the loan officers and computerized data systems which act as basic distribution channels are actually information and educational utilities. On the basis of this personalized-plus-computerized distribution capability, the company could then logically extend its business into new ventures in which this distribution combination is essential. Equipment leasing, home and car leasing, and travel leasing are examples of venture businesses which can meet a bank's distribution-oriented definition of its business base.

Finally, a bank can look to its borrowers' and depositors' life-style processes as a third venture base. It would find all life-style roles whose patterns involve personal or business financial management theoretically marketable. Based on market acceptance for this widespread money management capability, a bank could logically extend its business into personal financial planning, budgeting, and accounting as well as investment ventures.

Venture-Basing a Broadcaster

A broadcasting company like CBS is a processor of words and music. From a product point of view, the physical outputs of its processes are variety education and entertainment programs. If CBS wants to define its business on the basis of the processing of its products, it could say that it is in the business of creating, packaging, promoting, and distributing convenience-packaged programs of information. On the basis of this technological capability, the broadcaster could then logically extend itself into new programming ventures in the convenience-information processing business.

If the broadcaster looks to its distribution process, it can see how the original distribution medium, radio, and the current major medium of television are actually only two of potentially many media. On the basis of a capability to distribute information by means of a coordinated sales force and media system, a broadcaster could then logically extend its business into new media-based ventures utilizing motion pictures, phonograph records, musical instruments, electronic libraries, books, and toys. Even a baseball team can be regarded as a venture medium for the distribution of education and entertainment.

Finally, the broadcaster can look to its advertisers' and audiences' life-style processes as a third venture base. In their roles as profit-oriented businessmen, advertisers are concerned with profit improvement by means of cost-efficient market reach. In their roles as consumers of education or educational entertainment, their audiences are concerned with life enrichment. On the basis of this dual marketing capability, a broadcaster could define its business base as the profit improvement of advertisers' businesses and the enhancement of audience needs to learn or to relax. This would permit logical extensions of great variety into in-home and out-of-home education, advisory, and entertainment systems involving many media other than broadcasting.

Venture-Basing an Airline

An airline like American Airlines is a processor of real-time information. The output of its processes has been the identification, storage, and distribution of the people and goods which constitute its information bits. If American Airlines wants to define its business according to its traditional outputs, it could say that it is in the personal service business of convenience time-and-place processing. Based on its technical ability to convert energy that compresses time and place, the airline could then logically extend its business into new information distribution services. The convenience-information processing business could become an acceptable business definition for venturing.

If the airline looks to its distribution process, it can see how its sales forces, their local communications and transportation terminals which process information, and its ground and air equipment, which convert it from one state or condition to another, are actually a twenty-four-hour-a-day, 365-day-a-year real-time information utility. On the basis of this personalized, telephonic, and computerized distribution capability, an airline could then logically extend its business into new ventures in which this distribution combination is central. Venture businesses which match an airline's distribution-oriented definition of itself are most likely to cluster at information terminals, or stations, such as general aviation fixed base stations, automobile and boat service stations, health stations and nursing homes, travel-planning stations or agencies, real estate stations, institutional and public food service stations, employment and job opportunity stations, and educational stations modeled along the lines of its existing stewardess college. In all these cases, a common interface is created between people and computers.

Finally, an airline can look to its passengers' and shippers' life-style processes as a third venture base. All life-style roles whose patterns involve time or place conversion could theoretically be marketed to by a one-airline company which diversified its business into a variety of personal and business processing services such as public feeding, buying, selling, and renting commercial, business, or private aircraft, and land sales or housing rentals.

> Use Planning Pages 5/1, 6/1, 7/1, and 8/1 to work out definitions of your venture base according to its technological physical distribution, promotional distribution, and life-style marketing capabilities. Then use Planning Pages 5/2, 6/2, 7/2, and 8/2 to work out new markets into which venture businesses may be extended from each capability base.

DEFINITION OF VENTURE BASE
ACCORDING TO TECHNOLOGICAL CAPABILITY

NEW MARKETS INTO WHICH VENTURE BUSINESSES MAY BE EXTENDED FROM A TECHNOLOGICAL BASE

<u>DEFINITION OF VENTURE BASE</u>
<u>ACCORDING TO PHYSICAL DISTRIBUTION CAPABILITY</u>

<u>NEW MARKETS INTO WHICH VENTURE BUSINESSES</u>
<u>MAY BE EXTENDED FROM A PROMOTIONAL DISTRIBUTION BASE</u>

DEFINITION OF VENTURE BASE
ACCORDING TO PROMOTIONAL DISTRIBUTION CAPABILITY

<u>NEW MARKETS INTO WHICH VENTURE BUSINESSES</u>
<u>MAY BE EXTENDED FROM A PROMOTIONAL DISTRIBUTION BASE</u>

DEFINITION OF VENTURE BASE
ACCORDING TO LIFE–STYLE MARKETING CAPABILITY

NEW MARKETS INTO WHICH VENTURE BUSINESSES
MAY BE EXTENDED FROM A LIFE-STYLE MARKETING BASE

Knowing What Can Reasonably Be Achieved

Once the venture growth base has been satisfactorily defined, management can gain two insights into its business. One is what it has grown from. The other is what kind of general standards it can reasonably set for future growth.

Since no company can grow through internal development in excess of its capabilities or market acceptance, these two factors must be the foundation for corporate expectations about the quality of new-business development that can be achieved. If a company enjoys only limited acceptance in markets which its management knows best or only low levels of marketing or technical competence, it will most likely have to move its growth path away from internally developed businesses toward external formats for venturing. There will simply be no base for a logical extension of the existing business. In this type of situation, management will have to acquire or invest in someone else's internal development.

Knowing what can reasonably be achieved through venturing enables management to rough out a set of minimal base-line criteria for venture selection. For an opportunity to qualify as venturable, a small, select list of standards must be met if a venture is to be a realistic undertaking. "Given our base for growth as it exists inside our business and in our markets," management must say, "we can sensibly expect that each of our ventures will be able to exceed a 50 percent pretax return on funds expended and will be able to generate a minimum of 20 percent pretax return on total investment. We can also anticipate that our capability and opportunity mix will permit our ventures to establish an annual rate of $20 million in net sales by the end of a venture's third year of commercial life. Beginning from that point in time, we also have a right to anticipate a minimum 8 percent annual rate of profit growth through at least Year 5. No ventures which cannot promise to meet these expectations will be considered since they will not be capitalizing fully enough on our base of opportunity and capability."

These base-line criteria can then become the core standards for corporate venture selection. Each venture will incorparate them into its own set of criteria. In this way, management has the best chance of allocating its developmental resources with maximum cost efficiency. Furthermore, by using criteria for venture growth based on what it is actually capable of achieving rather than what it feels it needs, management can significantly reduce the risk of failure.

> Use Planning Page 9 to work out a set of minimum base-line criteria for venture selection.

MINIMUM BASE—LINE CRITERIA FOR VENTURE SELECTION

1. Minimum % pretax
   return on funds expended   ___%

2. Minimum % pretax
   return on total investment   ___%

3. Minimum $MM annual rate
   in net sales by Year 5 $___,___,___

4. Minimum % annual rate
   of profit growth through Year 5   ___%

Choosing a Growth Legend

The existing business base can be regarded as a company's common denominator for venture growth. Potential new-business extensions become its numerators. The way in which the denominator is verbalized is therefore extremely important, since the base for growth must be finite enough to provide a steering function for venture selection and yet broad enough to allow room for maneuver. The definition must express an essential truth about the business as it exists today in a way that still will permit extension into the near-term future.

The approach a company adopts in defining its business base for venturing provides it with its *growth legend*. This is the story line that unifies and directs the venture selection process.

A growth legend has three main characteristics: (1) It is short and concise. Each word is important and must be chosen with great care. (2) It lacks ambiguity. Many diverse minds can reach general agreement on what it means. (3) It positions the business to be grown in an industry that offers superior growth.

When Litton Industries began its diversification, it chose the growth legend of "a scientific-based advanced-technology company." Litton's legend positioned it on the leading edge of technological innovation, an exceedingly high-risk base for venturing. In quite another industry, Warner-Lambert chose the growth legend of "a health and well-being enterprise" to diversify into businesses that make and market eyeglasses, razors and blades, ethical drugs, cough drops, cold remedies, dental products, chewing gum, and mouthwash. Because health and well-being are both physical and psychological states, their combined use in a legend opens broad-scale opportunities for growth into health utilities like eyeglasses and health cosmetics like chewing gum and mouthwash.

Because the growth legend acts like a self-fulfilling prophecy, it biases the selection of venture opportunities according to their fit. The legend's semantics can be crucial. A food processor who defines his venture base as "convenience foods" will be predisposed to consider different growth businesses from those of another food processor who defines his venture base as "nutritional foods." A brewer whose growth legend positions him in the "refreshment business" will move in a broader manner toward diversification than he would with such legends as "liquid refreshment business," "alcohol-based refreshment business," or "refreshment and nutritional food and beverage business."

> **Use Planning Page 10 to work out a growth legend that will define your business base for venturing.**

GROWTH LEGEND

Obsoleting the Venture Base

As the venture process goes on, successive ventures which are each extended logically from previous ventures may eventually arrive at a point where they are considerably removed from their original venture base. A company may find that the numerator of one of its ventures is greater than the denominator; that is, a venture that was originally an extension has become a business base of its own. As such, it may threaten to obsolete, or at least significantly alter, the foundation of the company's established business.

No company can look forward comfortably to the prospect of obsolescence. Yet if a business can envision a way of obsoleting its definition of itself, the chances are good that other venturers elsewhere can achieve a similar vision. If so, they will have no reason to withhold it. When a business is scheduled to be outmoded, there are advantages if it outmodes itself. Ventures permit the deliberate courting of obsolescence. Over the long run, courting-type ventures can periodically rejuvenate a corporate image as well as underwrite its essential continuity.

Ventures which deliberately risk obsoleting the original venture base are dealing in the next generation of new profits. For a manufacturer of office products such as typewriters and dictation equipment, a venture may seek out the next-generation life-style of the business office, which may obsolete typewriters and dictation equipment. For a manufacturer of pots and pans, a venture may seek out the next-generation life-style of the kitchen, which may obsolete pots and pans. For a publisher, a venture may seek out the next-generation life-style of information retrieval, which may obsolete traditional print media.

An office products manufacturer's venture into the next-generation life-style is typical of the need to resolve a mosaic of subobjectives before the ultimate objective of the venture can be gained. The venture question "What will the life-style of the business office of the next generation be like?" immediately raises the corporate question "What kind of business will we then *have to be*?" This potentially self-obsoleting question raises the most dreadful hypothesis a company can face: "We may no longer be able to be the same kind of company we are now. Unless we change, we may have no business as we are used to defining it." Confronting a dreadful hypothesis like this is a quantum jump removed from confronting the comparatively simple issue of "What will tomorrow's typewriter be like?"

The office life-style of the next generation may not need typewriters. If it does, they can only be conceptualized by a protocol of questions like these:

"How can the office life-style of the next generation be visualized physically: what will it look like? How can it be visualized psychosocially: what will it feel like? What will be its human needs? What will be its machine needs? How, when, and where will they interface?

"Will office environments of the next generation tend toward greater centralization as single communal entities? Or will they decentralize into an interconnected series of "officettes" or even offices at home? In either event, what forms and frequencies of messages will be required? Will sound and sight need to be combined, perhaps by coordinating the functions of the dictation machine's microphone and the typewriter's keyboard with a push-button Picturephone so that words and pictures can be transmitted simultaneously? Once transmitted, will they need to be recorded by some form of xerography and retained by instant microfilming?

"What, then, will the messages produced by the next-generation 'typewriter' sound like? What will the next-generation 'dictating machine' type like? Or will both be obsoleted by a real-time, simultaneous-access display and interrogation information system that will supersede many if not most presently telephoned, dictated, typewritten, duplicated, and personally transmitted messages?"

No matter what the industry, the problem of confronting a dreadful hypothesis is a tough one. A breakfast cereal manufacturer may define his business as "mother-and-child convenience foods." But, at heart, he translates "convenience foods" into "cereals." After all, what could be more convenient than a convenience-packaged, conveniently distributed cereal that combines nourishment, taste rewards, and economy in each serving?

It often follows, then, that company *management* has a vested interest in the concept of breakfast, which forms the life-style context within which most cereals are eaten. But its *market* may have no such vested interest in breakfast. As a matter of fact, breakfast in the way we have long known it as the traditional first meal of the day may fast be becoming outmoded. As many as 75 percent of all American families no longer breakfast together five days a week. Many housewives, almost as many husbands, and a growing number of children eat their first meal of the day alone. Between 10 and 20 percent of all men eat breakfast outside their homes on a daily basis. If these trends increase, breaking the night's fast may be regularly accomplished through a number of alternatives to a life-style featuring a morning meal.

To prepare for such an eventuality, a cereal manufacturer must accept this premise as a dreadful hypothesis. This must be done in much the same manner as the petroleum refiner must accept the dreadful hypothesis of electric or natural-gas propulsion of automobiles, or the detergent manufacturer must accept the dreadful hypothesis of disposable household utensils which will not require aftermeal cleanup. In all cases, the venture attitude should be expressed somewhat like this: "We are working very hard to obsolete out present capability base because if we don't, someone else may." If a new base is found, a new definition of "our game" must be made and a new logic for extensions of it integrated into corporate operations. The best one-word description of this process is "growth."

> **Use Planning Page 11 to work out the most dreadful hypothesis that can obsolete your venture capability base.**

<u>THE MOST DREADFUL HYPOTHESIS</u>
<u>THAT CAN OBSOLETE OUR VENTURE CAPABILITY BASE</u>

how to pinpoint
venture targets

3

venture selection

The gross objective of venturing into new businesses is to increase the long-term value of the shareholders' equity. The net effect of venturing, however, is to increase the shareholders' short-term risk. Risk is the probability that a venture will fail to be commercialized. In these terms, the history of starting up new business enterprises shows that the probability of venture failure is extremely high. The venturer's rule of thumb warns that out of every 10 start-up businesses, 3 will turn out to be total losses, 3 will break even, and 3 will be marginally profitable. Only 1 will be profitable enough to make up for the 9 others and then some.

Most ventures fail because of poor market fit. The risk of market incompatibility rises in direct proportion to the difference between a venture business market and the established market with which corporate management is familiar. The stranger a market, the greater the number and complexity of its unknowns. The most difficult situation of all occurs precisely in the area where most venture marketing takes place. At this point, the combination of new products or services that must be sold to new markets by a supplier that is new to them presents the most severe challenge.

Venture Selection Processes

The scarcity and cost of corporate investment capital dictate that a process for qualifying venture opportunities must be found. Enough money is never available to satisfy everybody's favorite hunch about just what surefire big-winner opportunity should be investigated next. The margin for permissible error in money and time is small. Decisions are often irreversible. Even if they are not, money may be totally lost if it is put on the wrong ones. The opportunity cost of money which could have been invested more profitably may be the ultimate and insupportable loss.

63

The objective of a venture selection process ought to be to spot winners, not to avoid losers. The selection process must help ensure that the 1 potential big winner out of every 10 candidates is identified before it can slip away. Using a selection process to *screen in* the elusive big winners rather than to *screen out* the future failures gives venture management a positive approach to its mission. It allies venture selection to venture objectives, which are to seek out and commercialize profitable new businesses rather than to build an inventory of unprofitable ones. It achieves one more benefit, too. It deters venture managers from trying to beat the 9 to 1 odds against successes by providing a tool for operating within the odds and making them work to advantage. It teaches them that the major risks in venturing are never those posed by total losses, break-even businesses, or marginally profitable businesses. The truly unaffordable risk is the big winner that is not ventured.

Quite a few selection processes have come into being. They range from the utterly simplistic to the mechanistic. Some venturers have operated with a single criterion: "Since we sell through supermarkets, the products of any venture we get into must also be marketed there." At one time, Procter & Gamble expressed the belief that the common denominator for its new products had to be their ability to be flushed down a household drain or toilet after use. Another single criterion is the "top ten favorites" approach. As long as a venture business is one of this year's top ten growth businesses, it may qualify. This approach often leads management to venture into overly generalized target areas such as service industries, leisure companies, communications equipment, or information systems.

Even though venture capital corporations have different objectives from corporate management in developing growth profits, venture managers frequently find it useful to apply capitalist thinking to venture selection. They play the "What if we were a venture capitalist?" game with development opportunities. This may mean that they look for a minimum upside potential of 10 times their investment in five to seven years of venturing, arriving at this average through the realization that few venture businesses reach their potential, many fail, and still others merely break even. This kind of averaged-out thinking may lead venture management to prefer buy-out acquisitions of mature businesses or semimature businesses with a three-year history which present a small downside risk and may require only a few more years to maximize their objectives. The correlate of this preference is a diminished interest in providing seed capital for start-up ventures which require the financing of a new product or service concept totally lacking a prior track record.

Another venture selection process is the "answer machine" approach. Answer machines have been derived from engineering project-rating systems. They are often used to provide semiscientific support for a venture manager's judgment of business opportunity through modeling the probable environment a venture might face in the real world.

Westinghouse has worked with a venture-rating system based on a "formidable formula" which represents the estimates and knowledge of several contributors. The formula, which acts like a primitive model, reads like this:

$$\frac{\begin{array}{c}\text{Chance of}\\\text{technical}\\\text{success}\end{array} \times \begin{array}{c}\text{chance of}\\\text{commercial}\\\text{success}\end{array} \times \begin{array}{c}\text{average}\\\text{annual}\\\text{sales}\\\text{volume}\end{array} \times (\text{price} - \text{cost}) \times \begin{array}{c}\text{venture}\\\text{life}\end{array}}{\text{Total costs}} = \begin{array}{c}\text{priority}\\\text{category}\end{array}$$

The chances of technical and commercial success of a venture are expressed as percentages, with 100 percent equaling 1. Average annual sales volume is expressed in units. Price is the net sales price per unit in dollars. Cost is the total dollar cost per unit. Venture life is the square root of the estimated number of years of life of the venture business over which the average annual sales volume in the formula can be expected to remain approximately the same. Total costs are the total dollar investment in development, including research, design, manufacturing, and marketing. The higher the priority category the formula yields, the stronger the venture's claim to selection.

An example will illustrate how the formula works. Assume that engineering and research estimate that the chance of actually developing an acceptable venture product is 80 percent. Marketing estimates the chance of commercial success at 60 percent. Average annual sales are estimated at about 20,000 units per year during a nine-year life-cycle. Net selling price will be about $120. Total cost including materials, labor, and overhead will be about $87. Research has cost $50,000; design, $140,000; manufacturing, development, tooling, and facilities, $230,000; and marketing development, including advertising and promotion, $50,000. Total investment is $470,000. Thus:

$$\frac{0.8 \times 0.6 \times 20,000 \times (120 - 87) \times 9}{470,000} = \text{category } 6$$

Du Pont's answer machine is a business enterprise model of a venture which attempts to quantify the selection process. Built into the model are quantifiable factors and assumptions governing a business: price patterns, costs, sales volume, profit margins, investment requirements, plant capacity, consumption trends, and competitive information. Then the model is interrogated with various "What if" questions. At the end, an economic value is computed for the venture.

No matter what type of venture selection process is employed, it can only be as predictive as the criteria that provide its backbone. Unless an opportunity is compared with realistic and meaningful standards, criteria can only help justify a selection rather than channel it. Two types of criteria, sandwiched together around a situation survey of a venture's opportunity fact base, have demonstrated a superior ability to guide decision making to targets that pay out.

The Selection Sandwich

In many companies, the venture selection process is a sandwich. The top and bottom slices are composed of *management judgments*. The top slice calls for management to take an overall grand view of its business future and to judge two things, what rewards it requires to achieve its growth objectives and where rewards of this nature can be found. These criteria, which answer the policy questions of "What?" and "Where?" may be called "grandview criteria." The bottom slice of the selection sandwich calls for management to take an intensive, up-close keyhole view of potential business opportunities and judge whether they represent businesses "for us." These criteria are based principally on technical and marketing considerations. Because they apply the considerations of the grandview criteria to the short strokes of the venture process, they may be called "keyhole criteria." The meat in the middle of the selection sandwich is each venture's fact base.

The construction of the selection sandwich is weighted heavily on the side of judgment. Like all business decision making, venture selection is a judgmental process. This does not imply that facts are of secondary importance. It does say, however, that successful new-business building places no premium on facts. They are commodities, available to all diligent researchers. What distinguishes one venture manager from another and justifies the rewards of new profits is the ability to apply judgment in deciding what facts must be gathered and then how they should be interpreted.

Grandview Criteria: Deciding "What Rewards?" and "Where Shall We Grow to Find Them?"

When venture managers plan the direction they want their growth to take, most of them have strong subjective prejudices against certain businesses they want to avoid. One manager will say, "I don't think we should get into that," and an entire industry will be eliminated from consideration.

Someone else may have had an unsuccessful experience once or may have been in an industry some years ago and now warns that it is "a good one to stay out of." When it comes to answering the grandview question "Where *shall* we grow?" management is rarely so fluent.

The answer is never "Anywhere." To seek to grow anywhere is most likely to grow nowhere. At the other extreme, the answer is rarely to set growth targets that are only product or process line extensions of management's existing businesses. This type of consideration can lead to such pseudocriteria as "Since we are already well established in the indoor lighting business, we should venture into outdoor lighting to complete the picture."

Every management needs a set of grandview criteria to start the venture selection process. These are the criteria that set management's gross boundaries for growth in two categories: the dimensions of the rewards it requires as a return for its investment of resources and the type of businesses from which these rewards can be managed. A checklist of grandview criteria for an industrial manufacturer is shown in Exhibit 3-1. In Exhibit 3-2, a grandview checklist for a consumer products manufacturer is shown.

Each grandview criterion exercises a steering effect on where management looks for growth. The criterion of inflation resistance listed in Exhibit 3-1 is a case in point. The ability of a venture business to combine strong demand growth with price elasticity so that prices can be raised as costs become progressively inflated is regarded as vital by many venture managers. Once this criterion has been accepted, two major growth directions are set. One is away from regulated industries and commodity products. The other is toward three types of businesses which usually offer resistance to inflationary inroads: research-based businesses like ethical drugs and electronic instruments which are geared to a high level of premium-priced new-product development; businesses like computers, copiers, and biomedical equipment whose marketing is based on service rather than products and in which service and performance are more important to customers than price; and businesses like cosmetics whose price/value relationship is traditionally high.

As a second example, the criterion of a minimum gross margin of 35 to 40 percent on sales will tend to steer management to businesses in which a significant technical or marketing contribution is waiting to be made.

Every management will have to work out its own grandview criteria for growth. Each set of criteria must be authentically reflective of the corporation's personality, its industry background, and the degree of venturesomeness that characterizes its management style. One management's grandview may be another management's pettyview. A small capital requirement for entry may be philosophically and financially important as a criterion in one case. In another, management may seek out highly capital-intensive industries whose up-front investment makes it difficult for competitors to enter and thereby assures sufficient lead time for penetration.

> **Use Planning Page 12 to work out a set of Grandview Criteria for venturing. Refer to Planning Page 9 to allow your minimum base-line criteria for venture selection to stimulate your planning.**

exhibit 3.1

industrial manufacturer's grandview criteria

1. Reward characteristics

1.1. A minimum of 5 times capital appreciation over investment must be realizable during the first two or three years of venture commercial life, growing to a minimum of 10 times investment in a five-to-seven-year venture life cycle.

1.2. A minimum 35 to 40 percent gross margin on sales must be achievable.

2. Industry characteristics

2.1. The industry must offer a demand base which grows faster than the real average annual growth of the GNP during periods of expansion and which declines more slowly than the GNP during recessions.

2.2. The industry must display two or more inflation-resistant characteristics such as strong demand growth, low labor costs as a percentage of revenues, and small capital requirements, minimal investment in fixed assets, high profit margins, and the ability to protect them by raising prices as costs escalate.

2.3. The industry must not be dependent on scarcity-prone raw materials or consume unusually large energy resources.

2.4. A strong current market need must exist, and it must be susceptible to rapid development that can contribute substantial short-term profitable growth.

2.5. A specific preemptive market position must be achievable within three years, with the venture commanding a minimum 20 percent share of the market on the basis of product, service, and market superiority.

exhibit 3-2

consumer products manufacturer's grandview criteria

1. Reward characteristics

1.1. A business must offer a minimum annual growth rate of 8 percent over a projected period of five years.

1.2. A business must have the potential of developing a minimum of $25 million in net sales or $5 million in profit before taxes, or both, by the fifth year of market life.

1.3. A business must have the potential of yielding a minimum 30 percent return on investment on a before-tax basis.

2. Industry characteristics

2.1. A business must have a high potential acceptance for new branded products and services that have high consumer repeat rates and high retail turnover rates.

2.2. A business must position mass, middle-majority homemakers as its major customers and preferably also involve the homemakers' families.

2.3. A business must lend itself to standardization of products and services, yet possess opportunity for a meaningful product or marketing difference that can be mass-advertised and mass-merchandised.

<u>GRANDVIEW CRITERIA</u>

1. Reward characteristics

2. Industry characteristics

Keyhole Criteria: Deciding "Is There a Business Here for Us?"

When a candidate business for venturing meets a company's grandview criteria, venture management must get down to the nitty-gritty. This requires a much more finite set of standards that enable the venturers to obtain a keyhole view of a venture candidate's suitability for selection. These keyhole criteria help management answer the question "Is there a business here for *us*?"

The policy decision to grow new businesses that are logical extensions of the existing business base goes a long way to predetermine the nature of the keyhole criteria used to isolate opportunities. An existing business can extend itself logically by one or both of two pathways. It can work from its basic marketing capabilities and seek new businesses which appeal to its known markets or which can utilize its marketing expertise and experience. Or it can work from its basic technical capabilities. In either case, venture management will be operating from its greatest sources of strength.

It is therefore natural that, among the three categories of keyhole criteria, one category encompasses marketing criteria. The major marketing criteria for most logically extended ventures will include a set of standards for evaluating a venture's corporate marketing compatibility, market acceptability, and degree of consonance with product and service characteristics, sales and distribution characteristics, and competitive characteristics that management judges to be required for big-winner success. A model checklist of some keyhole marketing criteria is shown in Exhibit 3-3.

A second category of keyhole criteria that help ensure logical extension are the technical standards which a venture business must meet, along the lines of the model shown in Exhibit 3-4.

A third category of criteria for keyhole selection is composed of venture financial objectives. When venture objectives are used as criteria, they should be translated literally in the style of the following two examples:

1. To be venturable, a candidate business must promise a minimum average pretax return on investment of 30 percent over its first three years, with a minimum average aftertax return of 20 percent.

2. To be venturable, a candidate business must promise a minimum $10 million gross retail sales volume by Year 3, with a minimum $5 million net sales yield and a minimum $1 million profit before taxes.

exhibit 3-3

keyhole marketing criteria

1. Corporate compatibility characteristics

1.1. Product and service systems must be compatible with market perceptions of the corporate image in regard to ethical standards, social responsibility, and environmental protection.

1.2. Product and service systems must be compatible with corporate marketing knowledge and within the scope of corporate marketing management's capabilities.

1.3. Product and service systems must be free from socially restrictive or legally regulated limitations on marketing.

2. Market characteristics

2.1. The market must be in the growth phase of its life cycle so that a minimum 5 percent increase in gross sales volume can be forecast over a five-year time frame.

2.2. The market must conform to the demand characteristics of a major mass segment composed of a minimum of 5 million households which generate a minimum $50 million retail market.

2.3. The market value of each 1 percent share must be a minimum of $2,500,000.

2.4. The market must promise a noncyclical or countercyclical stream of earnings.

2.5. The market must not demand more than a maximum $10 million direct marketing investment during Year 1, or an investment that will not exceed a 1:5 ratio of spending share to market share in terms of dollar value.

2.6. Market acceptance must be strong enough to provide a minimum 10 percent share of the market by Year 3 and a minimum 20 percent share by Year 5.

3. Product and service system characteristics

3.1. Products and services must possess a brandable competitive difference that is patentable, that preempts satisfaction of an

exhibit 3-3 (Continued)

important market need, and that is advertisable in a way that allows user benefits to be perceived as superior to direct competition and therefore deserving a premium price.

3.2. Products and services must possess line and category extension capability into coordinated families of product and service systems. No venture should be a one-product business.

3.3. Products and services must be sufficiently future-oriented to promise a minimum five-year life cycle that will sustain a high rate of profitable sales against competition throughout its duration.

3.4. Products and services must not incur more than a maximum $2 million total development cost up to the point of national launch.

4. Sales and distribution characteristics

4.1. Products and services must be compatible with sales force capability.

4.2. Products and services must be compatible with existing channels of mass distribution.

4.3. Products and services must be compatible with mass advertising distribution.

4.4. Product and service systems must not require more than a maximum three-year period to achieve full national distribution from the time of national roll-out.

5. Competitive characteristics

5.1. To assure sufficient lead time of freedom from competitive replication, product and service systems must promise a minimum one-year period of proprietary marketing grace derived from technical or marketing preemption, patents, or regulatory agency sanction.

5.2. If an established market is to be penetrated, it must not be "owned" by a single supplier. The market share of the top two companies should not exceed 40 percent. If there are more than two leaders, their combined market share should not exceed 60 percent. Nor should the market be so atomized that there is no leader with less than a 15 percent share.

5.3. The market should not be subject to intensive price competition or to private-brand competition which holds more than a 20 percent share.

exhibit 3-4

keyhole technical criteria

1. The venture business must be dependent on proved corporate technical expertise and technological traditions and be completely free of dependence on technological breakthrough discoveries.

2. To prove affordable technical feasibility, a working product or system prototype must be producible for a maximum $100,000 investment within one year.

3. Patent protection must be achievable.

4. A maximum approval time of eighteen months by federal regulatory agencies must be achievable.

5. For early and consistent standardization to be achieved, maximum quality control must be assured for ingredients, process, and product engineering.

6. Adaptation of output to automated mass production must be assured.

Criteria Elaboration

Minimum Profit

Minimum profit is the foundation of venture capital budgeting. If the cost of capital is 12 percent, for example, a minimum-profit criterion for investment in a routine nonventure type of business would have to be at least 14 percent to be attractive. For venture businesses, which by definition are not routine, a more likely minimum-profit criterion would be about 20 percent. This figure is generally arrived at by adding the basic company cost of capital together with a 2 to 4 percent overlay for corporate overhead and a 3 to 5 percent venture risk bogey.

Minimum Growth Potential

A venture market should show or promise growth in gross sales volume of a minimum of 5 percent annually for at least five years. Growth at a lesser rate or sporadic growth on a cyclical basis makes a market less suitable or undesirable for venturing. A practical symbol of growth in an existing market is the strength and frequency of new-product introduction. The higher the gross sales volume generated by new products, the more vigorous a market's growth is likely to be. The growth potential of an existing market can also be judged by the dollar value which each share in it represents. A robust, vital market for consumer products, as an example, may carry a minimal $2,500,000 value for each share point. With a 10 percent share, a growth market of this type should yield $25 million in net sales. Ventures which are designed to create a generically new market have a more difficult time in evaluating market growth potential. In their case, the only signposts may be the growth records of somewhat similar correlate markets.

Maximum Years to Payback

Venture management should ask two questions in advance of each investment. The first question is "How much must I put in?" The second question is "How long will it take to get it out?" Getting venture investments back in the shortest possible time is vital to maintaining the cash flow of a corporate venture commitment. The return on each successful venture is the best possible seed money for continued venturing. Only in this way can the venture process become self-supporting. If ventures are assessed a maximum of five years to payback, with most paybacks expected in three to five years, income and investment may be able to run parallel to each other after Year 5 of the initial venture. Secondary refinancing of venture management can be largely avoided or at least minimized. Used in this way, the criterion of years to payback is a handy measure of venture risk. It can be roughly computed according to this formula:

$$\frac{\text{Initial investment}}{\text{cash flow per year}} = \text{years to payback}$$

$$\frac{\$10,000}{(\$1,000 \text{ profit} + \$2,500 \text{ depreciation}) \, \$3,500} = 2.9 \text{ years}$$

Minimum Share of Market

For a rapidly growing business, gaining at least a 5 to 7 percent market share by Year 3 may be vital to success. This minimal market share is often the breakpoint for profitability. In turn, profitability is a function of market penetration. Venture management resources must therefore be directed to achieving a market foothold as quickly as possible and then to attaining market dominance in minimal time. There are two reasons why this is so. First, there is the advantage of economy of scale. Since cost falls as the number of units produced rises, the venture with the highest production level should earn the economies of least cost. At premium prices or even at competitive prices, it should also earn the highest profit. Second, there is the advantage of cost efficiency. Since the learning curve of experience rises with the number of units produced, the venture with the highest production level should have the highest cost efficiency. It will also be able to allocate every dollar of its advertising investment over a larger number of units, reducing its cost per unit.

Systems Marketability

With rare exceptions, a venture business should not be based on a single item which cannot be bred into a related family, or system, of products and services. The ability to market systems is essential to achieving extensive market penetration. It is also necessary in order to maximize profit by serving comprehensive systems of interrelated market needs. By defining market needs carefully at a venture's outset, systems interrelationships can often become apparent even in the case of seemingly single product concepts.

Mass Advertisability

The ability of many consumer products or services to be distributed through mass advertising is crucial to their success. A venture product's competitive difference should be readily dramatizable in terms of user benefits which its market will accept as more meaningful than competitive benefits. If the benefits of a venture product or service cannot be advertised as meaningfully different, there probably can be no mass venture business. In this regard, the adage "If it's advertisable, it's probably marketable" is generally valid.

Use Planning Pages 13, 14, and 15 to work out your Keyhole Marketing Criteria, Keyhole Technical Criteria, and Keyhole Financial Criteria. Refer to Planning Page 9 in order to allow your minimum base-line criteria for venture selection to stimulate your planning.

<u>KEYHOLE MARKETING CRITERIA</u>

1. Corporate compatibility characteristics

2. Market characteristics

3. Product and service system characteristics

4. Sales and distribution characteristics

5. Competitive characteristics

KEYHOLE TECHNICAL CRITERIA

KEYHOLE FINANCIAL CRITERIA

1. Minimum average % pretax
   return on investment over Years 1-3   ___%

2. Minimum average % aftertax
   return on investment over Years 1-3   ___%

3. Minimum $MM pretax profit $___,___,___

Based on

4. Minimum $MM gross retail sales volume
   by Year 3 $___,___,___

5. Minimum $MM net retail sales volume
   by Year 3 $___,___,___

6. Minimum % market share by Year 3   __%

Allowing

7. Minimum # years to payback   #_

82

A useful supplement to keyhole venture evaluation is the Consonance Grid. A sample grid is shown in Exhibit 3-5. On it, the promise of a new-business opportunity is matched to its apparent consonance with three major corporate capabilities: marketing strength, technical competence, and management style and skills. Where the consonance is high, the opportunity is scored as 1. The lowest consonance is 3. A summary value is arrived at by adding the three scores. For the business opportunity shown in the exhibit, any score above 5 would probably not be in sufficient consonance with business capabilities to be successfully developed. When Consonance Grids are used, even one score in the 3 category should probably disqualify a venture from being selected or, at the very least, make sure that it receives special scrutiny. A minimum of a single 1 score is imperative.

> **Use Planning Page 16 to work out a Consonance Grid comparing your venture's promise of business opportunity with your marketing strength, technical competence, and management style and skills to capitalize it.**

exhibit 3-5

consonance grid

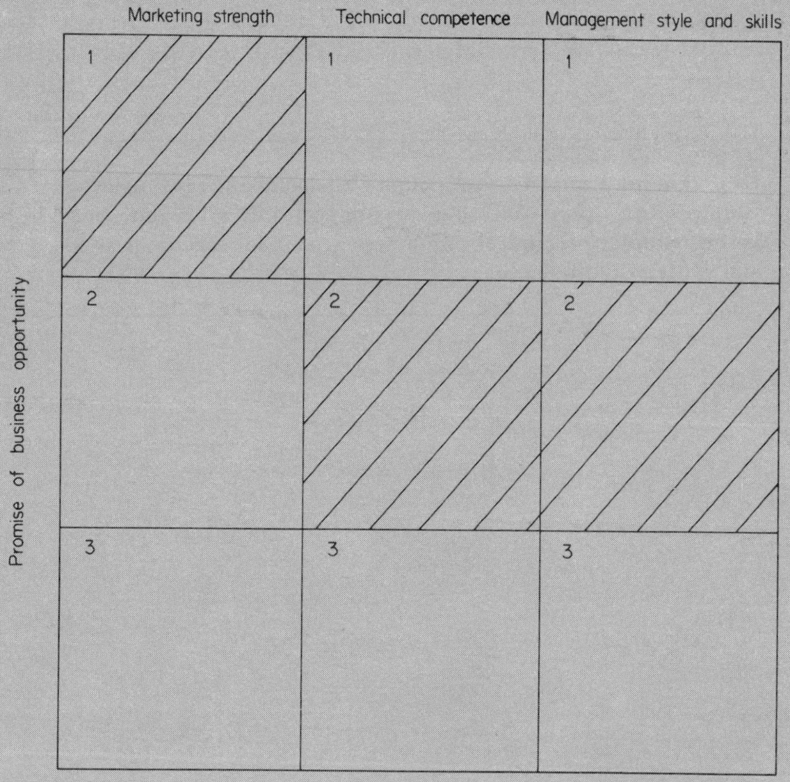

CONSONANCE GRID

	Marketing strength	Technical competence	Management style and skills
	1	1	1
	2	2	2
	3	3	3

Promise of business opportunity

Risk Hedging on the Near Venture

The "near venture" is a new-business candidate that almost, but not quite, meets minimal selection criteria. It is extremely interesting but slightly forbidding. It may have a single outstanding negative characteristic, or it may fail to meet an important positive characteristic. Yet it may still be attractive enough for management to want to take a chance on it. Through risk hedging, management can often have its cake and eat it too.

Risk hedging can be accomplished in two ways. One is by *risk division*, which separates high-risk ventures into a series of relatively small sausage-link commitments. The other hedge is achieved by *risk mixing*, which counterpoints one low-risk venture against every high-risk venture in a manager's portfolio. The low-risk venture can be run on an express-train, track-one basis while the higher-risk venture is run in parallel on a local-train, track-two basis which permits stops at periodic intervals for recommitment.

Making a venture's risk divisible can frequently make it acceptable. For example, a venture's total dollar risk may be projected at $100 million. The venture manager may calculate a 40 percent chance of losing it all, yet a 60 percent chance of returning as much as $500 million. In such a case, the venture manager may decide to divide the risk. The manager may invest $15 million to the point of first withdrawal if the venture is based on a proved technology and familiar market knowledge. If it is not, the manager may prefer to limit initial investment to $5 million on the basis of only a 20 percent expectation of success. If this initial investment proves out, the manager can invest a second installment of $5 million. A 40 percent expectation of success may then seem reasonable. At that time, the manager can put in another $25 million.

This is venturing on the installment plan. Cutoff can occur at any evaluation point. In common with all hedges, risk division trades off a demonstrable benefit for a potential deficit. By proceeding with risk-hedging caution, a venture manager may unwittingly permit a competitor to gain first entry. If that happens, a potential $500 million business may have to be shared at the $250 million level of penetration or lower. The venture manager will have to decide if an actual $250 million business offers a fair trade against a possible $500 million loss. The most important consideration may be that the manager has not bet the venture.

Use Planning Page 17 to work out a venture Risk Division Plan.

VENTURE RISK DIVISION PLAN

Total $MM at risk

    __% chance of total loss

    __% chance of returning $___,___,___

First installment

    $___,___,___ investment

         to point of first withdrawal by (date) __/__/__

Second installment

    $___,___,___ investment

         to point of second withdrawal by (date) __/__/__

Third installment

    $___,___,___ investment

The Selection Scenario

When a venture business proposition passes a first screening through its venture criteria, it should be written up as a "selection scenario." This is a terse narrative description of the venture treated on an as-if-basis: as if the venture had already been selected. The purpose of the selection scenario is to position the venture as a going business so that it can be visualized in the real-world context of its operations, its market, and its competition.

A model selection scenario is shown in Exhibit 3-6. The scenario should be supported by a pro forma statement of financial objectives and a summary of the key marketing strategies which can achieve them. These projections will necessarily be gross. No determination can be made about whether the venture will actually net out. But the selection scenario will serve its function admirably by affording venture management its initial opportunity to sense how a venture may gross out.

Use Planning Page 18 to work out a venture Selection Scenario.

---

exhibit 3-6

selection scenario

The "Personal Estate Management Company" is in business to improve the cost efficiency with which business executives, professional men and women, and other affluent individuals can manage their sources and distribution of personal income with the objective of maximizing their net worth. The company's service is performed by a staff of specialists in tax planning, insurance, securities investments, real estate, and exotic ventures in cattle breeding and oil exploration. Their services are marketed primarily to corporations and professional practice organizations and secondarily to individuals. The market is composed of a minimum of 1 million potential clients. In the absence of Year 1 direct competition, a minimum 30 percent pretax return on investment can be contributed by a minimum 12 to 15 percent share of the market.

VENTURE SELECTION SCENARIO

4

quick-screen
venture selection

Selection criteria tend to proliferate in direct ratio to the insecurity of venturers. Failure is avoided by avoiding venturing. To avoid criteria block, it is helpful to construct a "quick screen" composed of the minimal criteria that are absolutely essential to venture success.

A quick screen economizes the venture evaluation process. A potential winner which meets the minimal criteria can be looked at more intensively as soon as it passes through the screen. Similarly, venture candidates which fail to meet minimal criteria can be discarded without unwarranted appraisal or an excessive number of over-the-shoulder wistful glances.

A model quick screen for internally developed ventures is shown in Exhibit 4-1. It contains six criteria, or just about the upper numerical limit of what may be considered minimal. Three of the criteria are concerned with financial considerations. A fourth criterion ensures a venture's market orientation, a fifth forces an early judgment on the ability of a venture's product and service systems to become branded at a premium price, and the sixth relates a venture to corporate management's concept of itself as good citizens.

> Use Planning Page 19 to work out a venture Quick Screen.

Acquiring someone else's venture is a trade-off. Since the venture already exists in the real world of its market, it is open to close inspection rather than mere conjecture. This gives management the welcome opportunity to play physician by examining a live patient rather than act as a crystal-ball gazer conjuring up a vision. On the other hand, the price

exhibit 4-1

venture quick screen

1. Minimum 30 percent pretax return on investment.

2. Minimum 20 percent aftertax return after Year 3.

3. Minimum $10 million gross retail sales potential, to yield $5 million net sales and a minimum $2 million profit before taxes by Year 2, with growth potential to a minimum $25 million net sales and $5 million profit before taxes by Year 5.

4. Product and service systems marketable to a minimum of 5 million households through supermarket retail distribution and television advertising distribution.

5. Product and service systems brandable at a premium price/value relationship.

6. Business nature and style compatible with corporate image for ethical management and social concern.

VENTURE QUICK SCREEN

1. Financial screens

2. Market orientation screens

3. Premium—pricing capability screens

4. Corporate compatibility screens

that management pays for this advantage is reflected in the criteria which it makes sense to impose on the selection of an acquisition venture. As Exhibit 4-2 shows, the criteria are a good deal more narrative than an internally developed venture's quick screen. They may also have to be less finite.

> **Use Planning Page 20 to work out an acquisition venture Quick Screen.**

exhibit 4.2

quick-screen selection criteria for an ethical drug acquisition

1. Management capability

A youthful management capable of taking the business into the next decade in an entrepreneurial fashion, with an orientation to market need serving and an acute social and governmental sensitivity.

2. Sales volume capability

Minimum annual gross sales volume capability of $25 million as of date of acquisition.

3. Innovative capability

A future-oriented innovative capability to develop new product systems on the basis of next-generation technologies in aerospace, astrobiology, biomedicine, or medical electronics, as differentiated from traditional R&D capability.

4. Manufacturing capability

A broad-based manufacturing and testing capability, or the ability to develop or acquire it, to permit entry into a diversity of markets with a comprehensive product line.

5. Marketing capability

A customer-sensitive marketing capability, with specific emphasis on the ability of the direct sales force to create and maintain consultative relationships with customers.

6. Growth capability

An ability to develop the business significantly and to grow new profits so that the minimal incremental effect of the acquisition will be (a) a doubling of profitable sales volume over a three-year period, and (b) entry into at least two new markets in the same time frame.

7. Reputation

A high-quality reputation in the ethical pharmaceutical field among (a) the trade, (b) the professional medical market, and (c) governmental agencies, commissions, and other regulatory and certificating bodies.

ACQUISITION VENTURE QUICK SCREEN

1. Management capability

2. Sales volume capability

3. Innovative capability

96

4. Manufacturing capability

5. Marketing capability

6. Growth capability

7. Reputation

Quick-Screen Venture Potentiometer

It is often helpful to organize venture selection criteria in an evaluation guide that permits a quick screen of each candidate's business potential according to a standard set of weighted checkpoints. A screening device of this nature is called a "potentiometer."

Potentiometers are popular adjuncts to venture selection because most venturers seek quantification of their opportunities. But even quantified selection tools are essentially subjective. The criteria selected for emphasis and the numerical values assigned to them are both arrived at through personalized decision making. The major asset of a quantified screening system is that it focuses attention on the underlying judgmental beliefs of the venturers who create and operate it. This in itself is well worth the exercise. In the last analysis, it is the judgment of venture management that will determine the success of its business development operations.

Exhibit 4-3 shows a model potentiometer for quickly screening a venture product's potential candidacy for development. Each criterion on the potentiometer has been assigned values ranging from +2 to −2. The higher the value, the greater the potential candidacy of the venture product. On the model potentiometer shown in the exhibit, only products which pass its quick screen with a minimum value of 15 are to be considered further. This is an arbitrary cutoff point. Therein lies the potentiometer's contribution. For one thing, it gives an essential unity to the selection process. Further, it helps to personalize the company's individual approach to venturing by expressing management's sense of the business priorities which may distinguish it from competition.

A second model for a quick-screen potentiometer is shown in Exhibit 4-4. Each criterion has been awarded a single constant value. The combined values of all the criteria add up to 1.0. When a candidate venture is being run through them, a percentaged estimate is made of its probable ability to meet each criterion. The criterion's value is multiplied by the percentaged probability in each case. The net values for all the criteria are then added together to form a venture index. An arbitrary passing grade, below which no venture will be considered, is set for the index. In the exhibit, the venture index of 69 exceeds the passing grade of 51.

Use Planning Page 21 to work out a Venture Index Potentiometer.

---

exhibit 4.3

venture product potentiometer

1. Contribution to before-tax return on investment
+2 More than 35 percent
+1 25–35 percent
−1 20–25 percent
−2 Less than 20 percent

2. Estimated annual sales
+2 More than $250,000,000
+1 $100,000,000–$250,000,000
−1 $50,000,000–$100,000,000
−2 Less than $50,000,000

3. Estimated growth phase of life cycle
+2 More than three years
+1 Two or three years
−1 One or two years
−2 Less than one year

4. Estimated start-up time to high-velocity sales
+2 Less than six months
+1 Six months to one year
−1 One or two years
−2 More than two years

5. Capital investment payback
+2 Less than six months
+1 Six months to one year
−1 One or two years
−2 More than two years

6. Preemptive positioning potential
+2 Technical or marketing preemptive capability
+1 Short-term or partial preemptive capability
−1 Initial preemptive capability but susceptibility to easy knock-off
−2 No preemptive capability

exhibit 4-3 (Continued)

7. Business cycle effect

+2 Impervious to business cycles or countercyclical
+1 Reasonably resistant to business cycles
−1 Normally subject to business cycles
−2 Strongly subject to business cycles

8. Premium-price potential

+2 Superior perceived benefits that justify premium price
+1 Superior perceived benefits that may not justify premium price
−1 Equal perceived benefits that justify parity price
−2 Equal perceived benefits that justify only lowest competitive price

9. Ease of market entry

+2 Scattered competition that makes entry easy
+1 Mildly competitive entry conditions
−1 Highly competitive entry conditions
−2 Entrenched competition that makes entry difficult

10. Test-market time frame

+2 Moderate testing required
+1 Average testing required
−1 Significant testing required
−2 Extended testing required

11. Sales force compatibility

+2 Moderate or no sales force training required
+1 Average sales force training required
−1 Significant sales force training required
−2 Extended sales force training required

exhibit 4.4
venture index potentiometer

Criteria	Value	× % probability	= Net value
1. Minimum $10 million net sales by Year 3	.30	80	= 24
2. Minimum $50 million retail market potential	.20	70	= 14
3. Minimum one-year marketing grace period free from competition	.20	10	= 2
4. Proved technology	.15	100	= 15
5. Minimum 8% growth potential through Year 5	.10	90	= 9
6. Maximum $2 million development cost through national launch	.05	100	= 5
	1.00	Venture index =	69

VENTURE INDEX POTENTIOMETER

	Criteria	Value	×	% probability	=	Net value
1.		.--		---		--
2.		.--		---		--
3.		.--		---		--
4.		.--		---		--
5.		.--		---		--
6.		.--		---		--
		1.00		Venture index	=	--

102

how to organize
for venturing

5

the venture manager and task team format

A venture business task team is an intracorporate development group that has been "spun in" to the corporate organization structure to operate as a small syndicate within its parent company. It has its own charter, its own budget, and its own personnel, who are willing to accept unusual responsibility with its attendant risks and rewards.

A venture team may be described as a minimal group chartered with a maximal objective. It is imperative that a venture objective be broadly based to give the team sufficient room for maneuver. However, a broad base need not imply a vague mission. For a paper products manufacturer, a broad yet sufficiently directive charter for an internal venture based on paper clothing might read like this:

> To seek out the profit potential of a business in disposable wearing apparel and accessories of both a personal and an institutional type to be worn by men, women, and children. This search is to be carried out by (1) conducting a needs analysis for disposables within each of these market segments; (2) generating technical, promotional, and fashion concepts for market testing against each segment's needs; and (3) recommending a complete business plan for market entry to yield a minimal 40 percent pretax return on investment averaged over a ten-year life cycle.

In searching out entirely new business opportunities for their corporation, venture task teams must concentrate on developing the kind of large projects that can yield big winners. A portfolio of many little projects should be discouraged. If the task team concept of combining the small entrepreneur's flexibility and initiative with the backing of corporate financial and knowledge resources is to have a payout, truly forward-looking growth opportunities must be explored. At the same time, a task team must be free to ignore corporate staff services when they are parochial or are backlogged with regular assignments.

If a venture team needs a motto, it should be "New products and services for new markets." New products for existing markets and new markets for existing products should be left to operating divisions. These divisions exist to serve the marketplace. A venture comes into being to tempt it.

Because a venture task team is a temporary company, at some point it will come to an end in one of three ways. It will be terminated, adopted into its parent organization, or spun out as an autonomous business entity. In its precommercial life, it should be managed according to the principles of project management. It must have a manager, an organization, a plan, and controls. And it must have an objective common to all ventures: to make change. The major criteria of its management style and structure must therefore be ability to introduce change, implement it in the form of a commercial product or service, and sell it to management and to a market.

The project manager of a business development venture is the venture's single most important element. Management will be the venture's cause. Everything else will be an effect of what the venture manager is and what the venture manager does. The first step to venture growth is always "Find the manager."

A venture has often been compared to a horse. In this analogy, the venture manager is its jockey. In the ideal world, which rarely corresponds to the real world, management would field a good jockey and a good horse. Both selections would have excellence. But when trade-offs must be made, the rule of thumb is always to bet on a good jockey even if he is saddled with a mediocre horse. To bet on a good horse bringing a mediocre jockey home by itself is an undue risk. This does not suggest that management can be lax in its choice of venture opportunities. It does emphasize, however, the crucial importance of the venture manager and, to a lesser extent, the corporate support services that provide managerial backing.

A corporate venture manager is a paradox. He or she should not be entrepreneurial enough to want to start up a business outside the corporate environment. But the manager's personal style should be much too entrepreneurial for him or her to be content with operating an existing product line as a brand or product manager whose standard of performance is based on marginal renovations of an ongoing business rather than new business development. The ideal venture manager seeks all the attributes of entrepreneurial management except one, the initiation of a venture business by scrambling for seed money and then "working eighteen hours a day for peanuts." The corporate venturer prefers the corporation to be the venture's banker, consultant, and resource supplier. Within these boundaries, the manager wants to be as autonomous as possible and to run the show on an as-if basis, that is, as if it were independent.

Corporateur Characteristics

The quasi entrepreneur who makes a venture manager is best thought of as a "corporateur," an entrepreneurial corporate manager as distinguished from a true entrepreneur. Many companies try to prescribe a corporateur's characteristics. Some look for "self-starting, smart, imaginative marketing people with proved product management capabilities and entrepreneurial instincts." Others say they want "practical conceptualizers with inventive and inquiring minds who are sufficiently entrepreneurially oriented and profit-conscious to accept full responsibility for innovative application of technological concepts into viable commercial ventures." Exhibit 5-1 shows a consumer company's checklist of fifteen corporateur characteristics.

> **Use Planning Page 22 to work out the corporateur characteristics that are important to the management of your venture.**

Guidelines for Manager Selection

Venture capitalists have formulated guidelines for selecting and evaluating venture managers as the single most important form of insurance for their investments. Some of these guidelines are equally applicable to corporateurs:

1. The manager must devote full time to building the venture's business. No other demands must be permitted to distract the manager.

2. The manager must have some previous experience in the venture's industry. At the very least, the manager must speak the industry's language and know the way around.

3. The manager must have a strong personal stake in the business. Some form of financial stake is essential. An intense and unswerving emotional commitment is also essential.

4. The manager must agree that the reward is worth the effort. Since the effort is great, the reward must be acknowledged as being significantly greater.

5. The manager must build fail-safe organizational and operating procedures into the venture so that the manager's line

exhibit 5.1

corporateur characteristics

1. Ability to manage corporate assets to get maximum yield

2. Ability to manage the creativity of others

3. Practical judgment; ability to sense market opportunity

4. Energy and ego drive; a temperament not easily discouraged; stamina and stick-to-itiveness

5. High propensity to accept medium risk

6. Semiruthlessness in making necessary trade-offs

7. High tolerance for ambiguity and uncertainty; ability to work with a minimal fact base

8. Ability to initiate without supervision

9. Flexibility; ability to implement and innovate in the absence of ground rules

10. Ability to perform several functions alone if necessary without needing an organization for everything.

11. Ability as a good salesperson to keep top management sold

12. Market sensitivity

13. A winner's personality that expresses leadership and can motivate others

14. Desire

15. Luck

VENTURE MANAGER—CORPORATEUR CHARACTERISTICS

of succession is provided for as soon as possible. The venture must not be exposed to a leadership crisis.

Management Style and Functional Concentration

Of all the characteristics which may be necessary or simply desirable in a venture manager, omitting those that seem to call for a new Messiah, two major attributes appear from experience to be paramount. One is concerned with four aspects of a venture manager's *management style*. The second is concerned with three aspects of a venture manager's *functional concentration*.

Four aspects of management style

1. Emphasis on innovation to force a high rate of change within compressed time frames

2. Personal identification with the venture as "my business" by applying individual leadership styles and organizational formats

3. Insistence on superior rewards with early payout

4. Persuasive leadership, relying on personal decision making rather than on participative consensus agreement or working with and through others

Three aspects of functional concentration

1. Marketing concentration as the major source of venture growth

2. Short-term strategy planning, accepting short time frames for planning and executing venture development and market entry strategies

3. Management concentration on a few key people rather than on broadscale functions

Position Description Keystones

On the basis of the characteristics of management style and functional concentration which a venture manager appears to require, certain keystones of a manager's position description can be defined. These are the venturer's position responsibilities, the position options, and the standards of performance by which the manager will be evaluated.

Position responsibilities may range from creating a venture business concept and planning its market entry to going all the way by taking the venture to market as a full-blown commercial property. The specific responsibilities allocated to a manager will depend on the manager's individual capabilities and on parent company policy. Some managers excel in conceiving venture business opportunities, analyzing their market potential, and planning their penetration. These qualities may not be accompanied by an equal ability to manage the business they have planned in a competitive marketplace. Top management should be able to assign position responsibilities on an individual basis in order to utilize talent resources most ably.

Some managements are wary of what they regard as a turnover trap when a venture that has been planned and organized by a planning type of manager is turned over to a more entrepreneurial manager to carry it to test-marketing and into market launch. This is a procedure that can invite slippage. Even more serious slippage can occur if a nonplanner is made responsible for a venture plan or a planner is assigned chief executive responsibilities. If corporate policy cannot always predetermine the manager mix, the talent base of the managers on hand should be the basis of corporate policy.

The following excerpts from venture manager position descriptions illustrate position responsibilities for a planner-type manager and some position options and position evaluation standards for an entrepreneurial-type manager.

Position responsibilities

In response to self-created concepts for venturable business properties or in response to venturable property suggestions from management, the venture manager will charter a business development mission and organize a project team to create a market entry plan for its commercialization.

Position options

The venture manager may have access as necessary and desired to corporate capabilities on a consultative basis. The manager may have unrestricted access to external talent sources on a consultative basis and may engage external sources of materials and supply and processing capabilities consistent with quality control standards and cost efficiency. The venture manager may, with discretion, acquire external sources of planning and operating talent, materials supply, and processing capability and incorporate them into the venture.

Position evaluation

The standard of performance for the venture manager is met when the manager has completed an acceptable market entry plan for a commercial property whose objectives satisfy corporate requirements and whose property captures its projected profit and market share within the plan's time frame.

Compensation

Venture manager compensation must attract the unusually high-performing contributor and motivate an unusually high contribution. The rewards of venturing should be related directly to contribution and reflect risk. They should also provide flexibility in the way a manager chooses to accept the rewards so that venturers can acquire as much financial independence as their capabilities permit. The earnings environment that surrounds venture business development must be made so attractive that corporateurs cannot resist having a go at it.

Venturers are best compensated according to a cafeteria-style plan which offers an assortment of base salary bonus, profit sharing, and equity participation. Each venturer can assemble the optimal mix of these three types of compensation that is best suited to meet current life-style needs and future financial objectives.

Base Salary Bonus

Since a venture is a short-term, high-risk development, its manager may be motivated by a cash incentive bonus. The bonus may range upward from 50 percent of the manager's base salary to 10 times salary if 100 percent of the venture's objectives are achieved. Stock bonuses of similar value, either in parent company stock or in venture company stock, can also be provided.

Profit Sharing

In one way or another, it is essential that a venture manager share in the profits of his or her enterprise. Profit sharing is the essence of partnership, and the venture manager is top management's partner, not employee, in business growth and diversification.

One form of profit sharing is to award the venture manager a percentage of the venture's annual net profit after taxes in a three-to-five-year time frame following market entry. This period will generally encompass the higher-profit accruing years of the venture's life cycle. Sometimes a venture manager will be invited to share profits calculated in terms of pretax earnings. In either case, the manager's share reflects the venturer's status as a joint venturer.

Equity Participation

Stock ownership, either in the parent company or in the venture company, is a necessary element of venture manager compensation. If a venture is organized as a subsidiary corporation, the manager may be awarded something like an initial 20 percent ownership with a call on 10 to 15 percent more at a multiple of 5 to 10 times earnings. The parent company may retain the option to buy back the stock at the market or other price.

Phantom stock ownership is another agreeable form of equity participation for venturers. As its name implies, no actual stock shares are issued. The venture manager is therefore not required to make any up-front cash outlay. Books are kept on the phantom shares, however, just as if they were real. At the end of a specified period of time, cash or real stock can be awarded according to contribution either at market value or on a per-share earnings basis. Used in this way, phantom stock is a form of deferred profit sharing based on the venture manager's own performance. For this reason, phantom shares are sometimes referred to as performance shares.

> **Use Planning Page 23 to work out a venture manager Position Description.**

VENTURE MANAGER POSITION DESCRIPTION

1. Position responsibilities

These responsibilities will be met when:

2. Position options

These options will be properly managed when:

3. Position rewards

3.1. Base salary

3.2. Base salary bonus

3.3. Profit sharing

3.4. Equity participation

116

Venture Manager Resources

The venture manager's project team should be an organization with minimal resources. There are three resources which are vital to the venture manager. They are the core group around which the venture will be built. One is a *marketing resource* person whose technical expertise is forward-integrated with market needs and who possesses capability in planning and operating the marketing tools of distribution, sales, and advertising by which market needs are fulfilled. The second resource is a *product development resource* person whose technical expertise is backward-integrated with R&D and engineering and forward-integrated with manufacturing. The third resource is a *financial resource* person who can ride herd on venture costs and who can also work out volume/cost relationships, price/value relationships, and pro forma profit plans for the venture's products as they move through their development process. The venture manager's integration with these three essential resources is illustrated in Exhibit 5-2.

As a venture matures, its manager will be faced by recurrent make-or-buy decisions concerning the need for additional resources. In some cases, borrowing from corporate talent pools will be the best action. Otherwise, the manager will have to decide whether to make additions to staff or to buy outside consulting and operating services. The best rule of thumb to follow is "Never make what you can buy outside." Maintaining the leanness of the venture is one of the manager's principal tasks. Exhibit 5-2 shows a minimal venture team staff and some of its externally based support options which are available from inside and outside the parent company.

> Use Planning Page 24 to work out the staffing of your venture team by entering their names on the exhibit. Extend the exhibit to show the staff's relationships with internal and external support service options.

Venture Team Operating Prerogatives

In order to approximate the climate of true entrepreneurial venturing as closely as possible, it is wise for corporate management to grant three prerogatives to a venture team.

The team should, first, be allowed to position itself and operate as if it were a subsidiary spinout of its parent company. It must be conceived of principally as a marketer and only secondarily as a manufacturer. And lastly, it must be recognized as the sole steward of its market so that it can avoid the distractions of intracorporate organizational politics and concentrate on its mission.

exhibit 5-2

minimal venture team
and support services

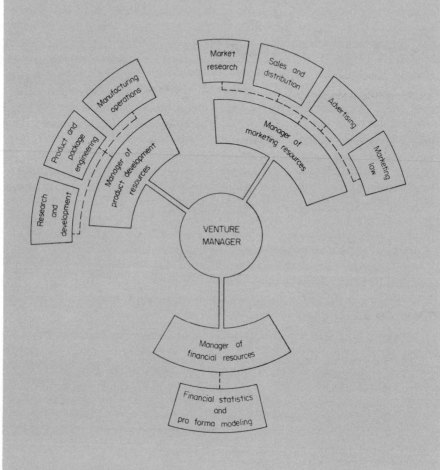

VENTURE TASK TEAM

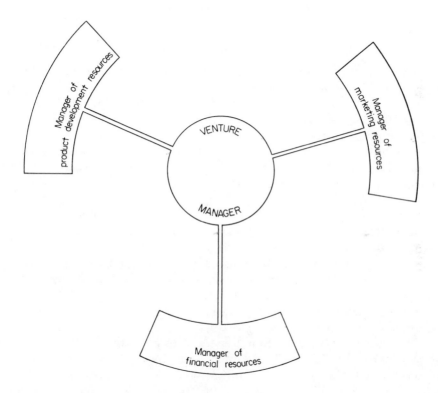

With these prerogatives, the manager and members of a corporate venture team stand the best chance of achieving their fullest realization. The implied status of corporate subsidiary confers autonomy. It acknowledges the venture mission to be considerably more complex than a new-product development team or acquisition team. Emphasizing the venture's marketing function places initial stress in the exact functional area where future stress, at the time of market entry and beyond, will be most severe. By keeping its ventures separate from the political structure of the corporation, top management can help avoid civil wars between the venturers and established corporate divisions or functions.

The Venture Relationship to Corporate Development

New venture business growth is part of an amalgam of management functions called "corporate development" that generally includes long-range planning, mergers and acquisitions, divestitures, licensing, joint ventures, and venture capital planning. Corporate development must report directly to the chief executive officer.

Venture management teams report to a director of corporate development, who is, in effect, their president. Some venture teams take a potential growth opportunity which has been initially screened by the corporate development function and analyze it, develop it into a business, and take it all the way through to commercialization. In other companies, the analytical and development responsibilities are kept separate so that venture staff operations like investigating new opportunities and styling one or more of them into businesses remain the ongoing province of creative imaginators, or "ideaphors." Venture line operations such as commercializing and managing venture businesses are then handed over to managers whose primary relationship to ideas is executive rather than generative.

As a case in point, the four-step venture process of a food producer shown in Exhibit 5-3 can be adapted by many other companies. A corporate Growth Council acts as initial screeners of industries which can offer unusual growth opportunity. The council, which some companies call a New Enterprise Development Group, screens largely in gross according to grandview criteria. It also acts as management consultants to its ventures and extends their lines of credit in its role as investment banker.

The Growth Council passes along its initially screened industry selections to a group of Business Development Greenhouses, each of which is directed by a business development manager. In a greenhouse, a more intensive secondary screening of industry opportunity takes place. Keyhole criteria are applied. Technical research may be commissioned. Business opportunities will be life-styled according to market needs so

exhibit 5.3

four-step venture development process

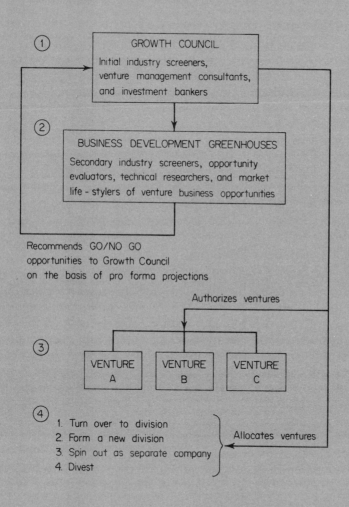

(1) **GROWTH COUNCIL**
Initial industry screeners,
venture management consultants,
and investment bankers

(2) **BUSINESS DEVELOPMENT GREENHOUSES**
Secondary industry screeners, opportunity
evaluators, technical researchers, and market
life-stylers of venture business opportunities

Recommends GO/NO GO
opportunities to Growth Council
on the basis of pro forma projections

Authorizes ventures

(3) VENTURE A   VENTURE B   VENTURE C

(4)
1. Turn over to division
2. Form a new division
3. Spin out as separate company
4. Divest

Allocates ventures

that they can be oriented to their most receptive market. The Growth Council is the wide mouth of the venture funnel. Each greenhouse is an exceedingly fine distillery where probable growth must be judged to be possible or impossible.

The food processor has organized three greenhouses. One is committed to grow business opportunities in new foods, another in nonfood grocery products, and the third in nongrocery products and services of above-average growth opportunity. Each greenhouse manager recommends to the Growth Council GO/NO GO opportunities based on pro forma financial projections of profit and return on investment. The council then authorizes ventures to develop the most promising opportunities. A new food venture might be commissioned to develop protein-based fabricated foods, adult mealtime beverages, nursery school foods, or high-nutritional health foods. A nonfood grocery product venture might be commissioned to develop therapeutic chewing gums, educational toys, and personal care products. A nongrocery product and service venture might be commissioned to develop lawn and garden care products and services, arts and crafts, or preschool learning centers.

Upon successful market entry, the Growth Council will turn over a venture to an existing corporate division, form a new division to accommodate it, spin it out as a separate company, or divest it.

Corporate Development Chartering

The corporate development function is a company's growth and diversification group. It centralizes policy decisions which give the fiscal authorization for ventures to receive their seed money and their secondary financing. A corporate development council always includes the president and vice presidents of marketing, research and development, and finance. It may also include the vice presidents of law and operations along with the directors of corporate planning and operations research. Some companies add two general managers or divisional managers for leavening with real-world attitudes.

Corporate Development Objectives, Responsibilities, and Relationships

If venture growth is to become a continuing corporate policy, the corporate development function will require a set of ground rules to govern the function's operations. In Exhibit 5-4, excerpts are reproduced from a consumer products manufacturer's statement of corporate development objectives, responsibilities, and relationships.

Decentralization with Coordinated Control

A corporate development function can keep new-business profits moving only if it can achieve decentralization with coordinated control. With

exhibit 5-4

corporate development council objectives, responsibilities and relationships

1. Development Council objectives

1.1. Primary objectives: Penetrate one major new domestic business every year through internal development. To ensure proper allocation of development resources, the Development Council will present an annual Business Growth Plan. This plan will provide broad guidelines for total corporate development.

1.2. Secondary objectives: Stimulate and help coordinate corporate growth and diversification. New ideas, concepts and technologies that result from the Development Council's creative concept development, consumer research, and interface with corporate research will be shared with the divisions through close liaison with division development.

To help ensure this coordination, the Development Council will chair a divisional development managers' group that will meet quarterly. Through this group, the Development Council will present its learning discoveries to operating managers throughout the corporation.

2. Development Council responsibilities

2.1. The Development Council will recommend areas of new profit opportunity and a plan for penetrating them. The Development Council will identify major new business opportunities that meet validated consumer needs through a combination of:
   a. Origination of creative new product and service concepts.
   b. Identification of future consumer needs.
   c. Screening of current growth industries.
   d. Close liaison with corporate research to determine emerging technologies that can benefit consumer needs in new and better ways.
   e. Evaluation of ideas and suggestions from outside sources.

2.2. The Development Council will act as the ultimate review authority for corporate development and ensure coordination of the

exhibit 5-4 (Continued)

total development effort. The Development Council will review and endorse:

a. The corporate development department's total growth program, which will be reviewed within the Council every three months.

b. The establishment of all major ventures and allocation of the resources required for their development.

c. The market test of each venture.

d. The national expansion of ventures.

2.3. Plans for the internal development of ventures will be prepared and executed by proved top-caliber venture managers. Internal development of ventures with high probability of success requires that venture managers (a) possess general manager potential, (b) have proved experience in generating new businesses, and (c) command a high degree of respect and acceptance within the corporation.

2.4. Venture managers will evaluate and develop new businesses all the way through to successful national expansion.

a. Once a broad area of interest for development has been uncovered, the Development Council will assign a venture manager to explore the concept. To stimulate involvement and commitment, the manager will be given the option of evaluating each venture against other growth options and recommending the venture which promises the greatest potential success.

   If a business appears to have a potential of at least $25 million in annual net sales, the venture manager will recommend to the Development Council:

   The venture, its anticipated profit return, and rate of return

   The venture's business strategy and plan for market entry

   The dollar and manpower resources required

   A timetable, including key decision and review dates

b. The venture manager will form a team and lead it through test-marketing. At the point of test-marketing, the venture team manager will recommend to the Development Council whether the venture and team should be transferred intact to a compatible division. If the venture does not appear compatible with a line division, test-marketing will become the responsibility of the Development Council.

c. Once a venture business opportunity has been tested successfully in the marketplace, the venture manager will recommend the best plan and organizational form to take the venture on a national basis. The venture manager will be encouraged to lead the venture through to national expansion.

3. Development Council relationships

3.1. Definition of areas of development responsibility: The key to successful growth must be a clear definition and understanding of divisional Areas of Development Responsibility to minimize unplanned overlap. This will help ensure a harmonious corporate effort focused on prime opportunities. It should avoid the conflict and duplication that can arise if (a) divisions use the work of the Development Council as an extension of their own new-product development or (b) the Development Council arbitrarily decides where division development efforts need backstopping.

3.2. No unplanned duplication of effort: The Development Council will not generally duplicate division development efforts. It will concentrate on developing businesses outside division areas of responsibility. Exceptions should be clearly understood, accepted, and coordinated by the organizations involved.

3.3 Ranking development opportunities: Divisions will set specific development objectives for their areas of development responsibility and rank them on a priority basis. The total corporate development plan will then be consolidated on a priority basis. The plan will be reviewed by the Development Council, and reallocations of development resources will be recommended for approval. The Development Council will recommend the ventures to be developed, the broad strategy for their development, and the time, manpower, and dollar resources required.

growth industry selection, priority policy making, and venture banking under their control, corporate development managers can afford to give their ventures broad operating autonomy with consultative guidance. Corporate developers must make sure that venture managers are on plan. They must counsel against a venturer's temptation to work on too many projects at once or on "Mickey Mouse" projects which have small substance but seem to show progress. And they must be alert to counsel against the assumption of many venture managers that everything should be carefully documented and highly detailed, with all options worked out in advance, before any action can be taken. Intellectual rationalization rather than empirical demonstration in every instance must be encouraged.

Most development committees will have to get used to living with looser controls over their venture operations than they exercise over their traditional line divisions. How far a company goes in decentralizing venture operating control will have to be each management's decision, tempered by the trade-off that must always be made between management's need for comfort and its faith in the quality of its venture managers. The paramount question which corporate development must ask is "Which business ventures are competitive investments?" This will determine how venture resources are allocated and when a venture manager's decisions must be overridden.

The Skunk Works Approach

One of the looser forms of control is exemplified by the "skunk works" approach to venture organizations, which originated at the Advanced Development Projects Division of the Lockheed Aircraft Corporation. A skunk works was initially a small team of highly trained specialists who came together to do a certain job that was defined only in general terms and who were then left pretty much alone to do it. The well-known U-2 reconnaissance aircraft is a product of Lockheed's skunk works. When applied to venturing, the skunk works concept frees a venture team from many traditional requirements such as overly close supervision by management, voluminous progress reports, and rigid, detailed development specifications that limit design or operational trade-offs. Skunk works venture teams have a general charter but a reasonably free hand in how they operate under it. The charter usually includes the following simplified rules, which are intended to prevent overorganizing, overmanning, and overspending:

1. The venture manager must be delegated practically complete control of his program.

2. The number of people having any connection with the skunk works team must be restricted.

3. Great flexibility for introducing innovation and making changes must be provided.

4. Only a minimum number of progress reports should be required.

5. A monthly cost review, covering not only what has been spent and committed but also all projected costs to the conclusion of the program, must be held.

6. Good performance must be rewarded immediately by money payments or other financial compensation.

The explicit freedom of a skunk works environment may be too rich for the blood of many companies. It is nonetheless a good starting point from which successive layers of controls can be added as they are deemed necessary or desirable. The point which the skunk works approach makes, however, is a critical one. In new venture business development, freedom is a vital ingredient.

Skunk works venturing holds out to a corporateur type of venture manager the second-most-compelling incentive after financial reward: freedom to manage according to the manager's own personal preferences and philosophies, unimpeded by close supervision and proscriptive policies. When coupled with financial reward, freedom should make a venture proposition virtually impossible for a corporateur to resist.

6

spinout
venture formats

Instead of a venture task team spinning itself into a brand new business from the ground floor up, a corporate staff or line function can be spun out into a venture corporation of its own. Spinouts are logical extensions of the profit center concept, going one step further to give a business unit its own capital base to fund its activities. Spinouts come in two forms. The *functional spinout* gives autonomy to an existing staff or line function by restructuring its departmental or divisional status as a corporate entity. The spun-out function may then serve its corporate parent and other companies as a supplier of its chartered functions from a new position outside its parent's body. The second form of spinout is the *divested operating unit*.

The term "progeneration" describes corporate growth by internal spinout. Progeneration is the development of venture business opportunities by marketing the income-producing potential of corporate units such as divisions, departments, and service functions outside the corporation. The venture businesses created by progeneration may take the form of wholly owned subsidiaries or of majority-owned public corporations. Even though spun-out ventures are controlled or invested in by their parent companies, they can maintain their own independent line of credit, market image, and investment community recognition and support.

From a structural point of view, there are two kinds of spinouts. Complete spinouts are venture corporations all of whose equity securities are traded publicly. A complete spinout may be an option of choice to enable a company to enter a new business when it has a division whose price/earnings ratio can be higher than its own, when an increased debt capacity for the parent company is desirable, when a division simply cannot be operated cost-effectively within the parent company's management style or under its attitudes toward risk, when its business is unfamiliar to the

129

parent, or when its management team can best be motivated by a small-company entrepreneurial environment and stock-option incentive plans.

Partial spinouts, in which the parent company retains a portion of the new company's stock, may be chosen to raise funds, reward entrepreneurial executives, or take the place of acquisitions when parent company stock is selling at a low price/earnings ratio.

Progenerative Growth Benefits

Growth achieved by either of these two kinds of spinouts allows a company to diversify in the safety of working with known quantities. Management possesses in-house expertise in operating and evaluating each operation, understands its manpower requirements and capabilities, and feels at home with the operation conceptually. Progenerative internal growth can offer three other benefits:

1. Increased opportunity for investment capital and decreased need for long-term indebtedness

If an operation which has been spun out is converted into a corporate subsidiary, it can be used to add demonstrable value to the parent corporation. This is accomplished by public sale of minority holdings in the subsidiary's stock. As an example, Armour & Company spun out its personal care subsidiary, Armour-Dial, Inc. Armour-Dial was a consolidation of two businesses, Armour Grocery Products Company and Armour Pharmaceutical Company. Formerly, these two businesses had been "obscured within the whole of Armour & Company." They were consolidated to "multiply the effectiveness of human resources, establish a market value for the business, and make available a 'currency' to facilitate growth." When Armour-Dial was spun out, the parent company achieved $33 million in new value from its own shareholders at the equivalent of $18.50 per share.

By spinning out subsidaries in this way, the parent company frees them to borrow money on their own without increasing parental long-term debt, restricting its own borrowing powers, freezing its working capital, or diluting stockholders' equity.

2. Spreading entrepreneurial opportunity and its financial rewards across the board

When a spinout is incorporated, its stock can be offered to key employees as well as to the public or parent corporation stockholders. Employee participation in the equity of a spun-out subsidiary can complement regular compensation. It is also a powerful means of attracting entrepreneurs and rewarding them for their performance.

3. *Spreading the profit burden*

As the number of new market-oriented businesses is increased through spinouts, the corporate profit burden can be spread across a larger group of moneymaking product and service systems. The total growth burden is also lifted from new-product operations and dispersed among a wider range of corporate assets.

Functional Spinout Ventures

Most medium-size companies and all large companies possess venture business potential within their own organizations in the form of service functions. Purchasing, personnel and industrial relations, sales, marketing research, R&D, pension fund management, and other typical corporate services are all businesses in miniature. In any major corporation, many services are larger in staffing and more sophisticated in expertise than freestanding companies which perform the same functions. By spinning out its service functions into subsidiary profit centers, a company may be able to capitalize on each spinout's income-producing capability, employ its human and technical resources more fully, and manage it as a venture to penetrate new businesses.

Most companies have had some experience with functional profit centering, either in their own businesses or through doing business with the profit-centered services of other companies. A familiar example is the rental of surplus production time. A company may make its own under-used manufacturing facilities available to other companies or, when over-scheduled itself, contract for the excess plant services of other manufacturers.

It has become relatively common for many companies with electronic data processing facilities to capitalize on some of their investment by renting surplus computer time to outside customers or marketing computerized information, programming, and consultation. Since very few companies utilize their EDP capacity fully on a consistent twenty-four hour, seven-day schedule, selling unused time on a service bureau basis is often a source of profitable business. Also, it is probably one of the easiest services to organize as a profit center. Since EDP is very expensive, the desirability of recovering part of its cost makes a spinout operation relatively easy to sell to management.

What is feasible for production operations and EDP is equally practical for other service functions. In every case, when a function has been spun out, a small skeletal staff is generally left behind in the parent company. As for top executives of the parent organization, their principal contribution is to supply management consultation services to their profit center managers, provide financial guidance and support, and maintain the desired overall corporate image.

Venture spinouts can take a variety of forms and enter a broad range of businesses. As they themselves proliferate to the point where they can become parent companies for their own second-generation spinouts, they can form an ever-widening profit base which enjoys synergies within itself and increased insulation from cyclical economic swings. Venture spinouts are limited only by capability and ingenuity. Some spinout possibilities, like a division or subsidiary that is already semiautonomous, are obvious. Other venture opportunities require greater imagination. Litton Industries, a conglomerate, has spun out a capability called Creative Marketing Management, a consumer products and services marketing consultancy to other companies. Other companies have considered spinning out their top management team as a consultant group to utilize the team's acknowledged executive talents on behalf of noncompetitive organizations.

The following six examples will help illustrate the method and advantages of spinning out an internal venture.

The Commodities Trading Company: a Purchasing Function Spinout

The purchasing organization in many companies is a prime candidate for spinout. As Exhibit 6-1 suggests, a profit-centered purchasing function can extend the range and flexibility of its commodity purchases as well as market its professional knowledge to other companies. By applying modern information-gathering and data processing techniques to the commodities its parent company regularly trades in—metals, grains, oils, fruits and vegetables, livestock, or whatever else—it can record and analyze the market interactions between production, consumption, prices, socioeconomic trends, and expectations.

It can then use this information to improve the long-range forecasts and investment actions of its parent company, noncompetitors, and even direct competitors who can be served on a time-delay basis. In every instance, the commodities company will sell its services at a negotiated price. In its purchasing activities for the parent company, the new profit center can take full advantage of opportunities in its own and related commodities, buying when seasonal, cyclical, or economic conditions warrant rather than just when short-term corporate requirements dictate. In addition, it can speculate in futures.

The Land Development Company: A Real Estate Function Spinout

Many companies are major landowners. For most of them—airlines, railroads, banks, paper companies, growers, and extractive industries—land has served as an object of passive custodial care except when it has been used as a borrowing security. Yet, in a major corporation land and depreciated buildings may represent 10 to 15 percent of total assets. But be-

exhibit 6.1

the holding company concept of functional profit centers

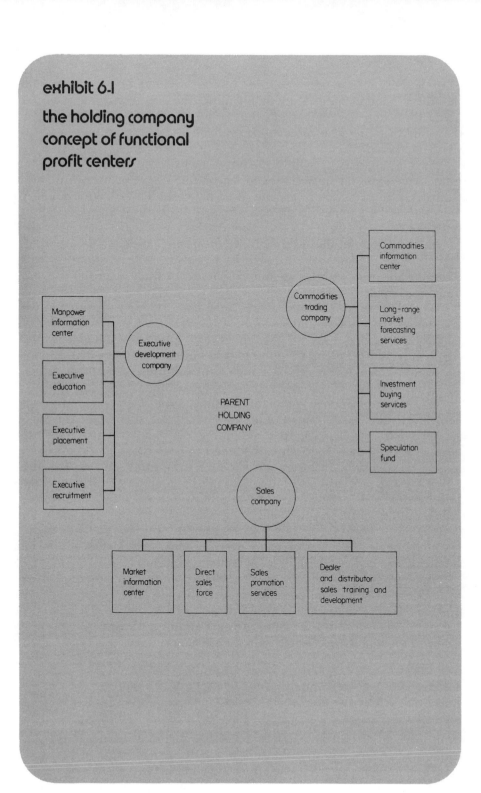

Commodities information center

Commodities trading company

Long-range market forecasting services

Manpower information center

Executive development company

Investment buying services

Executive education

Speculation fund

Executive placement

PARENT HOLDING COMPANY

Executive recruitment

Sales company

Market information center

Direct sales force

Sales promotion services

Dealer and distributor sales training and development

cause real estate is generally carried on the corporate books at cost, with buildings listed at their depreciated value, the stated worth is often far below the actual current market value. It is likely to be even further below the value that could be achieved if the land and buildings were aggressively marketed.

Several companies with a desire to realize the value of their real estate have spun off subsidiaries to manage it: Weyerhaeuser, Ford and Chrysler, Humble, Goodyear, and Westinghouse. The Chevron Land & Development Company is the real estate subsidiary of Standard Oil of California.

By spinning out the responsibility for managing the land and buildings it owns, a company can make its real estate organization a profit-centered business with far greater potentials for profit than the conventional real estate department.

The Norfolk & Western Railway sees real estate ownership and development as a natural adjunct of the railroad's function. On self-owned land long considered merely as right-of-way, N&W has undertaken four commercial and residential ventures on a partnership basis with experienced real estate developers. Through joint ventures, it has extended its diversification into deluxe recreational construction.

In a different industry, the International Paper Company has profit-centered its real estate department. It created a subsidiary land development company to manage its landholdings as vacation and recreation resources. Until then, the company's land had been thought of simply as a large flowerpot for growing trees to produce pulp, paper, and paperboard.

Boise Cascade has also formed a land development company. Like International Paper's subsidiary, this profit center was set up in business to buy land from the parent company at fair market value, prepare it for vacation homes or resort hotels, and then sell to a builder. Land development companies of this type can easily become major factors in on-site second homes as well as mobile and off-site homes.

Among the metal makers, United States Steel has committed itself to building an industrial park on company-owned land in Birmingham, Alabama. The Aluminum Company of America has created a potential spinout in the form of a division, Alcoa Building Industries, to consolidate and expand its real estate operations.

The Executive Development Company: A Personnel and Industrial Relations Functions Spinout

Whether a company grows its own manpower or obtains it in the recruitment market, executive search and development are inescapable costs. Either management supports an internal training and development program or the money goes into headhunting and the hidden costs of on-the-job training. This investment can also be profit-centered in one or both of two ways.

1. Recruitment and placement activities

A personnel department is a counterpart of the purchasing department. One buys the use of commodities, and the other buys the use of people. Under its typically narrow charter, a personnel department recruits only to meet its own needs. Normally, it processes more professional and managerial talent than it can market internally. Yet it does nothing with these marketable "by-products." At most, it stores information about sources of talent in seldom-retrieved, noncomputerized files which only add to its warehousing costs. From time to time, too, it spends money to help relocate the company's own surplus executives who outgrow or are outgrown by the company's evolution.

Combining the personnel and industrial relations departments is the first step toward manpower profit centering. Decentralizing the resulting organization into a subsidiary is the second step. The subsidiary can:

Find professional management for the parent company.

Find management for outside companies, even competitors.

Place the parent company's departing executives with other employers at regular professional fees.

Managed by a professional executive recruiter and operating from an electronically controlled manpower information center, one executive development affiliate is acting as a profit center for several investment banking firms. The New York Securities Company manages its Executive Development Corporation as a recruitment subsidiary for itself and other companies.

2. Educational activities

Just as a company must interview more executive talent than it hires, it also needs more trained entrepreneurs than it is likely to stock at any given time. The traditional in-house management education program is rarely more than a partial answer to the problem. Even when such a program is supplemented by infusions from outside experts or programs of various natures, it is apt to lose more in control and cohesiveness than it gains in professionalism.

An executive development company is a natural device for achieving both professionalism and profit. Some companies are taking initial steps by marketing educational courses. Union Carbide is selling an executive course in management science. Other companies have already created the organizational structure for an educational profit center. IBM's Executive Development Center, General Electric's Management Development Institute, the General Motors Institute, and the RCA Institutes are well-known examples. So are the Western Electric Company's Corporate Education Center, the Holiday Inn University, and Eastman Kodak's Marketing Education Center. The General Motors and RCA Institutes have been opened to outside applicants, in what may be a preview of things to come for other executive education companies.

Ling-Temco-Vought has approached the education center idea from another direction and for a different purpose. Three Texas business schools have been purchased to form one of the divisions of LTV Education Systems, Inc. A second division markets manpower and executive-training programs which the business schools test and sometimes buy.

Both the self-developed institute and the acquired school can meet the need for an educational profit center. The institute or university can be opened to executives outside the parent company in the broadly relevant areas of general management curricula. An acquired business school, on the other hand, is inherently multimarket in its orientation. It can enhance its profit potential by offering continuing courses in professional education for practitioners as well as graduate and undergraduate students. The business school subsidiary can also be a fruitful talent source for the parent company's organization.

The Information Company: A Marketing Research and Library Functions Spinout

Information is a central economic resource. A company's marketing research inventory is an information storehouse of product, promotion, and market knowledge that can act as cerebral capital for growth and development. When this knowledge is computerized for ready storage and retrieved on demand, the marketing research department can become a true information center. The department can act in this capacity for its parent company. It can also provide information services for a wide range of other companies that do business in or with its parent company's industry.

In serving its parent corporation, an information company can supply the information base for corporationwide decision making. Its two basic tools are primary marketing research studies to obtain original data and secondary research into the data banks of other information centers. Of course, most of each information center's primary research data will be proprietary, at least for a time. But every research exploration generates many by-products. These by-products tend to fatten files more than profits. When an information company takes on other customers, the by-products, as well as secondary research data and other knowledge that has become obsolete for corporate purposes, may become marketable.

Many profit-centered information companies have gone into business. McGraw-Hill operated an Electronics Management Center as an independently chartered satellite. Drawing upon the editorial and information resources of *Electronics* magazine, from which it had been spun out, plus those of the magazine's market research department and the corporate research abilities of McGraw-Hill and its subsidiaries, the Electronics Management Center offered information to companies that did business in or with the electronics industry. It made this information available in the multimedia forms of reports, financial and economic advisory services, and other communications.

The Creative Company: An Advertising and Sales Promotion Functions Spinout

Corporate investment in internal advertising and sales promotion services has followed contrasting patterns over the years. Historically, advertising departments have grown into creative centers or house agencies with about the same frequency that house agencies have become advertising departments. Some companies achieve a compromise with a fully staffed creative department that formulates basic strategic planning and product positioning but leaves media placement to an outside agency or media service.

Revlon, Yardley, and Lorillard are among companies which have operated highly sophisticated internal advertising functions. Full creative departments with supporting services have also been founded by a number of other businesses whose volatile nature, like that of the cosmetics industry, requires them to be highly responsive to dynamic consumer buying habit changes. In other cases, their pedestrian nature may make their work unprofitable for an outside organization to service. The Quaker Oats Company, whose cereal markets are highly dynamic, has a house advertising agency suitable for spinout. In much the same way, Pillsbury has organized its agency by consolidating a number of internal advertising, communications, graphic design, and consumer research functions. These agencies earn media commissions to amortize expenses. In a similar manner, United Air Lines spun out its *Mainliner* in-flight magazine as a profit center, including in it all the publication's business and advertising functions. To do this, United organized a subsidiary creative company which publishes its own medium. This company can also be reguarded as a publishing subsidiary with explicit creative company functions.

Spinning out a skilled, experienced advertising department or creative center into an affiliated company allows its talents to be marketed at a profit to other companies in similar or related fields. This also allows them to be made available to regional marketers who are not competitive. For many such clients, access to a professional advertising group with specific experience in its own field offers an otherwise-unavailable and consequently premium source of copy, visual design, account supervision, and press relations. In these areas, General Electric has taken two profit-centered venture steps. Its General Communications Services division, an internal advertising and sales promotion department, has been opened up to outside accounts. So has the General Electric News Bureau, formerly the corporate and product publicity arm of GE's advertising and sales promotion department. Its operations have been spun out to achieve the effect of an independent general public relations firm.

The Sales and Distribution Company: A Sales Function Spinout

Manufacturers' representatives and food brokers are organizations which are actually independent sales departments unencumbered by a manufacturing burden. Each has prospered by supplying sales staffs with an intimate knowledge of local markets. In this way, they can claim to reduce a manufacturer's cost of retail merchandising and allow him to serve wholesalers and retail outlets at a rate that is often about one-third of the cost of an internal sales force. This economic rationale is frequently strengthened by an array of professional marketing services which offer the special skills of setting up in-store or dealer and distributor promotions, displays, and cooperative advertising. In arrangements with jobbers and wholesalers, warehousing may also be made available.

Under the functional profit-centering setup, management seeks to capture the same economies for its own sales department, and to broaden its profit base at the same time, by spinning the department out into a subsidiary sales and distribution company. Uniroyal has done this with its USCO Services subsidiary, which it has established as "physical distribution specialists." USCO provides distribution and warehousing facilities and counsel specializing in such areas as materials management, order processing, and site location. It sees itself principally as a builder of corporate distribution systems.

Once a sales department has been granted autonomy, its services can be retained on a contractual basis by the parent company. Additional prospective clients can be other manufacturers of products that utilize similar distribution channels or must be passed on by similar retail buying personnel. Also prospective are manufacturers who depend on similar sales expertise but are not directly competitive. This enlarged source of "suppliers" broadens the sales company's access to profitable products, helps subsidize its administrative and staff costs, and enables it to offer a comprehensive range of manpower and support services.

Whether the products it sells are manufactured by its parent management or by others, a sales company regards them as essentially agents of exchange for profit. Sales force morale may be bolstered if a more marketable array of high-profit products dominates each salesman's line. His financial reward from selling them can be enlarged by increased salary and commissions. Furthermore, a wider range of products and services ought to mean new learning experiences for salesmen, which are themselves convertible into income.

The Development Company: A Research and Development Function Spinout

Surplus technology is always a potential profit-making spinout. American Standard, General Electric, Boeing, and National Cash Register are among the major companies which market their R&D assets. These assets are in the form of noncommercialized technological expertise or processes which they, as originators, either do not care to exploit further or are unable to market profitably because of shifting market demand or marketing strategies. Even technologies which are usable in-house can often be spun out. Almost every capability has a far wider potential than any one company can capitalize on fully. Furthermore, all companies pay for 100 percent of their R&D, but most of them utilize less than 25 percent of their investment, which, along with other corporate costs, has been rising steadily year by year. Spinning out R&D may be a way to preserve the function's staff capability and motivation in the face of cost squeezes which otherwise would force the reduction or even the dissolution of a research function. It is also a way to reverse the negative cash flow associated with technical staffs and at least break even on their support.

Technical transfers of surplus research may take several forms. All are variations of licensing or sale of patents, products, processing techniques, or even engineering or marketing research studies. Sales may be outright or on a down payment-plus-royalties basis, in which royalties run from ½ percent of sales to 20 percent.

Boeing operates its technology transfers through a subsidiary, Boeing Associated Products. General Electric's Patent and Technology Marketing operation is a function of its internal R&D Center. GE, American Standard, and National Cash Register also publish magazines which list their new product and processing availabilities. Sold on an fee basis, the magazines are additional ventures.

These steps can be viewed as precursors to the eventual spinout of some or all of the R&D function itself in the form of a venture business development company. In it, a unified grouping of technical, marketing, and financial expertise can be pooled. Marketing and R&D can at last be harnessed together organizationally.

The spinout approach has the critical advantage of freeing R&D people from the restrictive traditions of researching in one company. In addition, if the charter of the new subsidiary enables it to contract its abilities not only to its parent company but to noncompetitive clients as well, the scope of its innovative challenge can be considerably broadened. If the subsidiary is separately incorporated, its scientists and engineers can be given a personal equity in the profitability of their creations. They can be compensated for breakthroughs by means of stock options. Innovation can thus become more personally rewarding as well as more professionally challenging.

Operational Spinout Ventures

Any company with a vigorous R&D program eventually finds itself with divisions or departments based on new technologies, new processes, and new products that have somehow become stepchildren. Sometimes these are going but unprofitable businesses. At other times they are marginally unprofitable for years but always threaten to break through into the black. Frequently these stepchildren can be spun out as independent ventures to realize their full profit potential outside their parent company. Before they are spun out into the real world, they must have their businesses planned, market projections firmed up, physical assets such as inventory and equipment transferred, financing arranged, and their management placed in a position to operate. Management may be invited to invest its own money in the venture in return for equity. The parent company is a potential minority investor.

Expansion and diversification through operational and functional spinouts can take two directions:

A *horizontal* approach, which offers the same service to a number of markets.

A *vertical* approach, which offers a variety of services in depth to one market, thereby gaining the economies and efficiencies of synergy.

Horizontal Spinout: Multiple Markets for the Same Service

Multiple marketing is a method of amortizing the initial investment in a spun-out service by spreading its distribution horizontally across a number of markets. For example, the initial investment in setting up a creative company as a house advertising agency for an insurance company can be amortized by taking on related accounts in banking, underwriting, and other financial fields. A land development investment for a paper company can be amortized by marketing its services to individual home builders of vacation housing as well as to light industries interested in an industrial park complex. As Exhibit 6-2 shows, an airline's investment in a hotel reservation service spun out to serve vacationers can be recaptured on a multiple-market basis by offering its services to business convention groups. In all three cases, the same basic service is marketable horizontally across more than one market segment.

Use Planning Page 25 to work out a Horizontal-Spinout Venture Proposal.

exhibit 6-2

multiple markets for
the same airline service

Key

○ ◌ Airline originating service

⊏⊐ Markets

Business travel and convention market

Personal travel and vacation market

RENTAL CAR
RESERVATION
SERVICE

AIRLINE
RESERVATION
SERVICE

EDP
CAPABILITY

HOTEL-MOTEL
RESERVATION
SERVICE

Combination business, personal travel and vacation, and convention market

HORIZONTAL—SPINOUT VENTURE PROPOSAL

1. Spin out the (function) _____

2. To yield a return of:

        2.1. $___,___,___ net profit

        2.2. __% return on investment

        2.3. By Year (F19__–F19__)

3. By providing (the service) of _____

    _____

4. To the following market(s):

        4.1. _____

        4.2. _____

        4.3. _____

143

Vertical Spinout: Multiple Services for the Same Market

Multiple servicing is a method of amortizing management's investment in its basic corporate image by spreading its distribution upward and downward in the same vertical market segment. It is a means of multiplying the mileage of an undercapitalized image. Image value can be increased by enhancing its meaning in a market where image acceptance has already been established. An airline, for example, may already have a high image investment among businessmen. But the sole service it may be providing them is personal transportation. Its image, assuming it to be favorable, is being underutilized. That is, the market will accept more services from the supplier than are being offered. A credit balance exists that is not being spent.

As Exhibit 6-3 shows, an airline may be able to offer multiple services to its businessman market through spun-out functions such as sales and maintenance for the businessman's corporate aircraft or other companies dealing with fixed-base sales; service and flight instruction for the businessman in his life-style role as private aircraft owner and pilot; general or specialized automobile rental for the businessman as surface traveler; maintenance for the businessman's sales or materials-handling vehicle fleets; and corporate transportation consultation services to analyze company personnel travel patterns, evaluate the cost efficiency of the corporate travel mix, and recommend the optimal combination of vehicle and aircraft ownership or leasing. By offering multiple services to the same market in this way, a company can position its original business, and consequently its image, as the core of an overall system. An airline which defines its business as a distribution business can position itself broadly as a "one-airline distribution services company" which offers the distribution services of one airline plus other distribution services of a related nature to the same market.

A "one-bank financial management company" positioning allows a bank holding company to establish or acquire subsidiary money management services. Many existing bank departments can be spun out into such subsidiaries. Prime candidates for progeneration are a bank's equipment-leasing departments and its factoring and traveler's check functions. Other areas of bank expertise available for spinout include plant location services, acquisition and merger services, property management, and mortgage services. Trust services, estate-planning services, and automatic payment plans can be combined into an overall personal money management company. In a similar manner, a "one-brewery refreshment products company" can be created to serve diversified markets with related food and beverage businesses.

Use Planning Page 26 to work out a Vertical-Spinout Venture Proposal.

exhibit 6.3

multiple airline services
for the same market

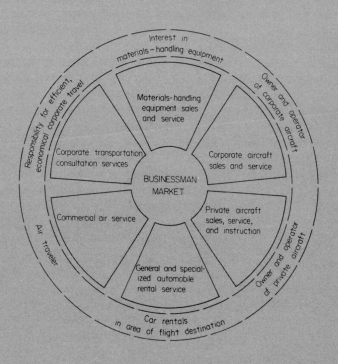

⬠ Airline-created services

⊏⊐ Interests of business
executives

VERTICAL–SPINOUT VENTURE PROPOSAL

1. Spin out the (function) ——————————————————————

2. To yield a return of:

        2.1. $___,___,___ net profit

        2.2. __% return on investment

        2.3. By Year (F19__–F19__)

3. By providing (the market) ——————————————————

4. With the following service(s):

        4.1. ——————————————————

        4.2. ——————————————————

        4.3. ——————————————————

146

Second-Generation Spinouts

Many spinouts perform so profitably that a second generation of satellites will be called for. Exhibit 6-4 illustrates one such corporate possibility. A sales department has been spun out of its parent as a sales company. The sales company has developed its markets so successfully that a second-generation spinout has taken place in the form of a company to help dealers and distributors recruit, train, motivate, and manage their own sales forces. In this case, a spun-out child has become a parent. Similarly, as the first-generation executive development company has succeeded, a second-generation organization for consultation in career planning has been formed. And as the first-generation venture company has moved into new development areas, the need for two second-generation venture specialist spinouts has materialized.

Parent-Child Relationships

Two characteristics distinguish the relationships of a parent company and its spinouts in a progenerative corporation:

1. The parent and each subsidiary are profit sources for each other.

2. Each does business with the other on a voluntary, contractual basis. It is inherent in the concept of a progenerative organization that its spinouts need not accept a work assignment from the parent company. Nor is a parent under obligation to invite project proposals from its spinouts. Profit, not proximity, determines who will work with whom. If a parent company can obtain a better price or performance elsewhere, it must reserve the right to allocate its resources to another supplier. And if a spinout cannot take a job for its parent company without sacrificing cost efficiency standards of its own, it must reserve the right to decline.

The eventual working relationship between the two types of organization should reflect the degree to which the parent has found a spinout to be a preferred supplier and to which the spinout has identified the parent as a good customer. The relationship works the other way, too. A spinout can be a customer of its parent, and the parent can be a supplier to its spinout. Here again, though, the working pattern should be free from the traditional pressures of reciprocity and the narrow economies of make-or-buy decisions.

There will be many cases, especially at the outset, when a newly spun-out subsidiary and its parent company will be heavy users of each other's products and services. But a long period of overly close marketing relations between a parent and its spinouts should be avoided if each spinout is to establish a true identity of its own. If it is to be able to enter each contractual negotiation with its parent from a position of strength, a spinout must command a sufficient market outside the parent company's business. Its right to refuse the parent's business or to improve its bargaining power in soliciting it will vary directly with the size and strength of its non-parent-company market. This puts pressure on every satellite to be an avid marketer.

Ideally, a spinout should attempt to develop up to 50 percent of its business from sources external to the parent corporation. This objective should be made explicit in the subsidiary's charter and be implicit in the parent's managerial policies. The market orientation of a spun-out service should be top management's first order of business.

Naturally, there can be disappointments in the performance of newly spun-out organizations. When such a case occurs, the management of the parent company should not commit itself to pumping business through a high-cost, low-efficiency venture satellite just to keep it alive. If the spinout is not viable in the competitive marketplace, it should be scrapped and a new spinout orbited in its place.

Use Planning Page 27 to work out a second-generation projection for the horizontal spinout you have proposed on Planning Page 25. Then use Planning Page 28 to work out a second-generation projection for the vertical spinout you have proposed on Planning Page 26.

exhibit 6-4

second-generation spinouts

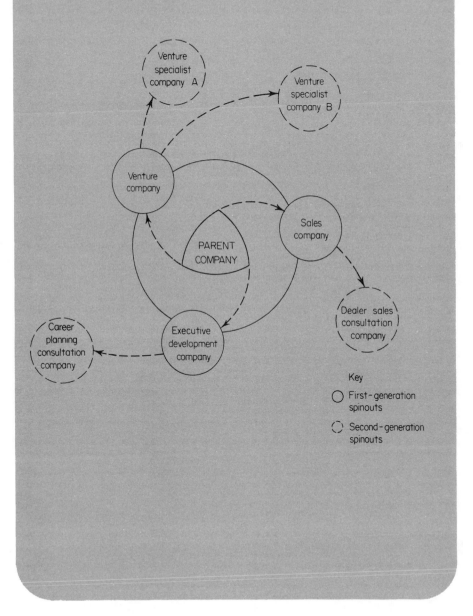

SECOND—GENERATION SPINOUT PROJECTION
for

(Horizontal—spinout function proposed on Planning Page 25)

1. Business definition

2. To provide (the service) _____

3. To the following market(s):
    3.1.

    3.2.

    3.3.

SECOND-GENERATION SPINOUT PROJECTION
for

_____

(Vertical-spinout function proposed on Planning Page 26)

1. Business definition

2. To provide (the market) _____

3. With the following service(s):

   3.1.

   3.2.

   3.3.

7

invertment, acquirition, and joint-venture formatr

A company that is not growth-based—that is, that has no technical or marketing leverage for entry into new businesses—must go outside for its diversification. But even when internal development is a feasible strategy, it can often be supplemented or complemented by one of three venture formats: minority investment in smaller companies, acquisition of footholds in new businesses through majority investment or buy-out, and cooperative joint ventures.

Minority-Investment Ventures

Minority investment is a cooperative format for venturing. One company, usually the larger one, makes an investment of less than 50 percent in a smaller or younger company. As a rule, the investing venturer will seek to control between 20 and 45 percent of each company whose growth it sponsors in its role as a minority venture capitalist.

A minority-interest venture investment can have one of three objectives. It can be a learning experience, enabling a company to feel out on a small scale what it would be like to be in a new business: what the technological requirements are, or what the marketing problems can be. Investment in this case is the same as financing a continuing market research project. A corporate venture team may be the actual investor. It may invest on behalf of exploring its chartered business area or one adjacent to its main interests or an area which might represent a logical follow on. Second, a minority investment can represent a foothold acquisition possibility. Finally, it can represent a short-term investment opportunity which may result in taking the sponsored business into public ownership. In this last instance, the venture investment is similar to a loan.

Alcoa, the American Can Company, General Electric, and Union

153

Carbide are among dozens of major corporations which have been active venture capital investors in smaller companies. Exxon Enterprises is interested in a wide range of venture opportunities. The Dow Chemical Investment & Finance Corporation seeks broad-scale opportunities to diversify and develop new products. The Johnson & Johnson Development Corporation is a venture capital company which invests in smaller health care businesses.

Sometimes the smaller companies are spinouts from their own investing parent companies. The parent companies divest themselves of them because they have been unprofitable but invest in them because they want to share in the rewards of what they suspect may be eventual commercial success. An investing company's interest may be expressed initially in the form of a client-consultant relationship. The company can then move to the private investment stage. A usual investment ranges from as little as $50,000 to $1 million or more. Sometimes an independent venture capital investor is invited to become a third party to the deal. In such cases, the venture becomes a three-legged stool on which the investing corporation, the outside investors, and the venture principals all sit in minority positions.

Since there are no formal reporting requirements for corporate venture investments, a high level of secrecy can usually be maintained. So can a high level of involvement. A worthwhile rule followed by many minority-interest ventures is for the gardener to follow the seed. Whenever seed capital is invested, the investor will safeguard its position by the additional investment of its own management talent. This may take the form of a board directorate and a consultative relationship with the venture, generally in the areas of marketing and finance.

While ground rules vary among minority investing companies, almost all of them look for certain characteristics in a venture investment. Typically, a gain of 5 times the initial investment over a two-to-three-year period, with a 10-times gain over three to four years, is desired. Within three to five years, a normally expected return on investment is 20 percent. A minimum patience time of three to five years will probably be required for most investment situations. Even then, as General Electric's investment subsidiary, Business Development Services, Inc., believes, "Out of every ten investments made, 2 or 3 will go down the tube, 3 or 4 will rock along, and the remainder may prove outstanding."

At the point where the initial investment has grown 10 times, buyout may be an option. If it is exercised, the company can then be merged into the investing corporation as a new department or as part of an existing division or be managed as a subsidiary.

Small private companies in an early developmental stage of growth, but still lacking an assured, long-term income-generating capability or broad market acceptance, are among the best prospects for investment venturing. This means that a company will have structured its administrative organization, completed its product or service prototyping, and initiated its maiden marketing over a two-to-three-year period. A sufficient track record of operating history then exists to provide a basis for judgment about the prime criterion of entrepreneurial management competence. It is squarely on management competence that further development will rest. Without it, it is unlikely that the business will be able to develop into a substantially larger enterprise which can obtain a significant share of a relatively large market. Management competence will also determine the ability of the business to yield a rate of return on its investment sufficient to finance much if not all of its further growth from internal funding, without additional borrowing, secondary investment, or a premature public offering. In exceptional cases, an investing venturer will consider new companies which have no previous operating record. Investments of this type depend wholly on subjective interpretation of a new company's business plans and the previously demonstrated managerial and technical experience of its principals. Taken together, they must outweigh the absence of an operating history as a going business.

> **Use Planning Page 29 to work out a Minority-Investment Venture Proposal.**

Foothold Acquisition Ventures

An independent company, preferably small and possessing an established product line and distribution system, can be purchased to give the acquiring company an immediate foothold in a venture business. Along with immediate entry, the start-up costs and many of the time lags associated with internal development may be avoided. In this way, foothold acquisitions or their smaller versions, toehold acquisitions, may represent a simplified means of entering new-business areas in high-growth fields.

A foothold acquisition made as a venture should be undertaken for operational reasons and not simply for short-term financial benefits. Generally, a venture acquisition represents a trade-off. On the one hand, there are the emotional and dollar values of the acquiring company's desire to get into a new business quickly and surely. On the other hand, there is the cost of buying someone else's successful venture experience. Another major consideration is the cost effectiveness of the acquiring company's R&D function, which sets a floor for make-or-buy venture decisions.

Acquisition criteria, like the selection criteria for internal venturing, vary significantly among venturers. Some selection standards are nevertheless fairly well agreed on. First, foothold acquisitions should be in businesses which the acquirer knows something about. This means that

MINORITY—INVESTMENT VENTURE PROPOSAL

1. Objectives of investment

    1.1. Business objectives

    1.2. Financial objectives

        1.2.1. Anticipated gain on investment of
            $___,___,___ over ____ years

        1.2.2. Anticipated return on investment of __%
            over ____ years

        1.2.3. Anticipated positive cash flow commencing in Year __
            (F19__-F19__)

156

2. Business name and definition

    2.1. Annual gross sales volume:
        2.1.1. Dollars: $___,___,___
        2.1.2. Units: #___,___,___

    2.2. Profit on sales: $ __,___,___

    2.3. Earned on capitalization of: $___,___,___

    2.4. Investment required for 5% control: $ __,___,___

3. Products or services and markets

they should be more or less natural extensions. Second, an acquired company must have proved management that is willing to stay on. Third, an acquired company should not dilute the acquirer's earnings.

Several other criteria are also common. A foothold's size should be large enough to provide all the necessary operating skills in sufficient depth so that it can continue to operate successfully without major intervention from the acquiring company. The foothold should also be well enough established to have strong industry contacts and customer relationships. It ought not to be so large, however, that it dominates its industry. No major parts of the foothold's business should be outside the acquirer's area of interest. If they are, their subsequent spinoff should be relatively well assured beforehand.

Most acquiring companies prefer acquisitions which offer the opportunity to increase their profits per share within a reasonably short period. Some acquirers also seek acquisitions whose capability base can put them into more than one industry segment or life-styled market. Almost without exception, acquirers insist on compatibility: a reputation with key trade, professional, and customer groups that is comfortably in keeping with the acquiring company's self-image. Furthermore, the acquisition's key people should be compatible with the acquirer's key people. Incompatibility is often the chief hang-up in acquisition venturing. Small-company entrepreneurs are frequently incompatible with large-company managers simply by nature. Nor is their accustomed autonomy easily yielded, no matter how gingerly the acquiring company infuses its management people and controls. As a result, many acquired venture businesses eventually become gutted after acquisition by the defection and dissaffection of their original key people. Often, only the corporate shells remain.

In Exhibit 7-1, model ground rules are summarized for a food-processing company's foothold acquisitions. Exhibits 7-2 and 7-3 show the company's evaluation criteria on a general industry basis and for specific candidates.

> **Use Planning Pages 30 and 31 to work out criteria for evaluating an industry for entry via acquisition and criteria for evaluating a candidate company within the industry. Then use Planning Page 32 to work out a Foothold Acquisition Venture Proposal.**

Joint Ventures

Joint ventures are typically intercorporate. The resources of one company are allied with those of another, which is preferably of similar size and stature in a noncompetitive industry. Each venturer puts up a 50 percent interest and splits the pie in the same proportion. Joint venturers are

exhibit 7.1

ground rules for
acquisition evaluation

1. It is not likely that an acquisition candidate will fully satisfy all our criteria. It is more important that the evaluation quickly establish which criteria are not met and whether those not met cannot be met and are essential enough to disqualify the candidate.
   a. Our efforts should be addressed to making a yes-or-no decision on candidate eligibility prior to investing time and effort in an intensified evaluation study.

2. We will not undertake an evaluation of any industry which will require more than three months' elapsed time to complete a pro-and-con study to determine our interest. There should be enough public data available or readily obtainable through preliminary fieldwork without engaging in protracted investigation.
   a. If an industry is of such a character that it does not meet the critical established criteria, we should avoid involvement.

3. Once we identify and get in touch with a company, we should have the stage set so that in the event of an expression of positive interest we can advance to final negotiations within thirty days of the initial contact. In the event of a clearly negative response, we should be prepared to move on quickly.

4. We will not reopen a previously rejected industry unless a significant new development that warrants a new review has been identified.

5. We will avoid industries:
   a. Which derive profits from an agricultural base
   b. Whose source of revenue is under federal, state, or local government control through a regulated rate or pricing structure
   c. Whose practice and ethics in any important way fall short of our own

6. Where and when feasible, a timetable should be established leading to acquisition. Should anything occur which delays this timetable (for example, more fieldwork or a reordering of our priorities), the delaying reasons should be clearly communicated.

exhibit 7.2

criteria for evaluating an industry
for entry via acquisition

1. The industry should be large and fast-growing.
   a. As a benchmark, the growth rate should exceed 8 percent a year.
   b. Embryo types of farther-out industries, while not entirely satisfying this criterion, should be considered for their latent profit potential.

2. Entry via acquisition should be free of unfavorable legal implications. We must avoid:
   a. Any food or beverage company
   b. Any other company selling products that are presold to consumers with advertising and promotion of the same general type used by grocery product companies if the acquired company is among the top eight producers in a product line or has more than 5 percent of a relevant market by geographic area or by product line
   c. Any other company which is among the leading producers in any concentrated industry
   d. Any other company which is in an industry composed basically of firms of relatively small size
   e. Any other company in an industry in which we can be considered to be a potential competitor
   f. Any other company engaged in a business in which combination with us may develop a substantial potential for reciprocity

3. Products or services should be broadly purchased.

4. We should be able to make a contribution to maximize profits by drawing on one or several of our principal resources:
   4.1. Marketing expertise
   4.2. Technical expertise
   4.3. Financial expertise in profit maximization
   4.4. Capital sourcing
   4.5. Product development
   4.6. Management organization
   4.7. International operations

5. The industry should be an innovation-oriented industry offering multiple new business or product development opportunities, or both.

6. The industry should be profit-oriented, have a consistent record of continued profit performance, and offer a satisfactory return on equity.

7. The industry should be compatible with our self-professed character and known reputation.

8. The competitive nature and climate should be sufficiently favorable for an acquisition to grow at a faster rate than our own industry.

exhibit 7.3

criteria for evaluating
a candidate company
for acquisition

1. The acquisition should be legally defensible.

2. A candidate should have the potential to increase our earnings per share in the first full year of ownership.

3. The purchase price should permit a 15 percent aftertax return on equity within ten years.

4. A candidate should have or be capable of producing a profit before taxes on net sales of 12 percent.

5. Products or services should appeal to broad masses of consumers and be compatible with demographic, economic, and social trends.

6. A candidate should offer the capability of developing a national consumer or industrial franchise.

7. The candidate's capable and motivated management will stay on after the acquisition with affordable and mutually satisfactory incentives. As an acceptable alternative, we can provide or readily obtain new management talent.

8. The personality of an acquisition candidate's management is compatible with that of our own management.

9. There is agreement with the acquired management on the broad approaches and direction for managing the business over the next five years.

10. Company products or services should have or be capable of developing a sound reputation for their price/value relationship.

11. The product line is expandable and responsive to new-product innovations.

12. The company is now, or has the capability of, operating profitably on a consistent basis.

CRITERIA FOR EVALUATING AN INDUSTRY
FOR ENTRY VIA ACQUISITION

CRITERIA FOR EVALUATING A CANDIDATE COMPANY FOR ACQUISITION

FOOTHOLD ACQUISITION VENTURE PROPOSAL

1. Objectives of acquisition

   1.1. Business objectives

   1.2. Financial objectives

      1.2.1. Anticipated return on investment of __%
over ____ years

      1.2.2. Anticipated net profits of $__,___,___
by Year __

      1.2.3. Anticipated average monthly cash flow of
$_,___,___ by Year __ (F19__-F19__)

164

2. Business name and definition

    2.1. Annual gross sales volume:
             2.1.1. Dollars: $___,___,___
             2.1.2. Units: #___,___,___

    2.2. Profit on sales: $__,___,___

    2.3. Earned on capitalization of: $___,___,___

    2.4. Investment required to acquire: $___,___,___

3. Products or services and markets

usually companies possessing uncommon technologies but a shared interest in serving a common market. Such an intercorporate venture might be organized between a cereal maker and a drug manufacturer to examine the technical feasibility and market acceptance of anticaries breakfast foods which would be nutritionally fortified and dentally therapeutic.

Joint ventures can also be put together between customers and suppliers. There is abundant precedent in many industries for this type of venture format.

In building its 1011 air bus, Lockheed Aircraft Corporation established a joint-venture approach. Lockheed made its avionics suppliers codevelopers rather than continuing to treat them solely as vendors who furnished systems to meet internally generated specifications. Lockheed's codevelopers acted traditionally in designing electronic flight control systems for the air bus. But they also assisted Lockheed in originating the way in which their subsystems were integrated into the airplane's overall operations. Not only were the suppliers involved in air bus design from its beginning; they were also on notice that, as Lockheed explained, they would "share a lot of the responsibility if the system doesn't work."

Joint venturers must overcome serious obstacles to make a mutual enterprise operational: problems of sharing with a supplier the proprietary thinking involved in an original equipment manufacturer's long-range planning, problems of maintaining confidentiality on both sides, and the mutual financial and legal hazards of commitment to a single supplier or customer. These obstacles are often counterbalanced by the risk of developing long-range projects independently. "What will you need from *us* over the next years?" is the supplier's key question that energizes his contribution to the joint venture. Since the answer to the return question "What can we expect from *you* over the next years?" is a vital factor in the original equipment manufacturer's long-range plan, a natural union of interest can exist.

The Continental Can Company and Ralston Purina formed a joint venture known as Ralcon Foods to produce and market soy protein products to be used as meat, poultry, and seafood analogs as well as animal protein boosters. In this venture, Ralston contributes vegetable protein technology. Continental contributes sales and marketing capability centered in its protein-casing business experience with the processed-meat industry. Continental has also formed joint ventures with brewers "to maximize the brewer's marketing advantages while minimizing his packaging and distribution costs by installing high-speed can-manufacturing lines on brewery premises, to be owned and operated by the can supplier, and to be technically serviced by him, under the auspices of a jointly created long-range marketing plan designed to optimize the profitable sales of its yield in canned beer." As in all customer-supplier joint ventures, lowered-risk financial and marketing advantages for both parties are the overriding objective.

Tax accounting practices sometimes favor the partnership form of business for joint ventures. Instead of forming a new corporation in which each venturer acquires 50 percent of the stock, the two companies setting up a joint business can each create a 100 percent-owned subsidiary. The subsidiaries can then create an unincorporated 50-50 joint venture. Initial tax losses can flow directly to the subsidiaries since they are now the joint venturers. Because each subsidiary is included in the consolidated tax return of its parent, current utilization of tax losses is permissible. If the joint venture has later profits, they can be taxed to the subsidiaries. In turn, the subsidiaries can remit the profits to their parents without paying an intercompany dividends tax. This arrangement can provide maximum tax advantages in the event of joint-venture tax losses or profits while still maintaining limited liability.

Use Planning Page 33 to work out a Joint-Venture Proposal.

JOINT VENTURE PROPOSAL

1. Objectives of joint venture

    1.1. Business objectives

    1.2. Financial objectives

        1.2.1. Anticipated return on investment of __%
over __ years

        1.2.2. Anticipated net profits of $__,___,___
by Year __ (F19__-F19__)

        1.2.3. Anticipated average monthly cash flow of $_,___,___
by Year __ (F19__-F19__)

2. Joint-venture name and technical capability

168

3. Common market to be served

4. Products or services to be offered

    4.1. Anticipated annual gross sales volume:

        4.1.1. Dollars: $__,___,___

        4.1.2. Units: #__,___,___

    4.2. Profit on sales: $ __,___,___

how to set
venture objectives

8

venture assumptions

Ventures are selected today for tomorrow. Inevitably, then, only some of the facts required to support venture objectives are knowable when the decision to go must be made. Other facts, and important ones, remain unknowable. They must be assumed. These assumptions about the unknowables become the most perilous commitment of the venture-planning process. When they are right, they may be the principal, if an unheralded, reason for venture success. When they are wrong, assumptions are the main reason why ventures fail.

An assumption is an attempt to assess the certainty of a future event. It is a venture manager's calculation of a risk whose exact time and probability of occurrence are unknown. In this sense, assumptions provide a venture's missing link. They fill the gap between the fact base, which, because it records the past, is entirely knowable, and the venture's objectives, which are pledged to become eventual facts. Between the knowables and the objectives is a small group of unknowables. Since they cannot be known, they must be dealt with in an as-if manner: as if they were known.

If a venture manager handles the as-if process poorly, venture breakdown may result. Sometimes a venture falls apart while it is still in its development process. From an emotional point of view, an early breakdown can be devastating. But from a cost effectiveness perspective, ventures that come unglued while they are in the house are the lucky ones. Three well-known examples of venture products that succumbed expensively in the real world because of incorrect assumptions are found in the recent history of the aircraft industry.

Penalties of Incorrect Assumptions

An Incorrect Assumption about Market Trends

General Dynamics produced the Convair 880 on the assumption that the preferences of the airline industry were moving in the direction of speed even at the expense of payload. To gain speed at the upper limits of the subsonic range, the 880 was built with a thin body which contained one less seat in each row over the entire length of the cabin. This reduced the plane's earning capacity by 18 percent, a price airlines found to be an unacceptable trade-off for a few miles per hour of extra speed. The Convair venture failed to break even.

An Incorrect Assumption about Competition

Lockheed produced the Electra on the assumption that competitors would permit it to squeeze one more generation of short-haul aircraft out of piston power before they could engineer sufficient economy into pure jet engines. The Electra's designers created an airplane that acceptably exploited the lower-cost capability of the turboprop engine. But competitive turbojet aircraft appeared on the market much sooner than Lockheed had expected. The performance characteristics of the turbojets made them cheaper to operate for short as well as long hauls. The Electra's life cycle was profitlessly foreshortened.

An Incorrect Assumption about Technology

Douglas produced the DC-7 on the assumption that the technological state of the art of engine design would progress fast enough to deliver a power plant to fit the airframe weight of the new plane. But the required lift capacity and range were not forthcoming. Because the DC-7 flew under constant strain, downtime from engine failure was frequent. Neither the speed nor the altitude necessary to fly the aircraft at a profit could be delivered with consistency.

Good Assumers: Rare Birds of Venturing

Good venture managers, in common with all good management men and women, are good assumers. The best of them make correct assumptions intuitively. They are credited with having a gut feeling for running a business. But the history of new business ventures, in fact, the history of business, demonstrates convincingly that good assumers are rare birds.

Boeing's William Allen assumed the jet aircraft engine could bring a unique business value to commercial flying. Donald Douglas thought so too but assumed the jet's unique values would wait. Along with Lockheed, he tried to milk one more generation of profit from piston-powered aircraft. As a result, Boeing captured the commercial airline market from both of them.

Allen had apparently learned from the experience of Baldwin Locomotive and American Locomotive, both of which had assumed that the steam engine would go on forever as the basic railroad power plant. While they were steadfastly rejecting the diesel engine as the successor to steam, General Motors became interested in applying diesel power to rails. Because GM was neither a railroad company nor a locomotive manufacturer, it was free to make assumptions based on market needs and not on steam. It came to dominate almost three-quarters of the United States locomotive market. Neither Baldwin nor American any longer exists. In similar fashion, General Motors was free to make assumptions about the improved cost efficiency which pure jet engines could bring to airplanes while Roy Hurley of Curtiss-Wright, a piston-engine manufacturer with a large aircraft market, did not want to believe the jet was here to stay.

The Boeing and General Motors examples, however, are exceptions to the rule. Their lessons were lost on Gillette, which assumed the stainless-steel razor blade to be an upstart innovation. Wilkinson saw its profit potential. As a result, Gillette's market share fell from 70 to 55 percent in less than eighteen months. In its own way, Gillette was repeating the history of the cigarette business, in which George Washington Hill's American Tobacco Company was the first to assume that a growth business could exist in blended cigarettes. Lorillard assumed it could not. It lost eight years of profit and market position before its Old Golds could begin to compete with American's blended Lucky Strikes.

Inability to foresee the future is not a monopoly of businessmen. Many technological forecasters and economists share it. Assumptions made in the late 1960s about the 1970 decade by a consensus of the world's leading economists show how wrong even professional predictions can be:

1. The economists assumed an increasing demand for raw materials. But they did not foretell the worldwide shortage in metals, timber products, food, feed, and fuel.

2. The economists assumed that demand for energy sources would quicken. But they did not foretell the development of a cartel of oil-producing countries that could force a fourfold price increase in crude oil. In fact, many economists were certain that the oil-producing countries were inherently unable to agree on anything, let alone form a cartel.

3. The economists assumed a continuing inflationary trend in prices averaging 4 percent per year. But they did not foretell an inflation rate of 12 percent.

4. The economists assumed the increasing intervention of government in the areas of safety, product quality, and environmental protection. But they did not foretell the scale of the regulatory programs that evolved or the costs they would impose on industry.

5. The economists assumed a rising demand for investment. But they did not foretell the total capital demand that would be created by combining needs for industrial expansion, modernization, compliance with governmental regulations, and rising prices due to inflation.

A System for Making Assumptions

Because good assumers are few and far between, most venture managers must hedge against the risk of being wrong by working within a system for making assumptions more or less scientifically. A good system will not turn off their intuitive feeling for the outcome of an unknowable event. Quite the contrary, it will encourage the manager to give free expression to subjective reactions with the heightened sense of security that comes from having a cushioning system of checks and balances. No system will replace the manager's foresight. A good system, however, will make it exceedingly difficult for even the most cherished preconceptions to lead the manager astray. To prepare the way for operating the system, the major unknowables must first be confronted.

The Eight Major Unknowables

For every venture, there are at least eight major unknowables about which the venture manager must make assumptions. They are (1) venture *staff* availability; (2) what the *business cycle* will do over the venture's early life-span; (3) how *competition* will react to the venture's products or services; (4) whether the emergent *market trends* which provide the need base for the venture's inauguration will continue to grow or will plateau off or even decline; (5) what new *technological developments* may become commercialized to preempt the venture's scientific base, obsolete its processes, or devalue the user benefits of its products; (6) what *legislative actions* may be authorized by federal, state, or local governments that can affect the acceptability of venture product ingredients or packaging, the venture's premium-pricing capability, advertising permissiveness, or environmental compatibility; (7) what *sociological reactions* may be directed toward the venture's business as a result of consumerism, life-style changes, or fads; and (8) how *energy and materials availability* can affect venture objectives.

Other unknowables may also force assumptions on the managers of specific ventures. A manager whose new business is labor-intensive will be forced to assume the continuing availability of the specialized labor pool he requires. If the business is capital-intensive, the manager will have to assume access to plant and equipment. If secondary financing at the "mezzanine" stage of the venture's development cycle will be necessary, the manager must look ahead to estimate the fluidity of the money market several years hence, the cost of debt financing in terms of interest rates and the opportunity cost of money, the probable attractiveness of equity financing, and other sources of investment in the venture.

Five-Step Process of Making Assumptions

In addition to their universal effect on all ventures, the eight major unknowables about which assumptions must be made share two other similarities. One is their ability to challenge the best individual minds. The other is their ability to resist easy consensus agreement among groups of experts. As a result, many venture managers have adopted a five-step process of making assumptions that is designed to reduce undue risk and orient the venture more harmoniously toward its forthcoming real world.

Step 1: Define the Elementary Unknowables

Every one of the major unknowables is composed of many smaller unknowables. In turn, these are made up of even lesser uncertainties. The first step is to catalog the major unknowables that will affect the venture and then to define the smallest uncertainties which can be assessed. Resolving small uncertainties is basic to the assumption process. An incorrect assumption about any one of them can be multiplied many times over as the venture moves along. For this reason, the small assumptions have come to be regarded as elementary events; they are the basic building blocks from which the composite events that form the major assumptions must be constructed.

Step 2: Surface the Trigger Variables

Within every venture's assumptive framework, one or more unknowns can be identified as trigger variables. These are uncertainties whose importance is large enough to trigger several other uncertainties. Their effect may be simultaneous or sequential. In either case, they will turn out to be the key events in the influence chain. They must therefore be surfaced and spotlighted. A single variable such as the assumed inflationary rate of the economy or the inherent overoptimism of a sales manager may trigger dozens of dependent assumptions to jump to the high or the low side. The venture manager may believe that each of these assumptions varies independently. In fact, however, they are influenced by the trigger which activates them in a more optimistic or a more pessimistic direction.

The perceived value of a venture product in the minds of its markets may be a trigger variable that can affect many assumptions about market trend projections. Assigning a dollar value based on market perceptions of added benefit value is therefore always one of the most difficult aspects of venture planning. Concept testing, use testing, and test-marketing can clarify price assumptions. But only marketing can validate them. Uncertainties about competition may also be a trigger variable. It is often impossible to assess whether a venture product will actually be competing with existing products, when improved products will be added to the competitive mix, and if new materials about which there is current conjecture will become commercialized within the high-profit–making years of the venture's projected life cycle. These uncertainties will be clarified only during venture marketing. In such cases as these, in which a single underlying uncertainty can trigger the reactions of several dependent uncertainties, there is no way that the risk of being wrong can be spread. A minimum plus-or-minus 20 percent variance is therefore often assigned to the end assumption of the venture's total business opportunity as reflected in its pro forma financial work-ups whenever formidable trigger variables exist.

Step 3: Analyze Allegedly Similar Situations

Most venture situations, almost by definition, have more differences from the past than similarities to it. This does not make past history useless as a basis for venture assumptions. It simply makes it unlikely that the future will be enough like the past so that straight-line projections into the venture's life cycle can be more than remotely relevant. The venture manager faces a companion problem in seeking analogous situations whose experience may be used as a guideline. If the venture is truly innovative, no genuine analogues should be available. The major problem in analyzing similar situations is the validity of the initial assumption that a situation is similar enough to be useful.

Assumptions of a venture's market penetration by the end of a specific commercial year are often based heavily on observation of similar situations, even though in many instances this practice is subconscious on the part of the venture manager. If, for example, five product launch and distribution situations are alleged to be similar to a venture product, their third-year penetration shares can be used as the basis for an assumption about the venture's probability of penetration. For the sake of the assumption, the venture's manager can believe that, on the basis of normal probability distribution, its product will behave similarly to any of the five historical cases. Thus, it may be assumed with a 50 percent probability that the product's penetration by Year 3 will exceed two of the historical cases, a 20 percent probability that it will exceed another two of the remaining cases, and a 10 percent probability that it will exceed the highest historical case and set a new record in the market.

In other situations, the degree of alleged similarity may be considerably less. Judgment will be required to determine what, if anything, they reveal. If it cost two competitors an average of $3.5 million to research and develop a new product, the venture manager of an allegedly similar product may assume that only three-quarters as much expenditure will be required by the venture's R&D because of its superior technical capabilities or of advances in the state of the art.

Step 4: Bet on the Outcomes

When the elementary unknowables and the trigger variables have been identified and allegedly similar situations analyzed for assumptive clues, the venture manager is ready to bet on what the outcome will be. The final step in the process will be to assign a probability to each outcome. This statement of probability will be the manager's working assumption.

There are two types of possible outcomes. One is a qualitative yes-or-no outcome. This means that something either will or will not happen. Yes-or-no outcomes are often extremely difficult to decide, especially if no situations allegedly relevant to the venture situation exist. On the other hand, this type of outcome is simple to express. When the probability of a yes and the probability of a no add up to 1.0, all possible outcomes are accounted for.

The second type of outcome is not an either-or situation. Instead, it must be expressed quantitatively in terms of how many or how much: how many product units will be in use by Year 3, and how much will each unit cost to manufacture at that time, when 80 percent of plant capacity should have been reached? To position this type of outcome for betting, the venture manager will have to make a sausage-link chain of assumptions about the probability of 0 units, 50 to 100 units, 100 to 500 units, and so on. If the probability of 50 to 100 units is estimated at 20 percent and if the probability of 100 to 500 units is 30 percent, then the manager's assumption can be based on what appears to be the most probable outcome.

Step 5: Issue Probability Statements

Probability statements are the language of assumptions. They serve to qualify the venture manager's subjective judgments about the venture's unknowables so that they can be assessed in common terms. A probability statement says, "I assume at the X percent level of confidence. . . ." This is a venture manager's betting talk. This quantified conversation operates within a relatively small range. If the level of confidence is 0 percent or

100 percent, the manager is expressing certainty and not probability. Top management will interpret either of these levels of confidence as facts. Hence, a probability of 0 percent will be interpreted as certainty of failure. A probability of 100 percent will be interpreted as either certainty of success or certainty that the venture manager ought to be replaced. For these obvious reasons, such levels of confidence never appear in venture assumptions.

Even a 50 percent level of confidence will rarely be acceptable. It represents pure chance. A manager is regarded as the influencer of chance; management is supposed to improve on fortune. The value which management adds over and above chance is often used as an index of its professionalism. If a venture manager cannot do better than come up with probabilities that are equal to chance, there is no need for the manager's role. Accordingly, venture statements of probability must generally operate at the 60 to 80 percent level of confidence. Only then can the assumptions they are attempting to quantify be accepted as if they were knowable foundations for the strategies that will be based on them. This exemplifies the pressure for certainty in the midst of uncertainty that constitutes the yin and the yang of the new-business venture process.

Assumptions about some of the unknowables that have been made for a service business venture are expressed as a package of probability statements in Exhibits 8-1 through 8-5.

Use Planning Pages 34 through 41 to work out a package of Probability Statements based on your assumptions about how staff probability, business cycle probability, competitive probability, market trends probability, technological probability, legislative probability, sociological probability, and energy and materials probability will affect your venture objectives.

exhibit 8-1

assumptions about effects of the business cycle on venture objectives

We assume at the 70 percent level of confidence that the national economy will experience a moderate-to-good growth rate when averaged out over fiscal years 1976–1979. There will be neither a boom nor a recession. Real GNP growth will average 4 percent per annum. Inflation will average 7 percent per annum. *Therefore, we assume that the business cycle will favor venture objectives*. Revenues from financial management services will continue to grow. Furthermore, because of the inflationary squeeze of rising labor rates against the inability to raise prices commensurately, the availability of merger candidates will improve.

exhibit 8-2

assumptions about effects of staff recruitment and retention on venture objectives

We assume at the 80 percent level of confidence that staff manpower will prove to be the single most limiting factor on venture objectives from fiscal year 1977 on. *Therefore, we assume that, unless corrected, lack of availability of required staff capabilities will detract from the achievement of venture objectives.* As a result, primary attention will be paid to recruitment from both off-campus and experienced sources of the types and numbers of staff personnel who can help achieve the venture's objectives as well as to their training and development; their retention through compensation, motivation, and promotion; and their meaningful utilization. Staff availability may improve if the assumed moderate economic growth inhibits the career advancement of desirable candidates who are employed by correlate industries and thereby makes them more readily available to recruitment.

exhibit 8.3

assumptions about effects of competitive activity on venture objectives

We assume at the 80 percent level of confidence that competition from both direct and indirect sources will become increasingly active after fiscal year 1977 by means of intensified industry penetration, by cannibalization of the venture's existing clients, and by price competition. *Therefore, we assume that competitive activity will detract from the achievement of venture objectives.* The venture will incur added costs from being required to behave more competitively to maintain the commitment of current clients and to attract the attention of new clients. The venture will also be required to increase spending in order to become publicly more visible.

exhibit 8.4

assumptions about effects of legislative action on venture objectives

We assume at the 70 percent level of confidence that new legislative action will increase the number of burdens on business as well as the strictness of their enforcement over fiscal years 1976–1979. *Therefore, we assume that legislative action will favor the achievement of venture objectives.* New business opportunities will be provided by requirements for more specific and validated performance forecasts, shorter-term reports, and increased disclosures.

exhibit 8-5

assumptions about effects of technological development on venture objectives

We assume at the 65 percent level of confidence that continued advances in computer technology over fiscal years 1976–1979 will provide the base for a cost-effective commercial capability in on-line management performance analysis. We assume it will also generate increased demand for specialized financial management planning services and management consulting services. *Therefore, we assume that technological development will favor the achievement of venture objectives.* Computerized financial planning, econometric modeling, and economic forecasting of the impact which various price levels can exert on revenues will become important income sources.

STAFF EFFECT PROBABILITY STATEMENT

I assume at the __% level of confidence that the most probable effect on venture objectives of <u>staff availability</u> will be to:

Because:

BUSINESS CYCLE EFFECT PROBABILITY STATEMENT

I assume at the __% level of confidence that the most probable effect on venture objectives of <u>business cycle activity</u> will be to:

Because:

<u>COMPETITIVE EFFECT PROBABILITY STATEMENT</u>

I assume at the __% level of confidence that the most probable effect on venture objectives of <u>competitive actions and reactions</u> will be to:

Because:

MARKET TRENDS EFFECT PROBABILITY STATEMENT

I assume at the __% level of confidence that the most
probable effect on venture objectives of emergent
market trends will be to:

Because:

TECHNOLOGICAL EFFECT PROBABILITY STATEMENT

I assume at the __% level of confidence that the most
probable effect on venture objectives of <u>technological
developments</u> will be to:

Because:

LEGISLATIVE EFFECT PROBABILITY STATEMENT

I assume at the __% level of confidence that the most probable effect on venture objectives of <u>legislative constraints</u> will be to:

Because:

SOCIOLOGICAL EFFECT PROBABILITY STATEMENT

I assume at the __% level of confidence that the most probable effect on venture objectives of <u>sociological reactions</u> will be to:

Because:

ENERGY AND MATERIALS EFFECT
PROBABILITY STATEMENT

I assume at the __% level of confidence that the most
probable effect on venture objectives of <u>energy and
materials availability</u> will be to:

Because:

Technological Forecasting

Making assumptions about the type and timing of technological change often is an important aspect of the venture process. Another aspect is assessing with reasonable accuracy the impact of a new technology. Both are difficult arts. The story of computer forecasting is well known. In the 1940s, it had become safe to assume that the computer had arrived commercially. It had achieved technical feasibility. Its economic viability was the next question. One knowledgeable assumption predicted that computers would be devoted almost exclusively to scientific calculation and that the world computer market would, at most, be able to absorb 1,000 computers by the year 2000. Instead, by only 1965 a total of 150,000 computers were operating throughout the world. The great majority of them were employed in routine bookkeeping, payroll record keeping, and billing rather than the predicted scientific calculations.

Predicting whether a technology is likely to become important, when this may occur, and what the effects will be can be helped by two types of assumptive methods. One is based on the subjective, intuitive estimates of experts such as the Delphi Procedure. The second group of methods is composed of explicit forecasting procedures like trend extrapolation, replacement rate estimation, step-growth forecasting, and breakthrough prediction.

Subjective Forecasting

Subjective methods based on expert opinion must be used for technological forecasting when historical data that can serve as the basis for trend extrapolation are lacking. They must also be used when external technological events, perhaps controlled by a competitor, are the dominant variables in decision making. A third condition for subjective forecasting is present when a venture manager believes that the conditions which have been producing a trend are about to undergo a type of change that would make extrapolation useless.

One of the most cost-effective methods of subjective forecasting is the Delphi Procedure. Delphi uses a committee of experts. Each expert is asked to make a subjective forecast in response to a carefully structured sequence of questionnaires. The experts never meet face to face. They may even remain unknown to each other. Their anonymous forecasts are distributed for reevaluation over and over again by the Delphi Director, who controls all feedback, consolidates similar forecasts, and summarizes agreeable and disagreeable arguments. In this way, all individual forecasts can be considered on their merits, and without regard to personalities. The Delphi Committee need not reach a consensus or prepare a majority opinion. The forecasts of the committee are presented statistically. All views, no matter how diverse, are included in the final assessment. The most common form of summary is to calculate the median committee estimate. This is the number that half of the committee forecasts are above and half below. Along with the median estimate, the lower and upper quartiles are also presented. The lower quartile is the value expressed by one-fourth of the Delphi Committee. The upper quartile is the value expressed by three-fourths of the committee.

The median estimate from the final questionnaire in a Delphi sequence becomes the forecast. The forecast's uncertainty is indicated by the interquartile range, which is the width between the upper quartile and the lower quartile. This provides insight into the degree of disagreement remaining among the committee's experts at the end of their deliberations. A final summary of arguments also helps identify factors that may have a bearing on the validity of the single-point estimate of when Event X will occur. An outline of the Delphi Procedure is presented in Exhibit 8-6. Two typical estimates that can come out of it are shown as Exhibits 8-7 and 8-8. In Exhibit 8-7, an individual expert has predicted a venture product's sales growth. In Exhibit 8-8, the combined predictions of the Delphi Committee of experts are shown. The circles represent their median estimates.

Explicit Forecasting

Trend Extrapolation

An estimate of the total market size for a venture's output is necessary for decisions affecting plant capacity, sales objectives, and market share. Trend extrapolation enables a venture manager to identify a probable pattern of continued growth based on past growth in market size. As a forecasting method, trending is reasonably straightforward. It is based on an assumption that whatever forces have been acting to produce a trend will extend it. Any significant change in a major variable can invalidate an extrapolated forecast. For truly new venture products, for which no historical trends exist, extrapolation may have to be based on the experience of related product categories.

Replacement Rate Estimation

In some cases, a venture product will be positioned as an almost-direct substitute for an existing product. It is helpful for the venture manager to be able to estimate the rate at which the venture product can replace entrenched competitors. If one of the entrenched competitors is marketed by the manager's own company, a replacement rate forecast will also be valuable in phasing the competitor out as the venture product establishes itself.

Replacement rates often obey a simple mathematical law. The law

exhibit 8.6

the Delphi Procedure

First round

Questionnaire 1 asks, "By what year is there a 50-50 chance that Event X will have occurred?" The Delphi Director receives each forecast and calculates the median and quartiles for the first-round estimates. The director then distributes them along with the same questionnaire for a second round.

Second round

Questionnaire 2 requires each expert to take into account the forecasts made anonymously by all the other experts and to make a new estimate. If the new estimate of the occurrence of Event X is earlier than the first round's lower quartile or later than the upper quartile, the expert must offer reasons why the majority of the committee seems to be making a more optimistic or pessimistic estimate. The Delphi Director again receives each forecast, calculates the median and quartiles, and summarizes the reasons provided by the outliers for advancing or delaying the date for Event X. He then distributes them along with the same questionnaire for as many additional rounds as are necessary to smooth significant shifts of opinion. Something usually happens by the fourth round. The final round's median becomes the forecast date for Event X.

exhibit 8.7

**individual expert's prediction
of sales growth**

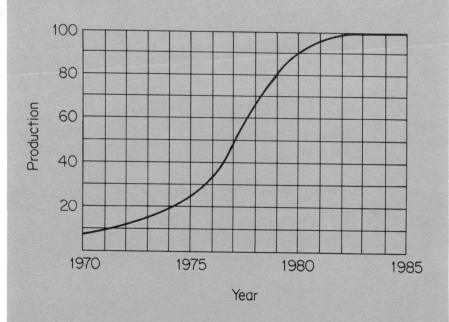

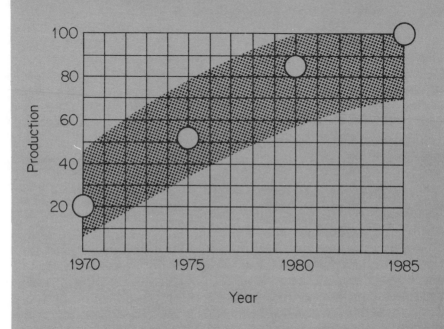

exhibit 8-8

combined expert predictions
of sales growth

says that if S denotes at least a 10 percent market share captured by a venture product, the ratio $S/1-S$ appears to grow exponentially. The slope of the trend is characterized by a takeover time period which is defined as the time for the venture product to grow from 10 to 90 percent of the market, that is, from $S = 0.1$ to $S = 0.9$.

Replacement rate estimation is usuable in essentially the same way as trend extrapolation. It depends on obtaining market share information on the existing product and making similar assumptions.

Step-Growth Forecasting

For a number of product types such as basic chemicals and heavy industrial equipment, there appears to be a fairly constant ratio between total production and the capacity of the largest single plant. Where this ratio holds true, the maximum capacity for a venture plant can be estimated. First, the venture manager must learn if there is a consistent pattern in the intervals of time steps between the introduction of larger-capacity plants in his industry. If there is, the manager should relate this pattern to the pattern displayed by the ratio of these plant capacities to total industry production. If a pattern match is discoverable, the manager may estimate at a reasonably high level of probability that it will repeat itself. Exhibit 8-9 shows how such a smoothed estimate would appear in graphic display.

Breakthrough Prediction

The greatest threat a venture faces is technical breakthrough by a competitive process before the venture has become fully commercialized. Venture managers often take comfort in one of two rationalizations. The first is the assumption that no breakthrough will occur. The second is the assumption that breakthroughs are inherently unpredictable and are therefore in the laps of the gods. Neither assumption is true.

No technology moves from laboratory to market overnight. Virtually every breakthrough breaks into awareness after as many as three or four decades of precursor events. These events suggest more or less clearly where a technology is going and when its arrival at specific stages of development may be anticipated. The jet engine was invented in the early 1930s. Because its performance was too low to make it competitive, most engine manufacturers assumed that it would always remain noncompetitive and stopped monitoring its successive developments. Meanwhile, its supporting technology improved, theoretical understanding matured, and new materials became available. Thirty years later, Boeing launched the era of the commercial jet aircraft while other airframe manufacturers still believed or hoped that the commercial jet would

exhibit 8-9

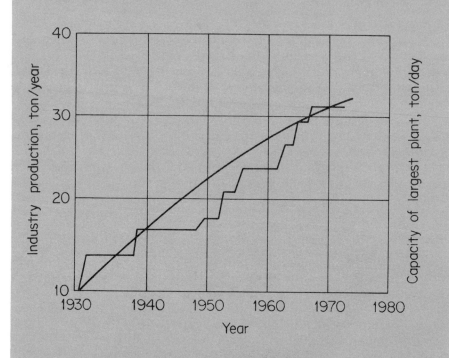

never fly. The transistor is another case in point. It was patented twice during the 1930s.

Breakthrough prediction, which is really anticipation of technological commercialization, is a result of persistent environmental monitoring. A number of precursor signals must be watched. One is the output from basic-research laboratories. A new chemical or a new reaction from old ones, a new synthesis of electrical components or effects, a new combination of chemical and electronic technologies may all be early-warning signs of a new product or process. Another signal is inventions, whether patented or not, that do not yet quite work. An important element may be missing. Supporting technology may still be inadequate. These inventions will bear monitoring.

Only rarely does one signal forecast a future commercial event. Signals that confirm earlier ones or supplement and complement them must be searched out. Each signal should be assumed to be an additional warning of impending breakthrough. As further confirming signals are gathered, a chain effect of precursors may point to breakthrough. In this way, environmental monitoring can help eliminate many surprises that are not simply technological events but can be economic, political, or social in nature.

The Toughest Nut: Interfacing Technology with Market Trends

Incorrect assessment of technological capability is a major cause of venture failure. When the venture is ready to go to market, no product exists. Sunk costs sink the venture. For this reason, many venture managers adopt the criterion of avoiding all new businesses which do not depend on proved technology.

While incorrect technological assessment can be extremely dangerous, correct assessment can be even worse when it is not interfaced with a correct assessment of market trends. This is one of the most difficult interfaces in venturing because it requires managers to relate two of the least ponderable uncertainties. A successful R&D operation can create an elephant in the barn for a venture manager. In order to feed the elephant, the manager can be strongly tempted to make venture decisions according to technical capabilities alone rather than their interplay with customer needs.

A familiar product will provide an example of the planning process which matches a correct technical assumption with an incorrect market assumption. In venture business situations as well as new-product situations, this paradox can totally negate commercial feasibility. The product is the 747 airplane, produced by Boeing in the 1960s to exploit what it could build rather than what would meet airplane passenger and cargo requirements in the air and on the ground.

Boeing had confirmed to its own satisfaction that it could build a radically new generation of aircraft during its unsuccessful competition for the C-5A military contract. By altering the variable-inflation landing gear required for soft forward military airfields, commercializing the supersensitive electronic equipment, and changing the nose-to-tail flow-through loading system to conventional side-door access, more than 100,000 pounds of weight were shaved. What was to become the wrong plane at the wrong time was offered to the airlines. By relating the 747 to the previously successful 707 series, Boeing positioned the new airplane as the latest member of the family, simply expanded in dimension, lift, and cubic capacity. Even the number of men in the cockpit was the same. True, the captain's salary would have to be raised by more than $10,000 a year to $50,000. But his higher cost could be distributed over as many as 500 passengers rather than the 707's fewer than 200.

Unfortunately, the passengers never materialized. The 747's cost per seat-mile became uneconomical. The aircraft became the first bigger, faster airplane in Boeing's entire 700 series that did not make more money. As the airlines have learned, it is far more cost-efficient to spread the services of a larger number of smaller aircraft over their markets in order to provide the benefits of more frequent and more flexible service. Even as a cargo freighter, the 747 lacked cost efficiency. Its payload was too small in relation to its cost and the investment it required in cargo hatches, materials-loading systems, special docking configurations, and other modifications of the standard airport handling environment.

In contrast to the imperfect interface of the technical capability to build with the market inability to consume that produced the 747, the Douglas DC-10 represented a more nearly perfect interface. It offered smaller unit capacity but greater operational economies. Because the DC-10 was designed with only three engines instead of the 747's four power plants, fuel consumption was reduced. There was also one less engine to tear down, inspect, and rebuild. Each time this periodic cycle occurred, it cost 25 percent of the acquisition price of the engine. Just in these ways, a DC-10 was able to save almost $5 million in maintenance costs a year. This attribute alone made the DC-10 far more marketable than the 747. It also makes a used DC-10 far more easily resalable to secondary markets and at a higher price.

The Final Analysis

The ability to make correct assumptions and validate them at levels of confidence with which top management will be comfortable is one of the highest skills of a venture manager. It is a complex skill because it requires a manager to be conceptual and analytical at the same time. Yet, in the final analysis, the ability to make assumptions about the viability of a new-business concept lies at the heart of the entrepreneurial traits which a venture manager must possess. This ability, no matter how strongly it may be buttressed by mathematical probabilities, is essentially a qualitative talent. Regardless of what the numbers seem to say, it always gets down to the gut feel of one manager or a small group of managers about whether or not a venture can become a profitable business. To have that gut feel, to be able to call upon it at a point of decision and find it ready, and, most important of all, to dare to trust it when it says "No" are the characteristics that separate the true venture manager from all the managers who operate ventures.

9

venture objectives

The concept of what a growth business is, and therefore of what a venture's objectives should be, is derived in large part by every management from its own experience in running a mature, established business. Accustomed profit is often the base line for venture profit. For this reason, specific objectives for venturing can vary widely from company to company. But the general objective for venturing is always the same: *to gain superior short-term incremental profit without impairing the value of longer-term future profits*.

Emphasizing superior short-term profit makes venturing big-winner–oriented. "Unless you can do much better than the GNP rate or the return from an established business, it isn't worth it" is a prevalent point of view. How much better "much better" has to be is the chief determinant of a venture's financial objectives. Venture profit must be significant. It must also represent an increment that would be unachievable if the venture's resources were allocated elsewhere.

Ventures are therefore properly regarded as strategies of accelerated capital appreciation. For a reasonably small company, a minimum growth factor of 3 to 5 times invested capital over a three-to-five-year period, or a 15 to 20 percent compounded growth rate, may be an acceptable venture objective. A larger company may require a minimum of 7-times appreciation of its investment over the first three to five years. In the second three-to-five-year growth period of a venture's life cycle, it may accept a 3-times multiplier. An 8 percent annual growth potential over a five-year life cycle is generally considered to be minimal, since it represents growth at approximately twice the traditional rate of normal GNP growth. Unless annual growth can be maintained at an average 8 percent rate, it will be impossible to justify a venture's reputation as a growth business.

True Venture Objectives

There are two true venture objectives. The first is the *minimum acceptable return on the venture investment before taxes,* which usually runs about 10 percent higher than return on investment after taxes. The second is the *minimum annual net profit before taxes,* which may be twice the aftertax profit. Each of these objectives must be expressed within a time frame for its accomplishment. All other objectives are supportive of these true objectives. A model statement of venture objectives, constructed in narrative form to show how it might be read as a composite of true and supportive objectives, is shown in Exhibit 9-1. A sample outline of ROI objectives for a venture and their supporting business goals is shown in Exhibit 9-2.

ROI and profit objectives can be planned as the beneficiaries of several supportive objectives such as sales unit and dollar volume, rate of annual sales growth, percentage share of market, and total marketing investment. ROI and profit can also be associated with several companion objectives such as increased earnings per share above the so-called good average of 8 to 9 percent, improved dividends and appreciation of net worth, growth of capital, and return on shareholders' equity. These should generally play a subsidiary role to the prime objectives of ROI and profit unless unusual circumstances dictate otherwise.

> Use Planning Pages 42 and 43 to work out a Statement of Venture Objectives in narrative form and an outline of the venture's return-on-investment objectives and their supporting business goals.

Charter-Based Objectives

Venture objectives originate in the charter. They are venture management's commitments, derived outright from the charter's definition of the market to be served by the venture and the type of business that will serve it best.

A charter is a quasi-legal document. For a venture business, it represents a contract between the venture's management and parent company management that certain incremental profits will accrue to the corporation in return for its investment. It also represents an implicit contract between the venture manager and the venture's market. For this reason, it is important to charter a venture business in the language of the market it will serve almost as if the charter were being dictated by the market's needs. Speaking on behalf of its steelmaking market, for example, a refractory venture business may charter itself to serve the steel industry

exhibit 9.1

model statement of
venture objectives

The minimum objectives of this venture are to yield an annual pretax return on investment of 30% over a projected 5-year growth phase of the venture life cycle, together with a $5MM cumulative profit before taxes by Year 5, representing a 30% net profit before taxes.

These objectives will be achieved by generating annual net retail sales at the rate of $25MM commencing in Year 3 from a minimum of 3 product and service systems, each with a projected minimum annual growth rate of 8%, based on a minimum 20% share of market.

Each product and service system must deliver a minimum of approximately $2MM in net profit before taxes as a result of a minimum annual net sales volume of $10MM.

exhibit 9-2

venture objectives

1. Return on investment

A minimum 20% return on investment by Year 3
A minimum 30% return on investment by Year 4
A minimum 40% return on investment after Year 5

2. Payback

100% payback by the end of Year 2

3. Operating margin

A minimum 25% operating margin to sales
A minimum average growth in operating margin of 10% per year

4. Operating income

A minimum 10% increase in annual operating income

	Based on target growth rate of 10%	
	$MM net sales	*$MM income before taxes*
1975	680	132
1985	1,764	344

5. Sales volume

A minimum 10% return on sales from Year 3

Year 1	$2.1 MM
2	2.7
3	3.4
4	4.2

6. Share of market

A minimum 20% share of market by Year 3

STATEMENT OF VENTURE OBJECTIVES

The minimum objectives of this venture are to yield an
annual pretax return on investment of __% over a projected __ year growth phase of the venture life cycle, together
with a $__,___,___ cumulative profit before taxes by
Year __ (F19__-F19__), representing a __% net profit
before taxes.

These objectives will be achieved by generating annual
net sales at the rate of $___,___,___ commencing in
Year __ (F19__-F19__) from a minimum of __ product and service
systems, each with an average projected minimum annual
growth rate of __%, based on a minimum __% share of market.

Each product and service system must deliver a minimum of
approximately $___,___,___ in net profit before taxes as a
result of a minimum annual net sales volume of $___,___,___.

VENTURE OBJECTIVES

1. Return on investment

    1.1. A minimum __% return on investment
                                    by Year 3 (F19__-F19__)

    1.2. A minimum __% return on investment
                                    by Year 4 (F19__-F19__)

    1.3. A minimum __% return on investment
                                    after Year 5 (F19__-F19__)

2. Payback

    100% payback by the end of Year __ (F19__-F19__)

3. Operating margin

    3.1. A minimum __% operating margin to sales

    3.2. A minimum average growth in operating margin
        of __% per year

4. Operating income

    4.1. A minimum __% increase in annual operating income

    4.2. Based on target growth rate of __%

	$MM net sales	$MM income before taxes
F19__-F19__	---,---,---	---,---,---
F19__-F19__	---,---,---	---,---,---

5. Sales volume

    A minimum __% return on sales from Year __

                Year 1 (F19__-F19__) $___,___,---
                     2 (F19__-F19__)   ---,---,---
                     3 (F19__-F19__)   ---,---,---
                     4 (F19__-F19__)   ---,---,---

6. Share of market

    A minimum __% share of market by Year __ (F19__-F19__)

with the benefit of lowered cost per ton of steelmaking. The charter will define management's objective as maximizing its profit by applying a combined product and service system of refractory brick and profit improvement consultants against a steelmaker's production problems. Consequently, the venture will be committed to act as a market-oriented benefiter of steelmaking profit needs and not as a product-oriented brick manufacturer.

Similarly, a materials-processing venture may charter itself to serve the homemaker market with preemptive benefits in meal cooking, serving, and storing. The venture's business will consist of supplying a combined product and service system of cooking utensils and food preparation and handling information. The venture will be committed to benefit convenience needs in the home rather than enter the pot-and-pan business.

A charter also attempts to outline the criteria by which a venture will select the ways it applies corporate funds and the basic strategies it will employ to convert these funds into profits. Thus, a venture charter ought to contain at least these three sections: "Business Definition and Objectives," "Selection Criteria Constraints," and "Operating Assumptions." An example of a venture charter which follows this outline appears in Exhibit 9-3.

Because a venture charter must be market-oriented from its outset, dedicating itself, for example, as in Exhibit 9-3, "to satisfy a broad base of mass, middle-majority homemaker needs, wants, and desires for improved psychic and physical well-being," a venture's objectives should be expressed first of all from its market's point of view. This means that a venture's ascendant objective is always external to itself: to render preemptive market service. Market service becomes the venture's reason for being in business since it is the market's prime reason for doing business with the venture. The result of being in business should be venture profit.

If a venture manager's innermost thoughts about venture objectives could be verbalized, they might sound something like this:

> My objective of being in business is to maximize the supply of preemptive benefits to my markets and thereby maximize the profitable rate of return I receive back from my investment in supplying these benefits.

> From my market's point of view, the optimal performance of my venture business will be obtained when further improvement in the benefits they receive from me is not possible by any changes I might make in their components while, at the same time, the value of future benefits they might receive from me is not being impaired. From my internal point of view, optimal performance will be obtained when further improvement in the profitable rate of return on my investment is not

possible by any change in its components while, at the same time, the value of future profits I might receive from my markets is not being impaired.

A venture's internal objectives are therefore corollary objectives, totally dependent on fulfilling its external objectives of market service.

An old management truism says, "Gross profits are the result of sales; net profits are the result of management." To this, the venture manager must add: "All profits are the result of market service." The charter formalizes this belief. Charter-based objectives answer the continuing venture question, "Why are we in this business?" and, by implication, "Why are we *not* in some other business?" The answers to these questions, in turn, enable the venture's management to plan its *direction* in terms of its objectives, its *definition* as a business enterprise, and its subsequent *diversification* into new venture businesses.

> **Use Planning Page 44 to work out a Venture Charter.**

The Return-on-Investment Objective

Return on investment relates a venture's expected profit to the investment risked to earn it. The basic ROI formula defines profit as the rate of profit on sales or, to say the same thing in another way, operating profit as a percentage of sales. Investment is defined as the total capital assets employed to produce sales. ROI compares a venture's profit margin with its asset turnover; that is, its earnings in terms of gross sales income and the capital assets employed to generate them:

$$\underbrace{\frac{\textit{Profit margin}}{\textit{expressed as}}}_{\textit{return on sales}} \qquad \underbrace{\frac{\textit{Return on capital}}{\textit{expressed as}}}_{\textit{capital turnover}}$$

$$\text{ROI} = \frac{\substack{\text{net operating profit} \\ \text{expressed as} \\ \text{income from earnings}}}{\text{sales}} \times \frac{\text{sales}}{\substack{\text{total investment in} \\ \text{capital assets employed}}}$$

$$\frac{\text{Profit}}{\text{Investment}} = \substack{\text{earnings as a per-} \\ \text{centage of sales}} \times \text{asset turnover}$$

exhibit 9.3

charter:
personal care
business venture

Business definition and objectives

The business objectives of this venture will be to satisfy a broad base of mass, middle-majority homemaker needs, wants, and desires for improved psychic and physical well-being by creating, testing and validating, and introducing to market a series of venture product and service businesses, each based on branded benefits to its distributors and users and each sequenced in an interrelated manner that will eventually build a major personal care business.

In return for this market service, the minimum market contribution to this venture is predicted to generate $5 million cumulative profit before taxes annually by Fiscal Year 5. In this way, an annual return on investment objective of 30 percent before taxes can be achieved. This rate of return will be achieved by maintaining and enhancing the corporate image for excellence as a manufacturer, marketer, and community citizen concerned for personal and public values as well as profitability.

Selection criteria constraints

To achieve the venture's objectives, each individual business will be selected for venturing under this charter only if it meets at least the

exhibit 9.3 (Continued)

following six selection criteria, which shall act as constraints against dilution of venture resources:

1. A minimum annual profit before taxes of $1 million
2. A minimum annual profit before taxes as a percentage of net sales of 20 percent
3. A minimum 8 percent annual growth rate potential
4. A minimum annual retail sales velocity of $10 million
5. A minimum annual net sales yield of $5 million
6. A minimum national life cycle of at least five to ten years

Operating assumptions

This venture will operate as if (1) it is a wholly owned subsidiary; (2) it is a supplier of branded product and service systems to a wide variety of market segments; (3) it is principally a marketer and only secondarily a manufacturer of its product and service systems so that the venture will be able to market even what it does not make and to draw upon external technologies for its product sources; and (4) it must conceive and develop its businesses internally, thus placing only secondary reliance on joint-venture activities and acquired businesses.

VENTURE CHARTER

1. Business definition and objectives
   The market service objectives of this venture will be to:

In return for this market service, the minimum market contribution to this venture is predicted to generate $___,___,___ cumulative profit before taxes annually by Fiscal Year 19__-19__ . In this way, an annual return-on-investment objective of __% before taxes can be achieved by:

2. <u>Selection criteria constraints</u>
   To achieve the venture's objectives, each individual business
   will be selected for venturing under this Charter only if it
   meets the following __ selection criteria, which shall act as
   constraints against dilution of venture resources:

3. <u>Operating assumptions</u>
   This venture will operate as if:

The classic formula for calculating ROI is shown in Exhibit 9-4. Because ROI accounts so comprehensively for the major activities of a business, it is generally the best way of expressing the yield on total venture capital employed, both human and nonhuman. It can be *determined* by comparing predicted profit with investment. But to understand how a venture's ROI can be *managed*, it is necessary to examine separately each of the two independent variables which contribute to profit and investment.

The first variable component of ROI, the profit margin expressed as the return on venture sales, is affected by all the elements included in the total cost of sales—elements such as sales volume, price, product mix, factory costs, marketing and administrative expenses, and any other factor affecting profit on sales.

But profit on sales is only one-half of the ROI equation. The management of venture capital turnover is equally important. A 20 percent profit margin multiplied by a capital turnover of 1 yields a 20 percent ROI. But a 10 percent profit margin can be managed to yield a 20 percent ROI when multiplied by a capital turnover of 2. This second component of ROI, the investment base, is affected by the movement in relation to sales of assets such as inventory levels, turnover of accounts receivables, and plant and equipment expenditures: in short, any factors which compose investment or affect its rate of turnover as related to venture sales. A venture's investment base is considered to be optimal when improvements in net profit are no longer possible by adding to or subtracting from the base.

Since either of the two ROI components may be manipulated independently of each other, ROI can be improved by two types of management strategy:

1. Maximizing the profit margin on sales without disproportionately decreasing turnover of investment, as through charging higher prices for the volume of goods sold or through selling a higher volume of goods.

2. Reducing the investment in capital employed without disproportionately increasing the cost of sales, as through lowering inventories, speeding the collection of accounts receivable, and controlling additions to property.

Each of the three components interrelated by the basic ROI formula —profit, sales, and investment—has a precise meaning within the ROI context. *Sales* is the simplest item to characterize. It refers to sales income, or net sales as billed. The other two components are somewhat more complex. *Profit* may be regarded as representing the supply of assets. *Investment* may be regarded as the demand on assets.

exhibit 9.4

return-on-investment formula

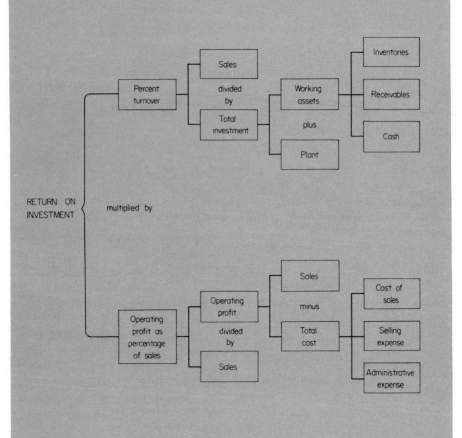

Venture profit is a net profit, the residual income from profit multiplied by turnover after deduction of operating costs and expenses. Since profit represents the usable earnings on investment, it is the venture manager's wage rate for the risk of capital. For most purposes of computing ROI, profit is usually considered as net profit after taxes, or NPAT. But in ventures in which problems of accounting for nontaxable income or nondeductible expenses are important considerations, net profit before taxes may be a more practical criterion.

Venture investment is the sum total of all capital assets employed to generate venture profit, figured at net book value. By "total assets" is meant more than just "invested capital" or "capital employed." Total assets include all the fixed, variable, and combination fixed-variable investments which contribute to profit: money, people, projects, and property.

The major investment expenses which form the base of most ventures can be classified in three categories:

1. *Fixed investments,* which include costs that do not change as the volume of venture production or sales change within existing plant and equipment capacity. General and administrative expenses are examples of fixed investments. So are property in the form of land, buildings, machinery, furniture and equipment, rents and taxes on such property, its insurance and depreciation costs, and basic light, heat, power, and communications utilities.

2. *Variable investments,* which include costs that change in direct proportion to changes in volume of venture production or sales. Selling expenses such as sales commissions and travel and entertainment expenses are examples of variable investments, as are materials and labor costs.

3. *Combined fixed-variable investments,* which include costs that change with changes in volume of venture production or sales, but not in direct proportion. Advertising and sales promotion expenses are examples of combined fixed-variable investments.

Establishing a Minimum Acceptable ROI Objective

There are five guidelines to establish a minimum acceptable standard of return on venture investment:

1. A minimum acceptable ROI objective may be an arbitrary rate fixed on the basis of wish fulfillment, historical data, and future projections. Hence, a venture manager can establish

as an objective that "new investments must pay back within a two-year maximum and offer a 20 percent minimum ROI."

2. A minimum acceptable ROI objective may be a rate set to equal or exceed the average 9.1 percent median rate of return of the 500 largest industrial corporations in the United States.

3. A minimum acceptable ROI objective may be a rate set to equal or exceed the popular rule of thumb that defines an aftertax range of 10 to 15 percent as desirable for a successful growth company.

4. A minimum acceptable ROI objective may be a rate set to equal or exceed the past performance of a business, the past performance of a major competitor, or the past performance of the overall industry to which the business belongs.

5. Instead of a single, minimally acceptable rate of return, a sliding scale of minimum rates based on risk which will be higher for larger investment and lower for smaller ones may be set.

There is often a sixth criterion of what constitutes a minimum acceptable objective. In setting a rate of return, many managements believe that the number should lend a shock value to the venture. To provide this added jolt, the rate ought to be a stimulating objective that is realizable only with all-out effort because it is pitched above a straight-line extrapolation of what seems to be the venture's momentum as it moves through its life cycle.

Limits on ROI as a Venture Objective

When ROI is used as the chief objective of a venture business, there is the danger (which applies in a lesser degree to the management of established businesses) that it may limit rather than accelerate the venture. There are several potential limitations. For one, the ROI objective may encourage short-term ventures and cause management to overlook opportunities with longer-term but greater payoffs. Perhaps, some managements believe, a more acceptable objective is a venture's ability to optimize a company's performance across a broad spectrum of activities rather than generate superior profits itself. Other managers feel that ROI is limited as a venture objective because of the difficulty in setting equitable profit objectives for a new business. Just one variable alone, the economic environment surrounding a venture, illustrates how complicated it is to answer reliably what rate of return the venture *should* earn, let alone what rate it *might* earn.

ROI concentration may also impose too narrow a framework on venture selection. Simply because a venture promises to yield less than a required ROI may not, in and of itself, be sufficient reason to pass it by. The experience of Du Pont when a 20 percent minimum rate of return was a standard new-business objective is worth remembering in this regard. While the minimum was in force, the company passed up xerography and the Land Polaroid camera. In these instances, emphasis on ROI provided a microview of opportunity rather than a macroview.

Another factor which may reduce the reliability of ROI as an objective for venturing is that a venture is top-heavy in new investment. In fact, a venture business may be nothing but investment for as much as a three-to-five-year period: a cost center which yields nothing but an annual loss before taxes. ROI may therefore be less than the best reflection of short-term to medium-term management performance. At the same time and for the same reason, it may also be less than a sufficiently exact instrument for venture financial control.

Venture objectives can rarely be set with the accuracy common in ongoing businesses. In addition, venture profit measurements are bound to be inexact because operating conditions vary more or less widely from the venture manager's going-in assumptions. ROI may therefore not always be the most satisfactory basis for determining the success of a venture or measuring its performance. As a result, venture managers often define ROI according to the real world of their situation. Instead of fixing a minimum ROI, they set a higher ROI objective when the risk appears greater and a lower ROI objective when the results seem more certain or when venture investment will also measurably benefit an established business. What they are doing is to set their expectations of a rate of return at a realistic level commensurate with the venture's degree of difficulty and the length of the time frame over which it can be expected to mature.

In spite of its venture limitations, ROI is still a reasonable if somewhat imperfect measurement of a venture manager's ability to use corporate resources to generate new profits. It has the additional advantage of being an accepted common denominator whose value can be compared directly between two or more venture opportunities. It can also be used to compare new-business ventures with established businesses. For the individual venture manager, ROI can be the surest guide to what may be going wrong. If the manager brings in less than the budgeted return, the business may be wrong. More likely, though, the manager may be incorrectly projecting its performance or operating it inefficiently and uneconomically. The venture's information resources may need to be improved, even at the risk of increasing costs. Or costs may need to be cut selectively or across the board. On the other hand, if a manager achieves a greater ROI than predicted, the venture may be spending too little on advertising and sales promotion, for instance. By spending more or spending funds more effectively, the venture might be able to increase sales volume and thereby improve cash flow.

The Three ROI Management Guidelines

Top management is a lender of capital to its venture managers. A venture manager is therefore an investor of borrowed assets. Venture managers, like their assets, are necessary evils. Neither exists for itself but only for its yield. Presumably, venture management plus assets will yield a more profitable contribution than unmanaged assets. The difference between these two sums is the value of venture management.

Top management is said to make growth policy, which is simply the determination of where, how, how much, when, and under whose management its assets will be invested. ROI guidelines are management's basic criteria for deciding on the investment portfolios it will acquire, that is, what businesses it will choose to enter. Once in, management can then use these guidelines to help maximize the profitability of each portfolio:

1. The *appraisal guideline* of evaluating current performance, which may be paraphrased in the question "Given an $80,000 yield on $500,000 worth of invested assets in venture portfolio A, for a return on investment of 16 percent, how can the management of these assets by venture manager X be judged?"

2. The *predictive guideline* of forecasting future performance, which may be paraphrased in the question "Given an increase of $250,000 worth of invested assets in venture portfolio A, what return on investment can be forecast by the management of these assets under venture manager X?"

3. The *incentive guideline* of motivating current and future performance, which may be paraphrased in the question "Given the objective of a 16 percent return on a $500,000 investment, what incentive for venture manager X will maximize his certainty of achieving or exceeding this objective?"

ROI as an Appraisal Guideline

Achievement of the ROI objective can be the ultimate measure of venture management. It allows current profit performance to be compared with its profit target. On a this year/last year basis, it allows immediate past performance to be compared with previous past performance. Among venture managers who are in similar businesses, it allows one manager's performance to be compared with another's. And within each market segment, it allows a manager to compare the performance of one optional mix of assets with others.

ROI as a Predictive Guideline

The ROI objective can also be an accurate forecaster of future management performance. It can serve as an index of future venture portfolio accumulation, based on the truism that investment goes where the return is. The ROI objective helps management forecast the individual strategy mixes which it will use to grow and develop each of its venture business portfolios. Will ROI be enhanced if the capitalization of the mix is increased? If so, by how much? Management may then forecast the need for incremental investment. Will ROI be enhanced if the product or service components of the mix are altered? Management may then forecast an altered product and service system mix. Will ROI be enhanced if the promotion components of the mix are altered in the form of advertising and sales promotion or in the form of the compensation, motivation or distribution of the sales force? Management may then forecast an altered promotion mix. Or will ROI be enhanced if the managerial components of the mix are altered by improvement of the venture manager as a result of a training and development program or replacement of one manager by another? Management may then forecast an altered administrative mix.

ROI as an Incentive Guideline

Because venture managers accept unusual risk, they merit unusual reward when they succeed or exceed their objectives. When the rate of return on venture investment is used as a prime venture objective, money or equity incentives can be pegged to each percentage point of ROI beyond which the manager can go in achievement up to the point at which incentive will be maximized.

Short-Term, Long-Term ROI Trade-offs

The investment base is more than just the denominator in the ROI formula. It is the planning base as well, since every plan incurs a cost which adds to investment. It is hoped that every cost will help yield increased profitable sales. But profit can be increased without increasing income. In this simple fact lies the managerial dilemma of the long-range versus the short-range strategy of venture management.

If the venture manager plays the game for the short run, many variable discretionary costs can be eliminated or reduced. Without adding to venture sales, the manager can produce increased profit. Simply by reducing the magnitude of the investment denominator, the manager can almost automatically increase the venture's profit numerator. There are many cost-reducing temptations. Sales force compensation and motivation investments can be postponed. Advertising can be cut back or cycled in periodic waves rather than directed continuously against a venture's market. Second-generation new-product development may be temporized. Marginal renovations of the venture's original product line may seem to suffice. New plant and equipment investment may be put off. Subjective decision making may replace investment in objective fact-finding.

The more successful these short-range strategies prove themselves to be in reducing costs, the greater the danger that they may also produce considerable long-range cost in the venture's competitive position. Although current profit may be immediately enhanced, three-to-five-year profit may be adversely, perhaps fatally, affected as the initial impact of innovation peters out, plant and equipment age and incur eventually increasing costs, and the momentum of marketing pressure slows. The short-range game plan may make the venture a peacock today. But the venture may become a feather duster tomorrow.

On the other hand, there are equal temptations to play the game for the long run in a flight from present profit. Substantial immediate costs incurred for speculative future profits will immediately penalize short-range profits. But because they do so in the guise of planning ahead, a manager's escape from the requirement to produce current profit may go unnoticed or at least unsuspected. While the manager is building for the future, the present can often be sacrificed so severely that the future is compromised before it arrives.

It is easy to say that the optimal course is therefore the middle course between the temptation to spend less in the short range and more for the long range. Such a middle course might average out failure, but it would probably also average out success. As a result, it might be the strategy of greatest risk.

The venture manager must appreciate that there can be low-investment years when the short-range game can be played profitably with safety. There is also the need for high-investment years which act as seeding years for the next cycle of cost-reducing opportunity. Nor must years necessarily be the basic unit of cost accounting. Costs may be allocated against the life cycle of a market need rather than a rounded-off unit of calendar months. Regardless of the basic unit of cost accumulation, the venture manager must be more deeply concerned with the rate of return's trend over a three-to-five-year period than with the absolute rate of return at any given time. It is on the basis of ROI trends that the application of strategic investments to achieving objectives must be evaluated. It is therefore on this ongoing basis that the venture manager must plan.

Any year can be a low-yield year because of deliberately incurred investment costs. Similarly, any year can be a high-yield year because of deliberately reduced or postponed investment costs. It is the trend that matters, so much so that a venture business may be said to be operating optimally when, over each three-to-five-year cycle, its profit yield could not have increased by means of any additions to or subtractions from its investment base.

Avoiding the Sales Volume Snare

Increased sales volume is one of the most pervasive pseudo-objectives pursued by venture management. The belief that increased sales volume contributes automatically to increased profits and therefore to increased ROI is often a fiction. Profits do not always improve with sales volume. Even if profits do improve, their rate of improvement may be so low that increased sales are being purchased unprofitably.

What is really important is not profit or sales but the rate of profit on sales. Unless the rate of profit on sales is maintained or increased as sales expand, increased sales volume may contribute nothing to maintaining or increasing ROI. In fact, if increased sales volume requires additional investment costs or reduced income because of lower prices, ROI will be reduced instead of increased.

If this financial fact of business management is not acknowledged by venture management's objectives, insidious pressure will always be generated for sales growth. If the business is not operating at capacity, the pressure will be phrased in the interest of utilizing underemployed assets. If the business is operating at capacity or very close to it, the pressure will be phrased in the interest of taking advantage of existing sales momentum. Both types of pressure generate their own type of added costs, which in the end may nullify whatever additional sales volume may be achieved.

As soon as new sales volume is planned, it is inevitable that additional investment will have to be made in inventories and accounts receivable. If expanded facilities are required, new plants must be constructed, power and utilities contracted for, and additional warehousing space and equipment provided to handle the increased inventories.

The added facilities increase costs by increasing depreciation investments. They also require additional employees, employee benefit costs, sales force salaries, and probably commissions. Added working capital may also be required to accommodate the expansion. This will have to come from one or more of three sources: borrowings from banks or in the open market through bond issues, stock sales, or moneys plowed back into the business from retained earnings. In any event, new costs will be incurred. If the required additional capital is borrowed, interest payments must be made. If stock is sold, more shares over which to spread earnings will be in existence, perhaps resulting in a reduction in dividends and a consequent lessening of attractiveness of the venture investment. If profits are retained to cover the additional investment, less profit is available for distribution and corporate or venture dividends may be further reduced.

Exhibit 9-5 shows the effect on ROI of an unwarranted pursuit of increased sales volume, although the objectives of more volume and even more profit are achieved. Increased sales volume can be, at best, a short-term index of successful venture business growth. In the longer run, it can prove to be a misleading goal unless it is accompanied by an increased rate of return on the total assets invested to support the increased sales.

Probability of Achieving Objectives

All objectives are set in the anticipation of achieving them. Minimal objectives are set to be exceeded. Yet, in reality, a different probability of achievement attends every venture's objectives. Probability of achievement is a key factor in venture decision making. While it is not always directly variable with the size of a venture's objectives, higher objectives generally have a lower probability of being achieved.

It is useful to express an objective's probability of achievement as a percentage of 100 or as a number of points based on 10 and directly correlated with a percentage of probability. Either method can yield a "PA Index," or Probability of Achievement Index. A PA Index will provide the venture's managers with a bogey on which to evaluate the rationale of the objectives they have set, to help rank competitive ventures in a rough order of priority, and to base one aspect of their eventual GO determination. A theoretical sure thing could be assigned a PA Index of 100 percent, or 10 points. A 90 percent probability would receive 9 points, 80 percent 8 points, and so on, down to a cutoff, for example, of 70 percent, or 7 points, below which no venture would be considered. The higher the PA Index, the higher the priority that can be attached to its venture.

Probabilities of achievement are a mixture of subjective feel and a blend of confirmatory experience and information. Not infrequently, members of a venture team will sense different probabilities of achievement for their venture's objectives. This very often results in lowering the venture's targets or raising the venture's controls. A consensus PA Index for a venture team as a whole is a useful tool for dramatizing the group's conviction to itself. Exhibit 9-6 shows a topographic map on which a venture team has positioned a venture it is considering according to the probability of achieving its objective of $10 million. The map suggests

exhibit 9.5

roi and the pursuit
of sales volume

1. Before the pursuit of increased sales volume

Profit margin of 15 percent × turnover of 2.5

$$\text{ROI of 37.5 percent} = \frac{\$150,000 \text{ profit}}{\$1,000,000 \text{ sales}} \times \frac{\$1,000,000 \text{ sales}}{\$400,000 \text{ investment}}$$

$$= \frac{\$150,000}{\$400,000}$$

2. After the pursuit of increased sales volume

The objective is to increase sales volume by $200,000. As a result, profits are expected to rise by an additional $20,000. To support these incremental sales, additional investments of $100,000 are necessary. Profits will therefore show an increase of 13.3 percent on a sales volume increase of 20 percent. However, these increases in profit and volume will be more than offset by the increase in their required investment, thereby decreasing the ROI by 3.5 percent.

Profit margin of 14.2 percent × turnover of 2.4

$$\text{ROI of 34 percent} = \frac{\$170,000 \text{ profit}}{\$1,200,000 \text{ sales}} \times \frac{\$1,200,000 \text{ sales}}{\$500,000 \text{ investment}}$$

$$= \frac{\$170,000}{\$500,000}$$

exhibit 9.6

probability of achieving objectives

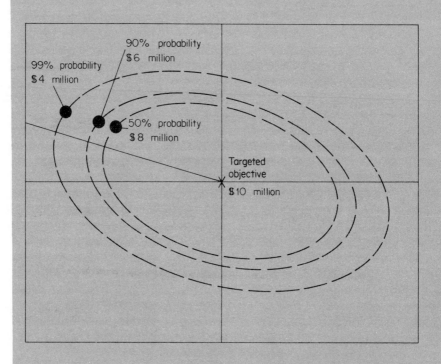

99% probability
$4 million

90% probability
$6 million

50% probability
$8 million

Targeted objective
$10 million

that the venture has been given a 50 percent chance of achieving $8 million, a 90 percent chance of achieving $6 million, and a 99 percent chance of achieving $4 million.

Finance Proposal Guidelines

When corporate management plays the role of venture banker, it looks at venture proposals as new-profit proposals first and as new-business evaluation proposals second. It is not difficult to understand why. Profit is management's universal language. It speaks in familiar numbers. A new business, on the other hand, may present management with a dictionary of foreign terms to comprehend before it can confront the essential growth opportunity it may offer. For this reason, venture-financing proposals should be structured along the following management-oriented lines as a means of ensuring their success:

1. Sell the venture's benefits expressed as an incremental new-profit and new-market position. Do not begin yet to sell the venture itself.

2. Compare the venture's profit benefits favorably with its principal risks. These risks always include the venture's budgeted costs, the probable value of alternative opportunities that must go unseized because of the venture's consumption of time and finite corporate resources, the degree of exposure to loss and the ability to cut loss quickly, and time to payback. Sell the benefits' favorable comparison. Do not begin yet to sell the venture itself.

3. Now, sell the venture in terms of its growth business opportunity, its expansive market, its ability to preempt competition, and the premium-price marketability of its product and service system.

Using Objectives to Secure Venture Financing

A company that plans to invest 5 to 6 percent of annual gross income in venturing, which is approximately equivalent to the long-term average annual investment in R&D, must be prepared for two types of financing. One is the initial financing required to see a venture through a twelve-to-eighteen-month period of gestation and get it off the ground. The other is secondary financing, which must be held at the ready to help a venture expand its initial foothold or to come to the rescue of a venture that has slipped behind in its time frame. The ability to provide secondary financing is often the margin between venture failure and venture success. In the world of noncorporate ventures in which secondary financing must be obtained from private or public funds, failure to plan for a second round of capital infusion is one of the largest single causes of venture mortality.

In-company venture financing is accomplished by the establishment of a line of credit by corporate management in its role as venture business banker. This allows each venture manager to draw funds on a demand feeding schedule up to a predetermined credit maximum. It is wise to establish two separate credit lines as soon as a venture has been commissioned. The first line will provide for the venture's initial financing through, for example, Year 1 of commercial marketing. The second line will be available for refinancing beyond that point. In this way, corporate management asserts its commitment to the venture as an ongoing business rather than as a passing fancy. With a cushion of secondary financing safely in the vault, the venture manager can concentrate on running up the business instead of politicking for future funds.

In its role as banker, corporate management must be shown the corporation's stake in the venture in order for it to become involved. New profits, superior to those obtainable in any other way, are usually the only sufficient motivation to encourage management to accept new risks. The best way to present the promise of new profits is through a five-to-ten-year profit proposal worked out on a pro forma basis, showing management what it can hope to add to its earnings and when. When a pro forma profit proposal comes up for management review, venture managers should anticipate that their corporate bankers will probably concentrate on getting answers to three major questions:

1. How much do we stand to *gain*, and when will it start to come in?

2. How much do we stand to *put up*, when will we need it, and when will we get it back?

3. How much do we stand to *lose*, and when can we get out to cut our loss?

Because these three questions are virtually every corporate banker's theme song, venture managers who negotiate for financing must come prepared to respond with satisfactory answers if they want to leave with their money. It is not difficult to predict the outcome in most cases. A venture manager can predict getting a turndown if any of his answers deviates too far from the ideal answers to the three major questions:

1. We stand to *gain* the sizable profit of $X, which will start to come in by Year 2.

2. We stand to *put up* the relatively small amount of $Y, for

which we will not be immediately liable, and we will get it back by Year 3 at the latest.

3. We stand to *lose* a maximum of $Z, and we can get out at any one of the following cutoff points at the following costs.

In many cases, because corporate bankers tend to be highly sensitive to the conservation of resources, the length of time to payback and the answers to the third question carry the greatest weight. Time-framing the venture's investment due dates to show cumulative costs sunk to each date can help reassure top management that it can get out without being too badly hurt if the venture turns sour. Exhibit 9-7 shows a Year 1 line-of-credit summary which has been time-framed on a quarterly basis and accumulated for the year. Exhibits 9-8, 9-9, and 9-10 show another useful approach to proposing a venture for financing. In these exhibits, an annual budget is proposed, and its coded categories, two of which are itemized, are broken out for detailed management audit.

Use Planning Page 45 to work out a Year 1 Line-of-Credit Summary for your venture. Use Planning Page 46 to work out an Annual Budget Proposal. Then, on Planning Page 47/1 through 47/8, break out from the Annual Budget Proposal as many individual Expense Budgets as you require to accommodate your principal codes.

---

exhibit 9.7
year I
line-of-credit summary

	Quarterly time frame	$MM	$MM cumulative
1. Start-up search and learn	April–July F1976–F1977	.1	.1
2. Find, analyze, and propose	August–November F1976–F1977	.3	.4
3. Develop for market entry	December–March F1976–F1977	.4	.8

exhibit 9.8

annual budget proposal

Code #	Type of expense	F1976–F1977 budget
250	**Manpower**	
	Employee transfer expense	$100,000
	Office temporaries	5,000
260	**Technical and professional**	190,000
270	**Information resources**	212,500
280	**Association memberships and meetings**	2,500
290	**Product development research**	50,000
320	**Office and general operating supplies**	2,500
330	**Communications**	3,500
340	**Travel and entertainment**	5,000

exhibit 9.9

technical and professional expense budget (code #260)

Type of expense	F1976–F1977	= First half	+ Second half
1. Venture business consultants, Smith & Jones Assocs.	$100,000 fee 2,500 expenses	$50,000 1,250	$50,000 1,250
2. Consulting chemists, Brown, Green & Co.	25,000	25,000	
3. One-shot consulting projects	25,000	12,500	12,500
4. Beautician and cos-metician Product purchases	25,000 3,500	12,500 1,750	12,500 1,750
5. Skin care panel	10,000	5,000	5,000

exhibit 9.10

information resources expense budget (code #270)

Type of expense	F1976–F1977	= First half	+ Second half
1. Secondary information searches	$50,000	$35,000	$15,000
2. Market segmentation study	50,000	50,000	
3. Product concept testing studies (10 at $5,000)	50,000	15,000	35,000
4. In-market validation screens (5 at $7,500)	37,500	. . .	37,500
5. Focus group panel sessions (5 at $5,000)	25,000	10,000	15,000

YEAR 1 LINE—OF—CREDIT SUMMARY

	Quarterly time frame	$MM	$MM cumulative
1. Start—up search and learn	_____-_____ F19__-F19__	__,___,___	___,___,___
2. Find, analyze, and propose	_____-_____ F19__-F19__	__,___,___	___,___,___
3. Develop for market entry	_____-_____ F19__-F19__	__,___,___	___,___,___

236

ANNUAL BUDGET PROPOSAL

Code #   Type of expense   F19_ _-F19_ _ budget

_____ <u>EXPENSE BUDGET</u>
(Code #   )

<u>Type of expense</u>   <u>F19_ _</u>-<u>F19_ _</u> = <u>First half</u> + <u>Second half</u>

238

_____ EXPENSE BUDGET
(Code #   )

Type of expense   F19_ _-F19_ _= First half + Second half

_____ EXPENSE BUDGET
          (Code #   )

Type of expense   F19_ _-F19_ _ = First half + Second half

240

_____ <u>EXPENSE BUDGET</u>
(Code #   )

<u>Type of expense</u>   F19_ _–F19_ _ = <u>First half</u> + <u>Second half</u>

<u>   </u>   <u>EXPENSE BUDGET</u>
(Code #   )

<u>Type of expense</u>   <u>F19__–F19__</u> = <u>First half</u> + <u>Second half</u>

_____ EXPENSE BUDGET
        (Code #   )

<u>Type of expense</u>   <u>F19__-F19__</u> = <u>First half</u> + <u>Second half</u>

_____ EXPENSE BUDGET
(Code #   )

Type of expense   F19_ _-F19_ _ = First half + Second half

_____ EXPENSE BUDGET
(Code #   )

Type of expense F19_ _–F19_ _ = First half + Second half

10

objectives through the venture life cycle

Every successful venture business has a three-phase life cycle. In the course of its life cycle, a venture business grows, reaches market maturity, and then begins a decline into obsolescence. For many ventures, perhaps for the majority, a three-to-five-year duration of prime "venturable life" is a safe planning maximum. After the fifth year of almost every venture's life, it will have become a mature business whose growth profits will be giving way to more normative profits. When the decline from market maturity begins to set in, as the idealized venture business life cycle illustrated in Exhibit 10-1 shows, a venture may enter into either a sharp or a more gradually prolonged period of senescence unless it undergoes rejuvenation. When rejuvenation is significant, a new venture life cycle may be initiated. When rejuvenation is only marginal, it may serve to plateau out the original life cycle's maturity phase and thereby to postpone the inevitable decline.

The venture life cycle's phases may be regarded as an interrelated series of three reductions: first, a phase of reduction of market inertia, followed by successive phases of profit reduction and cost reduction.

Growth is devoted to reducing market inertia, overcoming unawareness of the venture's product and service benefits, and establishing initial penetration. In the takeoff stage, demand must be accelerated and total market size expanded as rapidly as possible. Output grows, and unit costs fall, enabling unit profits to rise. If entry price has been set at a premium, profits can be accelerated even further by creaming the market. To continue growth, the market must be expanded among heavy users. New heavy-user candidates must be acquired. While distribution pipelines are being filled, the two severest threats to profit making are back ordering and its opposite, inventory buildup. If a true sweepstakes business is to be founded, early growth must be maximized by heavy investment.

247

Maturity is signaled by profit reduction when the knee of the life-cycle curve shown as point K in Exhibit 10-1 is reached. From this point on, premium price becomes difficult to hold. Price competition becomes intense, and sales volume generally plateaus off as competitors achieve market penetration based on marginal price or product differences. Advertising expenditures will have to be increased as venture products and services must maintain brand preference by more finite differentiation. The cost of sales will rise further as original distribution outlets must be held by price and service concessions and more extensive distribution must be sought out, educated, and supplied with products and motivation. While volume rises, profits erode as price falls and deals or free services give away additional earnings opportunities. As maturity ripens, market growth will slow down to the replacement rate. Venture "half-life," in which half of the commercial life of the venture has been lived, occurs. This is the point at which a technological or marketing advance may restore the venture to greater profitability. If not, the venture must begin to restructure its objectives to become a savings account type of cash-flow supplier for the funding of successor ventures.

Decline is the period of cost reduction in the face of increasing obsolescence and price competition. As profit on sales declines, marketing expenditures must also fall in order to contract the venture's base as much as possible. Growth becomes increasingly negative. Overcapacity may become evident, and the number of competitive suppliers may recede. Product line smoothing takes place. So do other cost control measures. The major management objective during decline is to make the venture self-financing so that its market share can be maintained without capital spending. In decline, the venture product or service has become a commodity of the blue-chip variety, with the low excitement and payout value of a bond.

The Profit/Investment Relationship

Investment and profit move in harmony with each other only when they are both in decline. During a venture life cycle's growth phase they are directly opposite each other. Investment is at its highest point, and profit is at its lowest. Generally, only losses are incurred, for profit is nonexistent. When investment is eased, profit rises sharply. In distinction to a venture's early growth, late growth and early maturity may be the high-profit phases in which, as Exhibit 10-1 shows, the widest disparity can exist between investment and profit returns.

In the high-profit phases, return on investment can begin. Each additional dollar of investment can produce many dollars in return. Never again in the venture's life-cycle history will this rate of incremental return

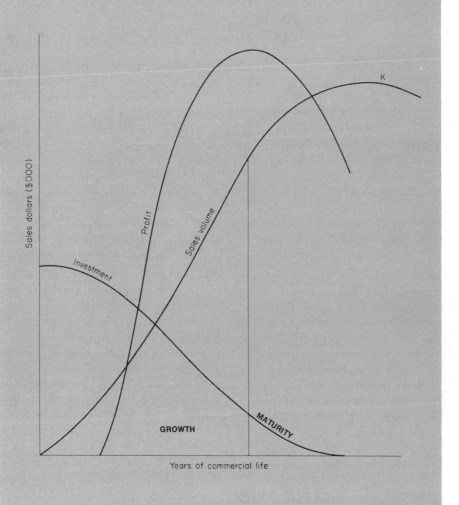

exhibit 10.1

interrelationship of investment, profit, and sales volume over the venture life cycle

K

Sales dollars ($000)

Profit

Sales volume

Investment

GROWTH

MATURITY

Years of commercial life

prevail. When the venture reaches the late stages of maturity, the incremental profit to be gained by additional investment diminishes. In fact, the point at which maturity begins to phase into decline is the point at which the cost of acquiring each incremental unit of profit reaches or exceeds the additional profit that can be acquired.

Up to this point of diminishing returns, the profit "output" obtainable by each additional unit of investment "input" rises geometrically in 2, 4, 6, 8 progression. This fact gives a venture its tremendous leverage. Beyond the venture's point of optimal rate of return, profit output decreases in arithmetic progression from 8 to 7, to 6, to 5, and so on. From point K on and sometimes even before, profit output may decrease in geometric progression. At this point, additional investment is no longer productive.

It is understandable from this analysis why most venture investments are made with the expectation of payback between Years 3 and 5 of venture life and why investors insist on a minimum gain of 5 to 8 times their initial investments for an average of four years at risk. Investment must stop when the cost of profit becomes too high, that is, when the profit return for each unit of incremental investment begins to decline. Ideally, investment will cease at the point at which the rate of return is optimal. Surely investment must cease by point K. If any investment is made beyond point K, it can only be in the hope of rejuvenating the venture life cycle by creating a new growth phase.

The profit/investment relationship over a venture's life cycle establishes two principles about a profitable rate of return on venture investment. First, venture profit accrues principally from emerging products and services whose rate of ROI is at its highest point. Therefore, a venture's ROI is chiefly return on the investment of products and services in their growth phase. Since emerging products undergoing growth return the bulk of profit, they must command the major portion of the venture investment base. Second, profit objectives must be set over a venture's accumulated life cycle. No venture can be expected to earn its maximum rate of profit every year. Once profit reaches its maximum point, it must inevitably decline. Annual profit objectives must therefore be oriented to the year's position in the venture life cycle, as in the following projection of ROI over a five-year venture life cycle.

Year	ROI %
F1970–F1971	8.2
F1971–F1972	34.6
F1972–F1973	19.4
F1973–F1974	18.6
F1974–F1975	12.1

The Profit/Sales Volume Relationship

Profit and sales volume do not proceed simultaneously over the venture life cycle. Profit objectives become possible only when market acceptance is achieved. It is in the venture growth phase that profit begins to be made if it is to be made at all. Once market maturity sets in, competition will attempt to restructure the venture's market. Even though sales volume may still be expanding, unit profits will start to shrink. In late maturity and decline, sales volume and profits fall together. Profit can be maintained only through product rejuvenation or cost reduction.

Over the venture life cycle, profit tends at first to lag behind sales volume, then to rise sharply ahead of it, and finally to fall faster than volume as the life cycle wanes. A venture's profit objectives must therefore largely be realized in its growth and maturity phases. These profit-making phases may occupy as little as two-fifths of a five-year life cycle's duration. When a two- or three-year development period precedes market introduction, a venture's life-span as a business investment is increased to a total of seven or eight years. This means that the profit phase may occupy only two-sevenths or one-fourth of venture life, a tightly constricted period in which the financial making or breaking of the total investment can occur.

> Use Planning Page 48 to work out your venture's probable life cycle. Enter on the exhibit the venture's projected sales dollar earnings on the vertical axis and the venture's anticipated years of commercial life on the horizontal axis. Then relate the venture's investment, profit, and sales volume over the life cycle by drawing their curves against the background of the idealized curves in the exhibit.

VENTURE LIFE CYCLE

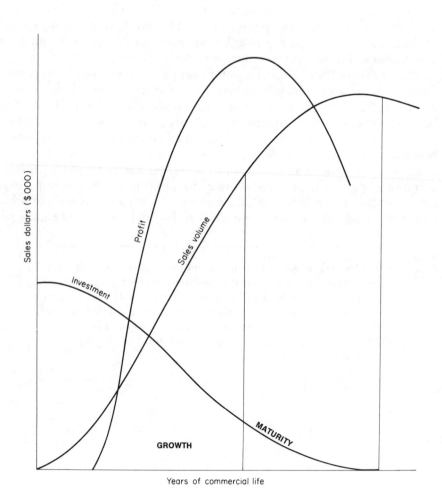

Pro Forma Financial Profile

A venture's minimum financial objectives must be proved to be realizable, or at least must not be provably unrealizable, before committing the venture to a GO decision. The device by which this demonstration of venture viability can best be shown is the pro forma financial profile. Exhibit 10-2 illustrates a pro forma based on minimum objectives and criteria for a venture in the personal care business. The pro forma projects the first ten years of the venture's national life as it can be imagined beforehand. Its purpose is to yield a rough idea of the major financial outcomes for the venture as if it were an actual operational entity.

The basic profit and loss relationships in the pro forma have been derived from secondary research into the personal care industry and firsthand information about internal development costs. These costs are detailed in the pro forma's attachment A, which is reproduced in Exhibit 10-3. Venture practice often encourages loading all development investments into Year 1 and using the national marketing launch date as the cutoff point for all developmental expenditures.

Use **Planning Page 49** to work out a **Development Cost Estimate** for your venture. Then factor this information into **Planning Page 50** to work out a **Pro Forma Financial Profile** based on your venture's minimal objectives and criteria.

---

exhibit 10-2

pro forma financial profile (based on minimal venture objectives and criteria)

Year	F70-75	1 F76	2 F77	3 F78	4 F79	5 F80	6 F81	7 F82	8 F83	9 F84	10 F85
Sales and related costs ($000)											
Total retail market (+5%/year)		550.0	590.0	620.0	650.0	680.0	715.0	750.0	790.0	830.0	870.0
(Our share)		(4.0)	(10.0)	(9.5)	(9.0)	(9.5)	(9.5)	(10.0)	(10.0)	(10.0)	(10.5)
Total A&P spending		70.0	75.0	80.0	85.0	88.0	93.0	98.0	102.0	108.0	113.0
(Our share)		(11.5)	(14.0)	(13.0)	(12.0)	(11.5)	(12.5)	(12.5)	(12.5)	(13.0)	(13.0)
Retail sales		22.2	59.0	59.0	59.0	64.0	68.5	73.5	79.5	85.0	92.0
Gross sales		10.6	26.6	26.6	26.6	29.7	31.8	33.0	35.6	38.3	41.5
Net sales		10.0	25.0	25.0	25.0	27.0	29.0	31.0	33.5	36.0	39.0
Direct cost		3.0	7.5	7.5	7.5	7.5	8.0	8.5	8.5	9.0	10.0
(% N/S)		(30)	(30)	(30)	(30)	(27)	(27)	(27)	(25)	(25)	(25)
Advertising		4.0	6.5	6.5	6.0	6.0	6.0	6.5	7.0	7.0	8.0
Promotion		3.0	4.0	4.0	4.0	4.0	4.5	4.5	5.0	5.5	6.0
Total A&P		7.0	10.5	10.5	10.0	10.0	10.5	11.0	12.0	12.5	14.0
(% N/S)		(70)	(42)	(42)	(40)	(37)	(36)	(36)	(36)	(35)	(36)
Overhead	1.0*	2.0	5.0	5.0	4.0	4.0	4.5	5.0	5.5	6.0	6.0
(% N/S)		(18)	(20)	(20)	(16)	(15)	(15)	(17)	(16)	(17)	(15)
PBT (LBT)	(1.0)	(2.0)	2.0	2.0	3.5	5.5	6.0	6.5	7.5	8.5	9.0
(% N/S)		(8)	(8)	(8)	(14)	(20)	(21)	(22)	(22)	(23)	(23)
Cumulative total	(1.0)	(3.0)	(1.0)	1.0	4.5	10.0	16.0	22.5	30.0	38.5	47.5

254

Development costs ($000)

Pretest	4.2	0.4	0.4	0.4	0.4	0.4	0.4	0.4	0.4	0.4
Test-market	3.3	0.4	0.4	0.4	0.4	0.4	0.4	0.4	0.4	0.4
Total	7.5	0.8	0.8	0.8	0.8	0.8	0.8	0.8	0.8	0.8
Total cost, PBT (LBT)	(8.5)	(2.8)	1.2	1.2	2.7	4.7	5.2	5.7	6.7	7.7	8.2
Cumulative total	(8.5)	(11.3)	(10.1)	(8.9)	(6.2)	(1.5)	3.7	9.4	16.1	23.8	32.0

Investments

	$MM
Average capital less depreciation over ten-year period ($10MM initial capital straight-line-depreciated over fifteen years)	$ 7.0
Average working capital (20% N/S basis)	6.5
Development expense plus Year 1 loss position (before tax)	10.5
Grand total investment	$24.0

Return

Average annual return over first nine profitable years (net of ongoing development costs)	$ 4.8

Before-tax ROI

Excluding F70–76 cumulative LBT position	36%
Including F70–76 cumulative LBT position	20%

* Depreciation and start-up expense.

255

exhibit 10.3

development cost estimate
(attachment a)

	F71–72	F72–73	F73–74	F74–75	F75–76	Average, years F76–85
Pretest	$624	$1,000	$ 800	$ 800	$ 800	$400
Test-market			800	1,050	1,300	400
Total	$624	$1,000	$1,600	$1,850	$2,100	$800

Assumptions

1. Test-market introductions:

#1	#2	#3
3Q/F73–74	1Q/F74–75	1Q/F75–76

2. Test-market cost assumptions:
   2.1. $800M, Year 1
   2.2. $250M/year prior to national launch

3. Pretest assumptions (F72–75):
   3.1. $700M base operating
   3.2. $100M per prototype (three in F72–73 and one each in F73–75)

4. Each year, F76–85: $400M for basic development (surveys, consultants, and prototypes), plus $400M to cover test-market costs of line extensions

DEVELOPMENT COST ESTIMATE

	F19__-F19__	F19__-F19__	F19__-F19__	F19__-F19__	F19__-F19__	Average, years F19__-F19__
1. Pretest	$ _,___,___	$ _,___,___	$ _,___,___	_,___,___	_,___,___	$ _,___,___
2. Test-market	$ _,___,___	_,___,___	_,___,___	_,___,___	_,___,___	$ _,___,___
3. Total	$ _,___,___	$ _,___,___	$ _,___,___	$ _,___,___	$ _,___,___	$ _,___,___

Assumptions:

1. Test-market introductions:

#1	#2	#3
_Q/F19__-F19__	_Q/F19__-F19__	_Q/F19__-F19__

2. Test-market assumptions:

2.1. $ _,___,___ Year ____

2.2. $ _,___,___/year prior to national launch

3. Pretest assumptions (F19__-F19__):

3.1. $ _,___,___ base operating

3.2. $ ___,___,___ per prototype

4. Each year, F19__-F19__: $ _,___,___ for basic development

plus: $ ___,___,___ to cover test-market costs

257

PRO FORMA FINANCIAL PROFILE
(Based on Minimal Venture Objectives and Criteria)

	Cumulative to date (F19__-F19__)	Year 1 (F19__-F19__)	Year 2 (F19__-F19__)	Year 3 (F19__-F19__)	Year 4 (F19__-F19__)	Year 5 (F19__-F19__)
1. Sales and related costs	\$_,___,___	\$_,___,___	\$_,___,___	\$_,___,___	\$_,___,___	\$_,___,___
2. Development costs	\$_,___,___	\$_,___,___	\$_,___,___	\$_,___,___	\$_,___,___	\$_,___,___
3. Investments	\$_,___,___	\$_,___,___	\$_,___,___	\$_,___,___	\$_,___,___	\$_,___,___
4. Return on investment	__%	__%	__%	__%	__%	__%

258

V

how to achieve
venture objectives

venture business positioning

A venture business can come into existence only through acceptance by the heavy users in its market. If market acceptance cannot be generated for a venture or if it is lost, the venture cannot live. For this reason, the positioning of a venture in the acceptance framework of its heavy-user market is a crucial event in the venture process.

Ideally, a venture will be inserted in its market as a round peg is welcomed by a round hole. Its business proposition will be understood, assigned credibility and value, and accepted by heavy-user customers. No "pernicious contraries" will blur the perceived value of the venture's benefits. The new business will be seen to fill an important need and will make its promise of fulfillment readily apparent. It will belong not just *in* its market but *to* its market. Ventures fail because they are negatively accepted as square pegs or find no hole in the market whatever their shape.

Positioning a venture in its market's need system gives the venture its style, or image. It provides the ultimate definition of the business, both to its market and, equally important, to venture management and top management. In its shorthand form, the business position is a marketing stance, summarizing the posture the venture chooses to take as a benefiter of needs.

Business-Positioning Statement

When the venture manager determines a position for the business that comes as close as possible to offering a premium benefit for an intense market need yet occupies noncompetitive space, a statement defining the nature of the venture business should be written for inclusion as the initial page of the market penetration plan. This statement answers the question "What business is being planned for?"

A business-positioning statement should contain three elements in this order of presentation:

1. The heavy-user market to be penetrated

2. The market problem to be solved or the market opportunity to be capitalized on

3. The premium benefit which is to be offered by the venture to solve the problem or to capitalize on the opportunity and which will be the basis for venture branding at a premium level of price

A potential venture customer can be defined as anyone who perceives the venture product's value to be equal to or greater than its price. In technical, industrial, or service markets, the definition of a potential venture customer can be pinpointed to include anyone who perceives the venture product's value as contributing more to the improvement of profit than its price. Customers who perceive value to be equal to price will probably be light or periodic users. They may comprise up to 80 percent of all venture product users. The remaining 20 percent or so will be the venture's heavy users. They will perceive value to be greater than price. This relatively small number of users will underwrite the venture's profit. They will be its most consistent, highest-volume customers. From the venture manager's point of view, the heavy users will be the market.

Because of their higher propensity to consume, heavy users are the only customers in each market segment which the venture should plan to serve. Only the needs of probable heavy users should be allowed to influence market estimates or product construction, formulation, and packaging. The needs of lighter, more sporadic users may be interesting, even intriguing, to the venture manager, but they are irrelevant to achieving the venture's objectives.

Heavy users exist in a tight time frame, the here and now. They are transient because the perceived values which mobilize them are transient. Each new competitive product carries the potential threat of rearranging the value perceptions of heavy users and thereby diminishing venture business opportunity. The manager must try to anticipate how the venture's targeted heavy users will react to new benefits, or to older benefits at new prices, offered by competitive products. In this way, it will be possible to make a reasonable assessment of how many heavy users the venture can project and for how long they may be counted on to keep using the venture product heavily.

The identification of a venture's heavy users is the single most significant aspect of positioning the venture as a business. A skin care venture acknowledges its heavy-user dependency by stating its business position in this manner:

> This business is designed to help teen-age girls, and to a lesser extent teen-age boys, to solve the physical and psychological problems accompanying juvenile and adolescent acne, and thereby to enhance the enjoyment of their life-styles, by providing a remedy for acne in the form of a self-applying product system manufactured under professional dermatological guidance and mass-marketed through supermarkets and drug stores. In the perception of the market, the business will be positioned as *the professional system of skin care available without embarrassment everywhere.*

A model positioning statement for an industrial security venture might read:

> This business is designed to help managers of business and professional offices, plants, warehouses and other storage areas, banks, and all other depositories of valuable real property to solve the problems of theft and unwarranted usage by providing a combined detection, apprehension, and alarm system based on the commercial adaptation of military radar electronics that will be prescribed, installed, leased, maintained, and upgraded by a single contract supplier. In the perception of the market, the business will be positioned as *the high-technology protection service that operates with military efficiency yet civilian cost.*

The business-positioning statement enables venture management to answer its cosmic question: "Is there a market for such a business?" If the answer is "yes," it will be contained in the venture market penetration plan. If the answer is negative, the venture manager will have to return to the corporate growth base capability and market opportunity mix and select another venturable proposition.

The Market Value of Business Style

Since the market accepts or rejects a business position in relation to its needs, a venture's positioning will become known to have been successful only after the fact. As market penetration takes hold, the venture's heavy users will peg the business for what they perceive its value to them as being. A venture which offers no perceived value will literally come to have no existence for its market. Ventures which are seen to offer value will take on a reputation for being "The people who . . ." or "The company that . . ." in the market's shorthand vocabulary. The words that complete these summary judgments describe for its customers or clients the net outcome of the entire venture process in the traditional twenty-five words or less.

The task of positioning the venture as a business is to put these words into the market's mind through every public act of the business. This procedure gives a market value to business style. Styling the venture means shaping and molding its public personality, including such diverse elements as its business name; the form and function of its product and service lines; their brand names; their promotional theming and media usage through advertising, sales promotion, publicity, and packaging; pricing; and the perceived attitude of management as being rewarding or difficult to do business with.

To style a venture business simply as "new" or "first" will rarely be a sufficient basis for positioning. It may even be detrimental in market situations where "new" equates with "unproved" and "unreliable." To lean on a high state of technological development can connote both positive and negative attitudes. Relating a venture business position to its parent company's positioning may be dangerous in certain situations and advantageous in others. There is no formula for successful styling except one: take the position closest to adding the highest perceived value for an intense market need that is also the position farthest from competitive offerings to benefit the same need. A rider to this formula suggests that if a compromise must be made, it is generally safer to move toward a competitive position, challenging a rival by offering a marginal rather than a gross difference in benefit, instead of moving away from a market need. In the final analysis, a venture's destiny will always be more strongly market-determined than influenced by competition.

> **Use Planning Page 51 to work out a Business-positioning Statement.**

Right-onness: The Concept of Market Fit

When a venture's business position can be said to fit its market's needs, four conditions will have been met:

1. The heavy users in the venture's market perceive that the venture's business offering fits one or more of their needs.

2. They perceive in themselves an intense motivation to satisfy these needs.

3. They perceive that the venture promises them optimal satisfaction because of its premium values, and they believe this

BUSINESS—POSITIONING STATEMENT

1. Heavy—user market to be penetrated
   by the venture

2. Market problem to be solved
   and/or market opportunity to be capitalized on
   by the venture

3. Premium benefit to solve market problem
   and/or capitalize on market opportunity
   offered by the venture

promise or at least suspend their disbelief enough to permit
a trial.

4. The promise of benefiting from the venture's premium
values is further documented by premium price.

A venture that meets these conditions should be right-on in positioning itself with its market. A failure to meet any one of the first three
conditions can foreclose the venture's opportunity by effectively depriving it of a market. A failure to meet the fourth condition can foreclose
the achievement of venture profit objectives by depriving the business of
premium-pricing capability at the growth stage in its commercial life
cycle.

**Use Planning Page 52 to work out a Venture Benefit/Market
Need Correlation Analysis.**

Positioning for Brandability

The objective of business positioning is to brand the venture, and accordingly confer branded status on its products and services, as a supplier of
premium value. Branding permits price leadership. It is also conducive to
establishing a transiently monopolistic role for the venture. This can grant
the venture the period of competitive grace it requires to recoup its investment and become a profit maker.

Branding, which is the opposite of commodity status, occurs when
premium value is perceived by the market. Just as the market endows a
venture business with its ultimate positioning, the market also attributes a
brand or commodity classification to it. Venture management must act to
endow its business with values its market will be willing to brand. These
values will come from the technical and marketing capabilities in management's growth base. If these capabilities do not contribute values that
will be perceived as additional to competitive values, management will
be unable to use the capability base of its existing business operations
as a jumping-off place for venture growth.

Premium-pricing capability is the result of brandability. It is the market's acknowledgment of added value. The degree of premium capability
which the market permits a venture business to possess is also a portent.
It enables venture management to approximate the margin of time it may
be able to count on before the market enforces the inevitable descent
into commodity pricing.

VENTURE BENEFIT/MARKET NEED CORRELATION ANALYSIS

Heavy-user market needs
as expressed by the market

Heavy-user market needs
as benefited by the venture

Competition as a Repositioning Force

The intent of a venture's going-in competition as well as its effect is to act as a driving counterforce to move the venture away from the right-onness of its positioning. Follow-on competition will have the same objective. Competition should therefore be regarded as a repositioning force. Its thrust is to drive the venture away from its branded status and thereby to deprive it of its premium-pricing capability.

To do this, competition does not have to capture the venture's market opportunity. All it has to do is to reposition the venture by nudging its business proposition off-center to its market. If this happens, the venture's heavy users will perceive its value as being less than premium. This is as good a way as any to interpret the functional role of competitive marketing in a rivalrous business situation: to devalue the market's perception of other suppliers' benefits. This can have the immediate effect of reversing a venture's value/price relationship and making price appear too high. The venture is then left with two options, each of which tends to diminish profit. One is to lower price to conform with the market's diminished perception of value. The other, which adds cost and thereby deflects venture cash flow that would go into profit, is to replot the venture business proposition back to a premium position.

The Gap Map

A useful tool for the venture manager in planning an optimal position for a new business is a "gap map," a plot board that shows the two critical determinants of positioning. One determinant is market needs. The other is positions of competitors who may already have staked out preemptive acceptance as suppliers of the same or similar benefits. A map of these needs and their preemptions will reveal where relatively unchallenged positioning opportunities may be located and where confrontation may be inevitable.

Market Needs: Hit Them Where They Are

The challenge posed by market needs is to hit them as close as possible to where they are. To be right-on a market need means that the venture's benefit value is perceived by its market as the best way to solve the problem or to capitalize on the opportunity that has created the need.

All successful venture businesses are built on fulfilling needs, but not all needs support venture businesses. Some needs are simply not intense enough to provide service by a commercial benefit at a high enough price or a high enough turnover to found a profitable business. Such second- or third-magnitude needs are understandable temptations to ventures, all the more so because they often show up on gap maps as unserved by competition. But, as a general rule, they are to be avoided rather than encountered.

Other needs are perceived by their markets as being best benefited by no benefit at all. Often, the benefit of doing nothing is a market's true preference. Although a need may be discoverable ("You really should do something about this problem or this opportunity," the venturer will say, and the market will answer, "Yes"), the market will not buy a product or service to fill its acknowledged need. Something called "nothing at all" is often the market's product of choice. Because benefiting its need is postponable by the market, it should be no less postponable by venture management.

A market need profile of the venture's potential heavy users is therefore a requirement. It should show what the needs are and the priority order of intensity with which each need is held. This profile pinpoints the venture's targets.

Competitive Positions: Hit Them Where They Aren't

The challenge posed by competitive suppliers who have already positioned themselves right on a market need can be dealt with in one of two ways. A well-entrenched competitor who is either a market leader or the number two factor in the market should generally not be taken on head-to-head. As a rule, a venture will be best advised to position its business value to one side or the other of a strong competitor. Yet its position must still be close enough to a major market need to be perceived as offering premium value. This is hitting a competitor in the gap. The key to success with this strategy is to make certain that there is an intense need in the competitive gap. Otherwise there will be no competition but no market opportunity either. There are many markets in which this is the case. Dominated by a single supplier or by two more or less identically positioned competitors, they may not be venturable. On the other hand, competitors who are less well established atop a market need can often be driven off by superior technical benefits or by superior marketing of similar benefits.

To appreciate competitive positioning and determine which positions are best to avoid or attack and try to win over, venture management should make two important estimates of each competitor:

1. What is each major competitor's present business position as perceived by our potential heavy-user market?

2. What positioning leverage does each competitor retain that could permit moving quickly to absorb or nullify our market entry position?

> **Use Planning Page 53 to work out a Venture Position/Competitive Position Disparity Analysis.**

Plugging the Satisfaction Gap

If a market is regarded as a group of potentially heavy users of a venture's benefit values, a market opportunity can be defined as a gap in their satisfaction structure. A satisfaction gap exists for one of two reasons:

1. A need is not being met by the benefits currently offered.

2. A need is not being met because no benefit is currently offered.

In the first instance, a venture opportunity may arise from offering a "new, improved benefit" with what is perceived to be a superior value/price relationship. In the second instance, a venture opportunity may arise from offering any benefit whose value exceeds the market's perceived value from doing nothing to satisfy its need. In neither instance, however, is an automatic venture opportunity implicit. A new, improved benefit may not meet market needs any better or enough better to command preference. Management may see the benefit as new and improved, but the market may regard it as a me-too replica. Needs that are not currently being met should always be approached with caution. There may be good reason. The best reason from the market's point of view is that its satisfaction is more postponable than the cost of satisfaction is disposable. This nets out to no marketable need.

It is the intensity of market need to fill one of its satisfaction gaps rather than the simple existence of need that is a venture's driving force. The essential business proposition of a venture must therefore be presented to its market in this way: "Your business (or your life-style) can add a superior benefit value to satisfy an intense need at the most favorable (or, at the very least, a favorable) value/price relationship by trading with our business." If such a presentation is accepted by the market, the venture can become positioned as the most favored supplier: the supplier of the greatest perceived value. This is optimal venture positioning. Less than optimal positioning, but nonetheless often acceptable as a profitable business base, is to be one of several favored suppliers. Anything less is probably fatally flawed.

In all cases, it is the market which positions a venture business on the basis of how well the business plugs one of its major satisfaction gaps. It is therefore more accurate to admit that a venture really cannot position itself. What it can and must accomplish is to offer its market the

VENTURE POSITION/COMPETITIVE POSITION DISPARITY ANALYSIS

<u>Venture value position
as a need satisfier</u>

<u>Competitors' names and value
positions as need satisfiers</u>

premium value around which its eventual positioning will be constructed. To position a venture, therefore, really means to position its *customer satisfaction proposition*. The market will take it from there and position the venture business on its measuring rod of comparative or absolute preference.

The Customer Satisfaction Proposition

The objective of a venture's proposal to deliver premium customer satisfaction is based on a simple formula: *Perceived value from doing business with the venture exceeds the cost (ideally, by the highest degree obtainable)*. This means that the venture's benefits must be perceived as being the highest, or at least very high, in relation to their price. This perception permits price also to be high. As long as values are perceived as higher, price can be maximized. As a matter of fact, the venture value/price concept should be stated in this manner to reveal its full importance: for values to be perceived as being truly of a premium nature, price must be premium as well.

A product's perceived value is the sum total of its benefits in use. For value to exceed price, one of three conditions must be met. (1) The user's cost of achieving his objectives must be lower with the venture product than with the best existing alternative product. (2) The user's benefits must be greater even if cost is not lower. (3) Deriving the benefits must be more important to the user than doing without them. End-user potential is the size of the market composed of all users for whom these conditions are met. Ideal price is the highest price at which the greatest number of potential end users can be induced to buy.

The extent to which perceived value is greater than price indicates a market's *thrust* toward the product. If a product is priced at value or near it, market thrust to acquire it will be low. If a product is priced below value, thrust can be high. Since low price is associated with lower profit margins and is incompatible with the market leadership image which a venture product should strive to achieve, it is not usually a viable alternative to produce thrust. This means that the best way a high thrust can be generated by a venture is to offer value that will be perceived as even greater than a premium price. This may be the venture manager's most difficult marketing challenge.

The venture's customer satisfaction proposition must offer a compellingly attractive trade-off between premium value and the premium price which is required to achieve venture growth objectives. This cannot be achieved by apologizing for premium price. The satisfaction proposal should not say that you get premium benefit values *but* that the price is also a premium. Quite the opposite, the venture proposal must make it clear that you get premium benefit values *because*, among other things, the price is premium too. Premium price can then be employed in its proper marketing role to document value and thereby add to market thrust.

A properly conceived customer satisfaction proposition establishes the venture as a supplier of greater value than its cost. This is the definition of a *bargain*. To be successful, a venture must be perceived as a bargain by its market. With premium pricing, it will be a high-priced bargain, to be sure, but a bargain nevertheless.

> **Use Planning Page 54 to work out a Customer Satisfaction Proposition (a Client Satisfaction Proposition if your venture is a service business) that will set a marketable value/price relationship for your venture's product or service benefit.**

<u>CUSTOMER SATISFACTION PROPOSITION</u>

1. The perceived value from:

    (Venture Product Benefit)

2. Exceeds its price or cost of $_____/unit

3. By an excess value of $_____/unit, or ___%

12

venture product and service lining

The two most difficult stages in the venture process are the selection steps at which, first, a venture business opportunity must be chosen and then its product or service lines determined. These two commitments give the venture its identity as a business. The fact that this is so, and that the venture is being shaped and molded in an irreversible manner, endows venture selection and product or service lining with the highest degree of importance and calls for the greatest demands on venture management skill.

The venture's products and services are the cash-flow sources that make the venture go. There are two basic questions that must be answered if venture motive power is to be high. One question concerns the total offering: "What makes a good venture product line?" The answer is "*a relatively wide choice offered to a relatively narrow market.*" The second question is, "What makes a good venture product?" There are three guidelines which can be helpful in predisposing venture product success:

1. A venture product is a transitory vehicle for an end-user benefit, not an end in itself. Today's superfine will be tomorrow's crude. Therefore, a quest for the perfect product is folly.

2. Product reliability means benefit consistency, a feeling of certainty by a market that the benefit will be consistently delivered. When a venture product is within specifications, it meets the market's requirements for benefit dependability. Venture product specifications must therefore be determined by market specifications.

3. The delivery of user benefits by a venture product confers a service. The service may be a positive reward which bestows an

advantage on a market. Or it may remove a deficit from a market. All product businesses are therefore service businesses which must be marketed for their service values.

The Challenge of High-Order Innovation

Venture product development is a case of high-order innovation. The products and services that come out of ventures must be perceived by their markets as significant departures from accustomed norms. This characteristic distinguishes venture products from the two lower orders of innovation represented by product improvements and product line extensions. Product line extensions are variations on a theme. They include new flavors, new sizes, and other minor alterations in the basic product concept. They lead to families of interrelated products. Product improvements are marginal modifications in the formulation, processing, or packaging of existing products. They represent the lowest order of innovation.

The rank ordering of innovation for venture product development is illustrated in Exhibit 12-1, which shows the six basic marketing environments. Venture product innovation is designed for Environments 3 and 6. Both of these environments are at the far end of investment in product and marketing technology. Environment 6 is the most challenging market. Investment and risk are maximized to their ultimate levels when a product's benefit concept and its intended market are unfamiliar to a venture management that, in turn, is unfamiliar to the market. This situation puts sizable pressure on the quality of venture product benefits.

Venture Product Concepts

Benefits exist only in the minds of markets. Unlike products, which are tangible, benefits are concepts. They are value attributes that markets perceive as able to satisfy their needs in a favorable relationship to cost.

All product concepts are promises to convey a beneficial service. The fact that a product concept proves to be marketable means that its promise of offering a solution to a problem fits the market's perception of its needs. This is ground for believing that a venture business opportunity may exist.

Exhibit 12-2 shows how a soft drink manufacturer can begin to work up venture product concepts within the close-in context of existing technical and marketing capability.

> **Use Planning Page 55 to work out close-in product concepts to satisfy your venture market's needs.**

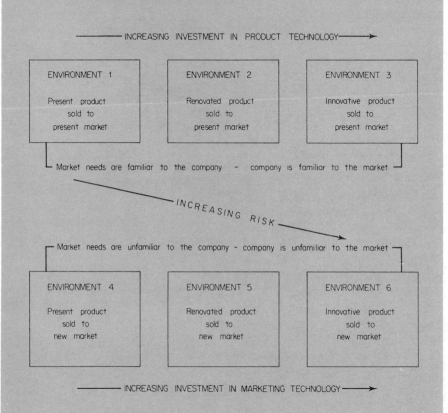

exhibit 12-1

the six basic
marketing environments

────────── INCREASING INVESTMENT IN PRODUCT TECHNOLOGY ──────────▶

ENVIRONMENT 1	ENVIRONMENT 2	ENVIRONMENT 3
Present product sold to present market	Renovated product sold to present market	Innovative product sold to present market

└─ Market needs are familiar to the company — company is familiar to the market ─┘

INCREASING RISK ──────▶

┌─ Market needs are unfamiliar to the company - company is unfamiliar to the market ─┐

ENVIRONMENT 4	ENVIRONMENT 5	ENVIRONMENT 6
Present product sold to new market	Renovated product sold to new market	Innovative product sold to new market

────────── INCREASING INVESTMENT IN MARKETING TECHNOLOGY ──────────▶

exhibit 12-2

cola product concept inventory

Potential market need	Product benefit concept to satisfy market need
1. Health and well-being	1.1. Vitamin-enriched cola fortified with vitamins B and C
	1.2. Protein cola fortified with essential body-building protein
2. Sophistication and personal flair	2. Cognac cola
3. Activity maintenance under stress	3. Energy cola
4. Sensual gratification	4. High-carbonated cola

CLOSE—IN PRODUCT CONCEPTS

Potential market need

Product benefit concept
to satisfy market need

In Exhibit 12-3, a more complicated challenge is illustrated for a breakfast foods processor. Three marketing environments are shown in terms of breakfast contexts. One is composed of breakfast eaters for whom the traditional concept of breakfast still fills a need as the first meal of the day. Another is composed of breakfast eaters for whom the current concept of breakfast has become transitional because they perceive a need for something different from what breakfast offers. In the third context, breakfast has become obsolete. To meet the needs of each market environment, many food concepts can be generated for testing. For example, instant breakfasts which offer the vitamin, protein, and mineral values of a complete snack-type minimeal can be positioned at point 3C on the matrix. This, with points 1A and 2B, may be the most promising area for venture product opportunity.

> **Use Planning Page 56 to work out a Product Use/Product Concept Matrix for three market use contexts, beginning with current use and ranging through transitional use to future use.**

exhibit 12-3

breakfast context/ breakfast food concept matrix

	(1) Current breakfast context "Breakfast is still the first meal of the day"	(2) Transitional breakfast context "Breakfast today is different"	(3) Future breakfast context "Breakfast is obsolete"
(A) New breakfast food concepts	(1A)	(2A)	(3A)
(B) Breakfast supplement concepts	(1B)	(2B)	(3B)
(C) Breakfast substitue and replacement concepts	(1C)	(2C)	(3C)

PRODUCT USE/PRODUCT CONCEPT MATRIX

	(1) Current-use context	(2) Transitional-use context	(3) Future-use context
(A) New product concepts	(1A)	(2A)	(3A)
(B) Product supplement concepts	(1B)	(2B)	(3B)
(C) Product substitute and replacement concepts	(1C)	(2C)	(3C)

The Attribute of "Good Concept"

A good venture product concept is an accurate relationship between *perceived market needs,* defined as needs which the market, not just the venturer, perceives it has, and *perceived product benefits,* defined as values which the market will prefer to satisfy its needs, not those which the venturer thinks it should prefer. This relationship is often determinable by concept testing in the venture's market. Concept testing can provide a venture manager's sole control against releasing nonproducts for rejection. The gateway role of concept testing in producing venture products that can be said to have "good concept" is shown in Exhibit 12-4.

When a venture product has good concept, it will be able to meet two test criteria:

1. It will demonstrate an acceptable level of market appeal for its value/price ratio so that it can mobilize sufficient heavy users to form a trial market.

2. On the basis of interest in the trial, it will be able to promise an acceptable level of sustained appeal to ensure repeated heavy use.

To achieve a good concept, potential venture products must possess two positive relationships: a benefit/deficit relationship that strongly favors the benefit and a price/benefit relationship that allows price to be perceived and promoted as a function of benefit value.

Benefit/Deficit Relationship

A venture product or service must possess a positive benefit/deficit relationship. It must be able to offer at least one demonstrable unique benefit. Beyond that, it must not be contaminated by any significant deficit. These are the minimum criteria for success.

A demonstrable unique benefit is the central requirement for marketability at a premium price. It provides the basis for the high perceived value that allows the market to attribute a good reason to buy the product. The absence of a good reason to buy is one of the most recurrent causes of venture product failure. An equivalent product which is as good as competitive products is rarely good enough to be a venture entry.

This does not mean that venture product development must always be a search for the unheard-of product. Fountainhead-type products which are on the leading edge of research are among the most dangerous ventures. They tend to be overengineered, based far more firmly on technical capabilities than on market need. They must often be sold at a price inflated by engineering costs that may be impossible for the market to recover through value in use. For these reasons, venture product developers may deliberately refrain from drawing fully on their state of the art of technical feasibility. They try to create products that are simple to operate and cheap to make rather than products that are as complicated as their engineering could permit.

In terms of its benefit delivery, a venture product does not have to be all things to all people. It must only be one thing to enough heavy users to create a market. There is a further requirement. The product must not blur its sharp benefit image by giving the market a good reason not to buy it in the form of a significant deficit. If such a deficit is perceived by the market, the product may become known by the deficit as if it contained no benefits at all.

Use Planning Page 57 to work out a Benefit/Deficit Analysis for your venture product or service.

---

exhibit 12-4

the gateway role
of venture product concept testing

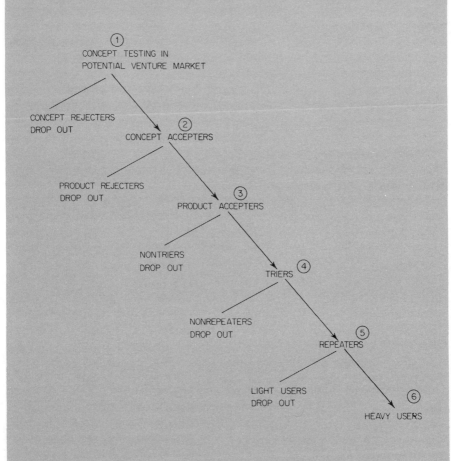

① CONCEPT TESTING IN
POTENTIAL VENTURE MARKET

CONCEPT REJECTERS
DROP OUT

② CONCEPT ACCEPTERS

PRODUCT REJECTERS
DROP OUT

③ PRODUCT ACCEPTERS

NONTRIERS
DROP OUT

④ TRIERS

NONREPEATERS
DROP OUT

⑤ REPEATERS

LIGHT USERS
DROP OUT

⑥ HEAVY USERS

VENTURE PRODUCT BENEFIT/DEFICIT ANALYSIS

Demonstrable unique benefit(s)
to justify premium price

Actual or potential deficit(s)
to be counteracted or eliminated

Value Maximization

Every product benefit decision carries its own risk and its own potential for reward. Value maximization offers a method of calculating the reward from a variety of product strategy decisions such as the following: What is the optimal benefit the product should deliver? How much of the benefit is enough? How many products carrying the benefit should there be in the line? A decision network for any of these questions can be created to serve as a graphic dialogue of a venture manager's question (for example, "What if we offered two venture products instead of one?") and an assumption of the risk/reward trade-off that could answer it. Exhibit 12-5 shows a decision network for maximizing the value of four product-lining strategy options. The network shows that a $10 million reward may be earned at odds of 2 to 1 by a single product entry. The odds steepen as other products join the family, rising to 3 to 1 with one combination of products, 5 to 1 with another, and 10 to 1 with a three-product family. Similar networks can be diagrammed for other "What if?" questions, both quantitative and qualitative.

Price/Benefit Relationship

Price is a venture product characteristic, not a benefit. As such, price itself cannot sell. What sells is the insight that price can give to a market about the value of a product's benefit. A premium price tends to support market perception of a premium benefit. In this way, premium pricing can be self-validating: a venture product's added market value acts to justify its premium pricing; in turn, premium pricing acts to imply added market value and thereby to reinforce the basis for a premium price.

An ancient marketing parable about hats can help define this relationship between price and benefit value:

> A hat is something a man owes to his head and his self-respect. A hat does more than keep his scalp clean, shade his eyes, ward off heat and cold, sun and rain. It conforms not only to his head and hand but to his ego. It becomes a part of him. It may tell where he comes from and where he's going. It signifies his status and his estimate of himself. A good man, with a good hat, stands a little taller in the world's eyes and his own.

These may be the benefits of hats. Price is not among them. If the benefits of hats cease to enjoy market value, hats themselves will cease to enjoy market value regardless of their price. Low price will not sell hats since no hat can ever be cheaper than no hat at all. And if no hat at all is what the market wants, then no price at all is what it will pay.

Because price is a function of benefit value, the proper role of costs in venture product pricing is to help determine the profit consequences of various pricing options. Costs represent the value added by manufacture.

exhibit 12-5

decision network for product-lining strategy

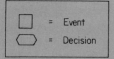

☐ =	Event
⬡ =	Decision

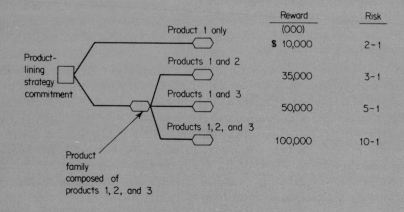

	Reward (000)	Risk
Product 1 only	$ 10,000	2 – 1
Products 1 and 2	35,000	3 – 1
Products 1 and 3	50,000	5 – 1
Products 1, 2, and 3	100,000	10 – 1

Product-lining strategy commitment

Product family composed of products 1, 2, and 3

They are a reliable index of manufacturing efficiency. Price above cost represents the value added by the market's perception of how well a product benefit is able to solve a problem or realize an opportunity. Price may therefore be regarded as a reliable index of venture marketing efficiency, that is, of a venture manager's ability to relate product benefit to market need. If product benefit is poorly related to market need, price may not be able to equal, let alone exceed, cost. Yet if product benefit matches market need, price may far exceed intrinsic worth. Price can therefore be defined as *the value added by benefit*.

Markets are not concerned with venture costs. After all, costs are the venture's burden. They may, but then again they may not, yield commensurate market rewards. Markets care only for rewards. In the absence of added reward, markets tend to reduce price to the level of cost. Price seeks the level of manufacturing efficiency since no marketing efficiency is apparent to the market. Commodity pricing is therefore a form of involuntary discount pricing. The difference between commodity pricing and premium pricing is, quite literally, the price a commodity marketer must pay to his market for his inefficiency in marketing to it. Because there is no price implication of superior value among commodities, their markets must shop for the best buy among them. This requires what may be termed the market's "effort after benefit." The function of venture product pricing must be to spare the market this effort and retain the reward for the venture.

The Nonproduct

A nonproduct is a product whose benefit value is perceived by its market as being less than its price. This makes the product "too expensive" no matter how low a price it asks. A nonproduct is a form of scrap: highly tooled, precision-made scrap perhaps, and often the only one of its kind, but scrap nonetheless.

Most nonproducts are created by the uncontrolled expression of venture management's technological capabilities. The more proficient these capabilities are, the greater the risk of producing scrap. Products that are made because they *can* be made or because "There is nothing like it on the market" are in danger of being in a prescrap mode. A case history of an electronics venture product will illustrate this point.

The electronics manufacturer possessed the technological capability to create a new high-speed magnetic stepping motor that was defined as "a method of converting pulses or current reversals into precisely positioned shaft alignments with exact incremental rotation of 18 degrees at speeds up to 1,000 times per second." In addition to its uniquely high speed and precision, the motor was miniaturized: it occupied as little as 1 cubic inch of space. It had only one moving part, the rotor. No directly competitive stepping motors existed.

On the basis of its physical characteristics and operating specifications, the motor was assigned the following alleged benefits:

Benefits	*Characteristics*
1. Versatility: multiple uses	1.1. Miniaturized: occupies as little as 1 cubic inch of space
	1.2. High speed: permits up to 1,000 steps per second
2. Reliability: dependable, troublefree performance	2.1. Simplified construction: only one moving part, the rotor
	2.2. Rugged: high shock and vibration immunity
3. Controllability: exact positioning	3.1. Precise: incremental rotation of 18 degrees

On the basis of its alleged benefits, the motor was assigned a rank order of four major "markets" where, it was felt, needs for accurate positioning at high-reaction speeds would provide demand for a new power source offering premium value at a premium price:

1. The tape, chart, and film drive market

2. The instrument drive market

3. The process control market

4. The business machine market

In three years of market penetration, the number of heavy-user customers buying 100 or more units increased from two to six. The total number of units sold rose from 1,000 to 2,100. Market acceptance was retarded by customer perception of "no clearly defined need." Alternatives already available were "reasonably satisfactory." Almost all the alternatives, while far less exotic in terms of unique benefits, were readily available, familiar, and less expensive. Unlike the new motor, the alternatives had all been proved out. The only way a potential customer could be certain that the new motor's value/price relationship would be superior would be to install a motor, design a drive and gear package for it, build the system, and evaluate it for a reasonable period under a full range of operating conditions. Since the time and dollar cost of obtaining proof of benefits was perceived as too high, the motor was perceived as both undervalued and overpriced.

Corfam: Deriving a Nonproduct through Incorrect Assumptions

Du Pont's venture into Corfam, a poromeric plastic material, cost the company $100 million and never yielded a profit. Introduced in 1963 with a $2 million advertising campaign, Corfam was discontinued seven years later. The material, which was produced as the result of more than 200 man-years of research and testing, appeared to offer significant benefits as a leather substitute.

Corfam was a victim of four market and product assumptions. Each assumption turned out to be wrong, leading the venturers to make their fatal mistake of overestimating the material's perceived value.

Du Pont's basic assumption, from which the other three assumptions were easily and harmoniously derived, was that the shoe industry would be Corfam's major opportunity. This assumption was based on projections which suggested that a substantial shortage of leather by 1982 appeared evident. Less leather would be available on a per consumer basis. Huge increases in footwear consumption were contemplated. This would create a "leather gap" for about 30 percent of all the shoes required in the 1980s.

Once the so-called leather gap was discovered, it was decided that the greatest opportunity to plug it with a high-priced leather substitute was in shoes selling in the $20 to $40 price range. In preparing to penetrate this market, Du Pont made the following three assumptions:

1. Assumptions about manufacturing benefits

Du Pont assumed that Corfam would offer a cost advantage to shoe manufacturers. At a price of $1.05 per square foot, Corfam projections showed an acceptable share of market could be conquered from leather even though initial use would thus be restricted to shoes priced from $20 up. But this price proved to be inhibitive, offering no significant cost advantage over leather and no compensating production cost advantage. Du Pont further assumed that mass production would lower the Corfam price. But, in scaling up from pilot operations, Corfam could never be turned out at the predicted cost and still retain its competitive benefits.

2. Assumptions about consumer benefits

Du Pont assumed that six very important user benefits would outweigh one moderately important deficit. Corfam promised shoes that offered breathability, water-repellency, scuff resistance, and a permanent shine. Du Pont also believed that durability was a major benefit, even though apparel markets were moving away from durability toward disposability, and that shape retention also was desirable. Unfortunately, shape retention, which was the result of Corfam's "memory," so effectively prevented the material from permanently stretching to accommodate the wearer's foot that Corfam shoes had to be broken in all over again after each wearing.

3. *Assumptions about competitive threats*

Du Pont assumed that Corfam's competition would come from domestic leather shoes. In fact, competition came from two unexpected sources: imports from Spain and Italy which offered Continental styling at low prices; and other synthetics, especially low-end nonbreathable polyvinyls.

It is, of course, highly unusual that unanticipated mass competition can come from low-priced imports, that nonbreathable vinyl can be accepted by a market that has always insisted on breathability, that the relatively slight discomfort in use caused by a material's memory can cancel out several genuine benefits, and that technical problems in a high-technology company can prevent predicted-cost projections from being realized over a seven-year time frame. The assumption is that compensating factors will occur in all situations so that multiple problems or errors do not fall on the same side. The major contribution of the Corfam experience may very well turn out to be to disprove this fifth assumption.

Life-styled Product Development

In most cases of venture product failure, inadequate market appraisal has prevented venture management from properly understanding end-user needs and has resulted in serious misjudgment of the number of customers prepared to accept the product. This is why the lowest risk is offered by venture products for an existing market. Conversely, risk increases with a market's remoteness from venture management's experience.

The risk and attendant cost-effectiveness of venture product development can almost always be increased by a strategy that assigns priority to defining, understanding, and serving existing markets first, adjacent markets second, and new markets last. This approach can accomplish three things: (1) encourage existing markets to reveal more of their needs than are now being served and to reveal known needs more meaningfully, (2) allow adjacent markets to disclose needs similar to those which are now being served in existing markets, and (3) enable new markets to be seen in terms of their familiarity to existing markets rather than their strangeness. "Life-styled product development" is an approach to seizing the concept of a market according to its most meaningful, repetitive patterns of attitudes and activities and then custom-tailoring products, services, and their promotional strategies to fit these patterns.

Life-styling the venture's product development, that is, deriving it from the needs contained in a style of consumer or business life, is a systems approach to conceiving a market. It is concerned with the patterns or systems of interrelated attitudes and activities that recur most frequently in a customer group, looking for acted-out expressions of a way of life that regularly culminate in heavy purchases. At the same time, it identifies the thought patterns and self-images that accompany these activities so that promotion can be efficiently directed to them.

Within each pattern of attitudes and activities, a life-styling product developer looks for three major attributes in each market group to be explored:

1. Its *psychographics*, expressed by its major needs that seek commercial benefits

2. Its *product usage* and *media usage* habits, especially the ways in which it perceives and evaluates the various product and media categories it consumes

3. Its *demographics*, such as age, education, and income

Target Attitudes and Activities

The attitude and activity patterns for which life-styled products can be conceived are, for the most part, openly perceptible in the real world. A market's activities are overt. For life-styling purposes, they can be categorized as *discretionary* and *nondiscretionary*. Many attitudes are also overt. They are expressed either in action or as accompaniments to action. Other attitudes, including some which can predispose in favor of or against purchase, are also overt. In Exhibit 12-6, some real world attitudes and activities are set forth for life-styled targeting.

To translate target attitudes and activities into life-styles, five criteria for assigning life-style status can be used:

1. Each life-style must represent a *marketable entity*. That is, it should represent a pattern of attitudes and activities which is meaningful enough to its practitioners to be reasonably exclusive of other patterns. This criterion attempts to guarantee a consistent, definable market.

2. Each life-style must have needs which are *commercially exploitable*. This criterion attempts to make certain that a market is being framed for profit-making products and services rather than, say, for philanthropic activities.

exhibit 12-6

real-world attitudes and activities for life-styled targeting

1. **Real-world attitudes**
   - Overt
     - Expressed in action
     - Expressed in words that accompany action
   - Covert
     - Noncommercializable
       - Political
       - Religious
     - Commercializable
       - Personal

2. **Real-world activities**
   - Nondiscretionary
     - Career work for sustenance
     - Routine self-maintenance
     - Emergency reactions and adaptations
     - Social expectations and obligations
   - Discretionary
     - Self-entertaining play
     - Leisure time "work"
     - Rest and relaxation
     - Being entertained
     - Moonlighting supplemental work

3. Each life-style must be *active and decision-making*. Passive roles in which products and services are imposed on a market, or must be accepted without the exercise of preference, are rejected. This criterion attempts to underwrite a marketing approach that can achieve results from individually directed persuasion.

4. Each life-style must be lived out by a middle-income *mass market* or an upper-income *specialty market*. This criterion attempts to ensure the cost effectiveness of developmental and marketing functions by directing them against populous or affluent targets.

5. Each life-style must, insofar as possible, be based on *repetitive attitude and activity patterns* that have a high rate of turnover in the market and that occur on either a predictably frequent schedule or at least a randomly recurrent basis. This criterion attempts to warrant an active, busy market with a high rate of repeat purchase.

Setting Up Life-Styles for Product and Service Development

Consumer product ventures, industrial product ventures, and service ventures can use these criteria to set up life-styles as contexts for product and service development. As an example, one important market pattern of attitudes and activities that has relevance to a health and beauty aids manufacturer can be called a woman homemaker's life-style role as family physician. In this role, which is spelled out as a scenario in Exhibit 12-7, the homemaker is acting, thinking, and feeling like a nonprofessional practitioner of nursing and medical functions. Many of her concerns are the same as those of medical doctors and registered nurses in a hospital environment. But because she is in the home, the homemaker must deprofessionalize them. Profitable new-product opportunities exist for health and beauty aids venturers who can commercialize her needs within the context of this life-style role—who can, in other words, get inside the role with her, act it out and emotionalize it with her, and look for commercial opportunities in health care products and information services that they otherwise might not have seen, or might not have seen as vividly, or might not have seen in a systematized manner.

The same concept of a market, the life-style role of family physician, can be useful to venture food product developers. Food processors are accustomed to relating their market of women homemakers as they play their role of family dietitian. When many of the same women are newly considered in the light of their physician-in-the-home life-styles, product ideas can be generated for functional foods that contain a health or nutritional market benefit. This approach can yield seasonal foods to prevent winter health problems, foods designed for people who are recovering from major illnesses, foods that provide quick energy, or foods that give added values to people when they need to react under stress. In a similar manner, venture product developers for insurance companies or for manufacturers of furniture or disposable wearing apparel can utilize the family physician life-style as a development base.

In Exhibits 12-7 through 12-13, the life-style role of family physician and several other roles are explored in some detail to show the stimulation that life-styling can provide for venture product and service development.

> **Use Planning Pages 58/1 through 58/3 to work out the market life-style roles that can provide useful contexts for venture product and service development.**

exhibit 12.7

family physician life-styled scenario

The mass, middle-majority married woman homemaker in her life-style role as family physician is concerned essentially with the feeling, the appearance, and the substance of her family's health. In short, she wants family members to feel healthy, look healthy, and be healthy. Her primary role is health maintenance. In this aspect of her role, she thinks and acts very much like an insurance agent for her family. Her concerns are principally *preventive*. The second aspect of her role is acutely critical, generally overtaking her with little or no warning. This is the emergency *therapeutic* aspect of family health care. Insofar as possible, she places her reliance on routine maintenance to ward off emergencies. When they happen anyway in spite of her best efforts, she needs to feel prepared with appropriate products and information services as adequately as possible.

The attitude and activity pattern of family physician is extremely sober and serious. Health is never a laughing matter. The married woman homemaker is therefore best addressed when she is in this role as a rational, caring, protective, and businesslike person who carries a severe responsibility. Accordingly, products and information services designed to serve her must be exemplary in their dependability, reliability, and guaranteed performance.

exhibit 12-8

life-style roles in home economics management

1. The married woman homemaker in her life-style role as family dietician.

The middle-majority homemaker, aged nineteen to forty-nine, in her roles as food selector and meal balancer, daily menu planner, and culinary artisan and food stylist.

Product and service system categories compatible with this role include foods, functional foods, and food analogs; meal-planning and menu-planning consultation services; recipe services; food-styling consultation and education services; fast-food franchise services; computerized food ordering and delivery services; and televised or franchised cooking schools.

2. The married woman homemaker in her life-style role as food systems engineer

The middle-majority homemaker, aged nineteen to forty-nine, in her role as skilled operator of food storage, cooking, serving, and disposal systems; meal-planning and menu-rationalizing systems; and utensil-cleaning, maintenance, and storage systems.

Product and service system categories compatible with this role include household appliance systems; appliance layout consultation services; appliance operation consultation services; appliance maintenance and repair services; service contract consultation service or books; disposable utensil product lines; detergents and ultrasonic cleaning systems; and appliance rental services.

exhibit 12.9

life-style roles in personal care management

1. The married woman homemaker in her life-style role as personal health care manager

The middle-majority homemaker, aged nineteen to fifty-nine, in her roles as family physician and nurse and family physical health and mental health educator.

Product and service system categories compatible with this role include internally and externally applied drugs, health foods, and functional foods; computerized health care and consultation services; self-diagnostic kits; clinics and care centers; disposable products; health education services and media; and feminine hygiene products and services.

2. The married woman homemaker in her life-style role as personal beauty and grooming care manager

The middle-majority homemaker, aged nineteen to fifty-nine, in her roles as socially attractive woman in public situations and seductively attractive wife or lover in private situations.

Product and service system categories compatible with this role include internal beauty care products such as beauty foods and beauty drugs, including psychedelic drugs; external beauty care products such as hair, face, and body cosmetics; fashionable apparel and accessories; and beauty care services such as beauty consultation and product prescription services, computerized complexion analysis, self-styling systems of beauty care, and shops, salons, or shopping services.

exhibit 12.10
life-style roles in environmental management

1. The married woman homemaker in her life-style role as internal environment creator and manager

The middle-majority homemaker, aged nineteen to fifty-nine, in her roles as interior decorator and mood stylist for the home; cottage craftsman; equity-building collector; communications systems manager; home repairman and service contract negotiator with external repair and manufacturing services; and family maid and sanitary engineer.

Product and service system categories compatible with this role include interior decoration consultation services and media; home repair kits and manuals; home furnishings for sale or rent; in-home communications systems; home repair contractual and insurance services; modular home study centers and work carrels; rental maid services; bathroom equipment and fixtures; saunas; household appliance and furnishings insurance services; and service contract consultation services.

2. The married woman homemaker in her life-style role as external environment creator and manager

The middle-majority homemaker, aged nineteen to fifty-nine, in her roles as architect and home builder; gardener and landscaper; outdoor living equipment and systems planner; general property value manager; and service contract negotiator with external repair and manufacturing services.

Product and service system categories compatible with this role include home rental or purchasing consultation services; home improvement products and services; home repair kits and manuals, property value maintenance instruction and information services; gardening tools, seeds, and planning services; synthetic lawns and other home decoration products and services; landscape rental services; disposable landscaping; landscape insurance; children's yard and porch structures and exercise equipment; pools and solaria; and service contract consultation.

exhibit 12-11

life-style roles
in travel and
entertainment
management

1. **The married woman homemaker in her life-style role as family travel agent.**

   The middle-majority homemaker, aged nineteen to fifty-nine, in her roles as vacation selector and planner.

   Product and service system categories compatible with this role include vacation-styling services; vacation packs of portable foods, drugs, and cosmetics; disposable vacation apparel and accessories; and computerized vacation-planning services.

2. **The married woman homemaker in her life-style role as family entertainment director**

   The middle-majority homemaker, aged nineteen to forty-nine, in her roles as amusement selector and censor, leisure-time planner, toy and game buyer, arts and crafts hobbyist and buyer, and family athletic director and coach.

   Product and service system categories compatible with this role include leisure-time planning services; toy, game, and craft products; hobbyist products; athletic equipment and instruction services; athletics-oriented cosmetics and quick-energy foods; first-aid equipment and preventive or remedial products such as suntan lotions and sprays or pills, aerosol bandages, and hot and cold packs; picnic and camping equipment; outdoor patio and backyard living equipment; sporting clubs and groups; country clubs; boats; and skis or ski-mobile manufacturing and rental services.

exhibit 12-12

life-style roles in training and education management

1. **The married woman homemaker in her life-style role as baby mother and trainer**

   The middle-majority homemaker, aged nineteen to thirty-nine, in her roles as baby entertainer and teacher.

   Product and service system categories compatible with this role include baby care instruction and education books, films, classes, and other consultation services; toys and games; baby accessories, apparel, and disposables; and reward-type foods.

2. **The married woman homemaker in her life-style role as child trainer and educator**

   The middle-majority homemaker, aged nineteen to forty-nine, in her roles as child entertainer and teacher.

   Product and service system categories compatible with this role include child care instruction and education books, films, classes, and other consultation services; children's toys, games, and crafts; children's preschool educational services and tools; children's accessories, apparel, and equipment for school; disposable training and education aids; child health insurance; and children's college enrollment insurance.

3. **The married woman homemaker in her life-style role as pet trainer and educator**

   The middle-majority homemaker, aged nineteen to forty-nine, in her roles as animal and bird purchaser, feeder, teacher, entertainer, and health manager.

   Product and service system categories compatible with this role include franchised kennels and aviaries; pet foods; pet accessories, disposable apparel, and toys; pet care instruction services; pet health insurance; and pet care and maintenance services.

exhibit 12-13

life-style roles in family business management

1. The married woman homemaker in her life-style role as family money manager

The middle-majority homemaker, aged nineteen to fifty-nine, in her roles as family treasurer and credit manager; family accountant and budgeter; and family estate executor.

Product and service system categories compatible with this role include household budget-planning educational services and computerized budget-keeping services; investment advisory services; and food budget–planning guides.

2. The married woman homemaker in her life-style role as family purchasing agent

The middle-majority homemaker, aged nineteen to forty-nine, in her roles as comparison shopper, buyer, and order taker within the family.

Product and service system categories compatible with this role include shopping consultation services; buyer education classes, books, films, and television programs; product comparison services; labeling and packaging guides for smart shopping; and gift suggestion and purchasing services.

LIFE—STYLE ROLE(S) IN _____

1. Title of role(s)

2. Description of role player's attitude and activity pattern

3. Product and service categories compatible with this role

<u>LIFE—STYLE ROLE(S) IN</u> _____

1. Title of role(s)

2. Description of role player's attitude and activity pattern

3. Product and service categories compatible with this role

<u>LIFE—STYLE ROLE(S) IN</u> ————————————

1. Title of role(s)

2. Description of role player's attitude and activity pattern

3. Product and service categories compatible with this role

venture market penetration plan

Venture market penetration occurs when a potential product or service value, still unproved, becomes accepted by an alleged group of customers, still unverified. Penetration validates the venture and brings it into the real world of business enterprise. Although it is true that penetration is no guarantee of success, without it a venture remains an academic exercise. For the venture manager, market penetration is the crux.

The problem of penetration can be reduced to two essentials. The first is a knowledge of the alleged market. Ventures, like all businesses, originate with market needs. The manager's ability to qualify these needs and then to quantify their intensity is the first essential requirement for venture penetration. The second essential requirement is a planned approach to the market which offers benefits whose perceived value is greater than the direct cost of buying or the hidden cost of doing without. It is an accurate oversimplification of the venture process to say that any manager who commands these two essentials can venture. The manager's basic command tool is the venture market penetration plan.

Penetration Planning

A new business venture requires a very succinct, straightforward plan. The plan should be viewed as a document of constraint. Its purpose is to set a limit on the venture's market service. The name of this limit is "optimal profit." The plan should therefore be a guide to operating the venture in an exceedingly businesslike manner. From the venture manager's first pass, colloquially known as the 01, one safeguard above all should apply: no unexplored alternatives should be omitted in the search for optimal profit.

A format for this type of market penetration plan contains three major operating sections which commit the venture to the things it will *do*: the

307

objectives it will achieve, the *strategies* that may achieve them, and the *controls* that will help make sure that the strategies are working toward the objectives. These operating sections can then be supported by an appendix which stores the venture's key information resources about what it *knows:* the profile of *market opportunity* on which the venture is based, the *technological source* of the venture's properties and its modification by energy and materials availability, the venture's *competition*, and the venture manager's *assumptions* about the future, which cannot yet be known.

Exhibit 13-1 shows an outline of this approach to venture planning, which highlights the four action elements of the venture that are doable and relates them to the four information elements of the venture which are knowable or must be assumed.

Objectives

Objectives, strategies, and controls are the plan's three action directives. The objectives answer the main question for which the venture manager is accountable: *Where are you taking the business?* The manager's response should be in two forms. One is the form of the venture's financial objectives, which are its primary missions. These are expressed as return on investment and net profit contribution. The second form of expression for venture objectives is offered in terms of the sales achievements that must be earned in the market if the financial objectives are to be reached. These are expressed as dollar and unit sales volumes and percentage of market share.

In the venture plan, objectives can be calculated and presented on a best-case, average-case, worst-case basis. The average-case objectives are the ones the venture manager must go with. Best-case objectives represent an ideal: everything will have to work out exactly according to plan for best-case objectives to be achieved. No venture should be commissioned if only its best-case objectives are acceptable. Worst-case objectives represent the minimum promise of venture accomplishment. There is great comfort in believing that the worst case will never occur. But because it may, no venture should be commissioned if its worst-case objectives are unacceptable.

Strategies

The second action directive, venture strategies, commits the venture's manager to answer the next question: *How are you going to get the business to reach its objectives?* This section of the venture plan calls for the manager to construct the most cost-effective strategy mix that has the best chance of fulfilling the venture's promise. There are two types of strat-

exhibit 13-1

venture market penetration plan

Subject section of plan	Planning pages to be included in this section
ACTION DIRECTIVES	

1. Venture charter

1.1. Charter	44
1.2. Growth legend	10
1.3. Business-positioning statement	51
1.4. Selection criteria	1, 2, 9, 12, 13, 14, 15, 18, 19, 20, 21, 25, 26, 27, 28, 29, 30, 31, 32, 33, 52, 53
1.5. Capabilities	3, 4, 5/1–8/1, 5/2–8/2, 11, 16

2. Objectives V2

2.1. Financial objectives	42, 43, 48, 50, 61, 62
2.2. Sales objectives	59, 60
2.3. Forecasts	

3. Strategies to achieve objectives

3.1. Market penetration strategies	V3.1 series
3.1.1. Product and service strategies	55, 56, 57, 58/1–58/3
3.1.2. Promotion strategies	54
3.1.3. Pricing strategies	
3.2. Business capability strategies	V3.2 series
3.2.1. Staff and organization strategies	17, 22, 23, 24
3.2.2. Facilities strategies	
3.2.3. Budget strategies	45, 46, 47/1–47/8, 49

(Continued)

309

exhibit 13-1 (Continued)

Subject section of plan	_Planning pages to be included in this section_

4. Controls and contingencies

4.1. Appraisals	63, 64, 65
4.2. Controls	V4.2 series
4.3. Contingency strategies	V4.3 series
4.4. Revised objectives	V4.4 series

INFORMATION BASE

5. Situation survey

5.1. Factual information base	V5 series
5.1.1. Market opportunity profile	
5.1.2. Technical capability profile	
5.1.3. Competitive profile	
5.2. Assumptive information base	34, 35, 36, 37, 38, 39, 40, 41

egies to be planned for. One is the venture's market penetration strategies, which are the external actions that will impact directly on the market. The other is the venture's business capability strategies. These are the internal actions that will provide the support and substance required for market penetration.

For most ventures, market penetration strategies can be conveniently planned in three categories. The first category is the venture's product or service, or system of products and services, that will be sold. These are the venture offerings that will enter into physical distribution. The second category is the venture's promotion system which correlates sales and distribution strategies, advertising and sales promotion, and publicity. A venture's product and its promotion strategies are correlates of each other. In separate forms, each represents the value in use that the venture can deliver to its market. The third category of market penetration strategy is price, the reflector of value in use.

The second type of venture strategy is its business capabilities. These are the internal actions that provide the staff, the organization, and the facilities which support the venture's market penetration strategies.

Controls

The third action directive is provided by the controls which will monitor the venture's strategies. Controls are the manager's answer to this question: *How will you make sure your strategies are working toward your objectives?* A control system must have two parts. A reporting method of periodic audit, preferably over a thirty-day period, is necessary to highlight problems within tight time frames so that they can be spotted while they are still young. Then an inventory of corrective strategies, created in advance and held as contingencies against need, is required to provide remedies for strategies that are not working or for assumptions that are found out to be unreal.

The venture control system should allow the manager to "manage by exception." This permits the venture to proceed with only exceptions to its plan becoming red-flagged for attention. Exhibit 13-2 shows a control system decision key to be used with a venture market penetration plan.

The Four Information Elements

Underlying the venture plan's action elements is its knowledge base. This is made up of three knowable elements and several unknowables. The first knowable input is the venture's market opportunity profile. This is the key venture information resource. It contains an analysis of the major characteristics of the venture's probable heavy-user market, infor-

exhibit 13.2

control system
decision key

Green flag
  Decision 1

    Performance is on plan.

Yellow flag
  Decision 2

    Performance is on plan, but alterations in the situation
      require monitoring.

  Decision 3

    Performance is off plan, but variance is self-correcting.

Red flag
  Decision 4

    Performance is off plan, and remedial action is required
      to alter strategies.

  Decision 5

    Performance is off plan, and remedial action is required
      to alter strategies and objectives.

  Decision 6

    Performance is off plan and turnaround action is required
      to rescue the business.

mation on how the heavy users buy or how they may buy, and the reasons that appear able to motivate buying behavior.

The second information element is an inventory of the venture's technical capabilities that are the source of venture products and services and the energy and materials on which their production will depend.

The third area of venture information is an analysis of actual and probable competitors, both those who compete directly for the same disposable dollar and indirect competitors whose dissimilar products or services offer benefits for the same needs that the venture serves.

Finally, the fourth element in the information base is the unknowables, whose impact on the venture must be estimated in the form of assumptions.

The As-If–What-If Planning Process

To the venture manager, the venture market initially is unreal. It does not yet exist. Yet it must be visualized *as if* it were tangible. Its composition must be structured, its buying potential estimated, its needs itemized in detail, and beneficial values put forth to meet them. By modeling the alleged market (and it is best to regard it as alleged until it demonstrates its actuality), the venture manager can come to grips with it and realize it on an as-if basis: as if it were already mobilized. This as-if representation of the venture market is the manager's *market model*. It represents the venture's potential opportunity. Within each market group, the heaviest users must be spotlighted as the venture's core customers.

Against the as-if model of the market, the venture manager can then play the "What if?" game of positioning strategy options to determine which ones can yield the best profit objectives. The eventual result of playing "What if?" is a venture *marketing model* which contains its product options, its sales and advertising options, and pricing parameters with the best ability to penetrate the venture market.

Venture Market Model: Acting As If

The venture market is beyond the venture manager's control. Its size, expressed as units and dollars, determines the venture's sales opportunity. A model of market size and composition can help the manager act as if he could accurately forecast venture sales and thereby gain some measure of control over the market.

The key inputs for modeling a venture market are the venture's products and services and their end-use applications. The most important relationship between them is *product potential*, which is the sum of all the end uses for a venture product in which its perceived value appears greater than its price. Each of these end-use categories may become a

heavy-user market segment for the venture. Once they have been identified, their probable heaviness of use can be projected on a segment-by-
segment basis.

End-user trial purchase will be influenced by the growth pattern of
the user's market as well as by perceived value. Perceived value will
move users into the venture's market. The market's growth pattern will
determine venture dynamics. In some markets, size will be proportional
to the rate of population growth or disposable income. The growth pattern
of such a market will tend to be a straight line of moderately progressive
upward slope. Venture product growth can be expected to parallel it. In
other markets, saturation or technological preemption may be predicted
to occur early after venture entry. The growth pattern of such a market
will be an initial upward curve followed by negative growth. Perceived
value in this case may be high at the outset but short-lived.

Venture Marketing Model: Playing "What If?"

A venture's marketing model is its game plan. It develops as the result
of evaluating a wide range of alternatives which appear capable of delivering the highest perceived value to the greatest number of the venture
market's heavy users. The ultimate evaluation of every venture market
planning alternative is its effect on venture profit and rate of return on
investment. The evaluation game that venture management plays is called
the "What if?" game. It is played by asking, "*What if* this action were
commissioned? What impact would the action have on venture earnings
and expense?" For each system of alternative strategy actions, a pro forma
income statement, balance sheet, and operating ratio projections can be
put together to arrive at an answer.

The venture manager's "What if?" game smokes out the alternative
strategy options which appear available to the venture. The principal
options are the venture's product and service mix, their promotional
strategies, and their pricing. The one best bet must be made about each
of them. Then the one best bet must be made about their optimal mix.
All these bets of the single most feasible alternatives must be made by
working with assumptions that can be, at best, imperfect representatives
of what will later turn out to be reality.

Two bases for framing "What if?" alternatives are open to the venture
manager. Some bets can be made as expressions of the manager's subjective preferences. The manager may simply favor one option over another
on the basis of gut feel. At other times, when the focal point of feeling
about a decision is located elsewhere, the feeling is called "seat of the
pants" reasoning.

The second basis for deriving strategy options may be somewhat
more scientific although not necessarily superior. This is called value

maximization. Through the use of decision networks, like the one shown in Exhibit 12-5, an attempt is made to calculate the reward from each strategy decision along with the probable risk of obtaining it. The decision with the best risk/reward ratio can then be selected, qualified perhaps by gut feel, as an alternative strategy for the "What if?" game.

Unlike the venture market, which is beyond the manager's control, venture marketing is controllable by the manager's decisions in favor of one or another alternative strategy. The venture manager must learn the minimum number and minimum cost of the strategies which can help control the market's choice. All markets have three choices: buy the venture product or service, deal with competitive offerings, or do without. A model of the product and marketing factors which may be able to encourage market choice can help the manager design the most cost-effective penetration plan and predict the unit and dollar sales that may be earned. On the basis of this prediction, the manager will be able to show how the best perceived value/price relationship can be created for the venture product.

Venture Strategy Scenarios

A venture market penetration plan is the sum of many destructions. Each destruction is a "What if?" scenario whose answer has turned out to be negative or not sufficiently positive to take the venture to its objectives. In the strategy-making phase of the venture process, the venture manager's greatest talent is the ability to produce miniature off-Broadway plays that rehearse the probable market effect of various strategy mixes. "What if I put these strategies together?" the manager will have to ask. "What penetration will occur in the market?" If the answer is "Not enough," "Not soon enough," or "Not long enough," the next level of questions must ask, "What if I substitute this strategy for that strategy or introduce this new strategy that I haven't used before into the mix? Now what penetration will occur?"

Venture strategy scenarios should follow the principle of the minimix: the fewest strategies that will produce the highest perceived value at the lowest cost should be mixed. Such a minimal strategy mix for a personal care venture could read like this:

> To penetrate the skin care segment of the personal care market to a net profit yield of $X by Year 3, there will be directed at the market a strategy mix consisting of (1) an initial three-item product line, extended to twelve items by Year 3, to be sold through supermarkets and drug stores; (2) a network of twelve company-owned treatment salons and at least twenty-four franchised salons in major metropolitan markets; and (3) two schools to train salon operators. This mix will cost $Y and will be promoted by an advertising, sales promotion, and publicity budget of $Z. Rate of return will be R percent.

The plot of every "What if?" scenario has the same cast of characters. The hero is the market. It must win perceived values if the venture manager is to receive new profits in return. "If the market gets these added values, the venture will get these added values" is the common scenario theme. The manager's eventual market penetration plan will be the scenario which appears to deliver the best balance between these two sets of values.

The Five Key Assessments

A venture's market penetration plan must draw its resources from five key assessments: market potential, market penetration, probability of product acquisition at various prices, cash flow, and the impact of generic competition on lead time.

1. Assessing Market Potential

Market potential is the venture's upside sales opportunity if every qualified heavy user becomes a venture customer. As such, market potential is a mythical figure. But it is nonetheless valuable as a gross target in estimating the extent to which market development may be expanded.

2. Assessing Market Penetration

Penetration is the fraction of total market potential that is actually being planned for realization at an annual rate. Penetration may be expressed in sales units or sales dollars. In either case, it tells the rate at which share of market is being accumulated. Sales in dollars can be projected by multiplying unit sales by unit price. These projections form the basis for venture profit projections which the market plan must try to optimize.

Penetration is a volume concept. It answers the question "How much?" It is also intimately connected to time. It answers the question "How long will it take to achieve our volume objectives?" For every market, there is an average number of years that are required for a product to top out the penetration level on its life cycle curve. When this number is known, penetration can be used as an index of venture maturity, since it reveals the extent to which qualified prospects for the venture's products are entering the market and reaching their heaviest usage rate.

3. Assessing Probability of Product Acquisition

Probability is an expression of the likelihood of product acquisition in the near term at various value/price relationships. It is based on two inputs:

1. Needs, which may range from low to high

2. Benefits perceived for each need, which may be derived from one or more product features

The ideal venture product is one that is seen by its market as fulfilling a high degree of need with high perceived benefits. A venture product that is not ideal but still acceptable fulfills a high degree of need with a medium benefit. Venture products probably contain an unacceptable risk of failure if they are perceived as delivering high benefits for low needs. These are the products about which their manufacturers usually say, "There has never been anything like it."

A second error to avoid is the belief that the more benefits a product contains, the better. Only one or at most two interrelated benefits are necessary to meet market need. One strongly motivating reason for buying is more effective than several moderate reasons. But there is no substitute for a strongly felt need. When it exists, even a moderately beneficial product may prove profitable.

Price and probability of acquisition are closely related. Initial penetration should be planned at a premium price. As penetration expands, price can be used to test the elasticity of the market's further probability to acquire venture product benefits at successively lower costs.

4. Assessing Cash Flow

A market penetration strategy mix must be responsive to the venture's return-on-investment objectives. The investment on which the return is expected will be the total venture investment. A major component will, of course, be the cost of the venture's marketing plan. Market penetration planning must therefore strive for the maximum cash flow that is consistent with return on investment so that the venture can be as nearly self-financing as possible.

Cash flow is the cash proceeds from venture earnings minus venture cash outlays. The projected cash-flow patterns of two alternative market penetration plans illustrate how ventures with similar returns on investment can generate different streams of cash over a three-year life cycle:

Cash flow

	Preentry	Year 1	Year 2	Year 3	Three-year cumulative net cash flow
Plan A	(−$20,000)	+$16,000	+$16,000	+$ 4,000	+$16,000
Plan B	(−$20,000)	+$ 4,000	+$ 8,000	+$24,000	+$16,000

Both plans predict the same average three-year return on investment of $5,334 per year, or 53 percent. On an ROI basis, there is little to choose between them. But the flow of cash earnings from Plan A promises to recover venture marketing outlays earlier than the flow from Plan B, enabling the venture to be placed on a more nearly self-sustaining basis beginning with Year 1 instead of waiting until Year 3.

5. *Assessing the Impact of Generic Competition on Lead Time*

Generic competition is direct competition in kind with a venture product or service. A generic competitor markets a physically or functionally similar product or one whose benefits are perceived as similar and obtainable at a comparable value/price ratio. Direct competition on a generic basis is inevitable for a successful venture. Penetration projections should plan for such competition from the outset. The only real variable is *when* it will occur, not *if*.

The entry of generic competition marks the end of venture lead time. During lead time, the venture may own its markets. Penetration may be low, but profit can be high because premium pricing can prevail. With the onset of penetration by generic competition, as shown in Exhibit 13-3, pricing at branded levels may have to give way to commodity pricing and correspondingly lower profit. Because of competition's effect on venture price, it is important to estimate not only the terminal date of lead time but also the most probable replacement rate at which venture penetration will be eroded. This will permit profit projections to be based on relative annual market shares under competitive conditions.

The approximate date of the end of lead time can be reasonably well assessed in advance. One method is based on the time when patent privacy opens up. Other methods are related to past evidence of competitive interest, present competitive capability, and the demonstrated amount of time each probable competitor requires to reach commercialization. When lead time disappears, venture marketing disappears with it and competitive marketing strategies suitable for established products or services must take over. The venture game plan must be revised. It must switch its approach from concentrating on fast penetration to a far more flexible strategy mix designed to maintain market share or expand it marginally, trade some of it off for improved profit, or supplement it with second-generation venture products.

Probability theory may also be applied to estimate the end of venture lead time. Three assumptions may be made: a zero probability that competitive entry will not occur for four or more years, a 50 percent probability that competition will enter the venture market within two years, and a zero probability for a competitive end to lead time within Year 1 of commercialization.

Use Planning Pages 59 through 62 to work out your assessments of market potential, market penetration, probable product acquisition, cash flow, and competitive lead time for your venture.

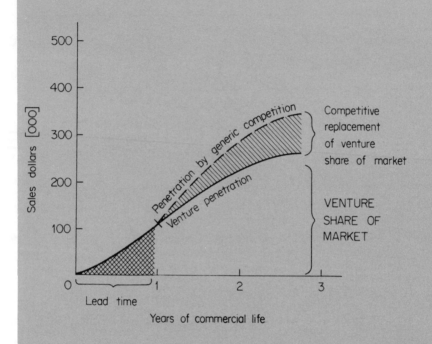

exhibit 13.3

competitive onset

Sales dollars [000]

500
400
300
200
100

Penetration by generic competition

Venture penetration

O   1   2   3

Lead time

Years of commercial life

Competitive
replacement
of venture
share of market

VENTURE
SHARE OF
MARKET

MARKET POTENTIAL ASSESSMENT

1. Total number of heavy-user venture customers
   in Year 1 (F19_ _-F19_ _)   = #_ _ _,_ _ _,_ _ _

2. Total % market share in Year 1   = _ _%

MARKET PENETRATION ASSESSMENT

1. Annual \$ sales volume in Year 1 (F19__-F19__) = \$___,___,___

   at unit price of \$_,___.__

2. Annual unit sales volume in Year 1   = #___,___,___

3. Probable product acquisition to generate sales volume:

PRODUCTS	CONTRIBUTION (\$00)
3.1. _____	_,___
3.2. _____	_,___
3.3. _____	_,___

CASH-FLOW ASSESSMENT

Preentry		Year 1		Year 2		Year 3		Three-year cumulative net cash flow		Three-year average ROI
(F19__-F19__)	+	(F19__-F19__)	+	(F19__-F19__)	+	(F19__-F19__)	=	(F19__-F19__)		
($__,__,___)		$__,__,___		$__,__,___		$__,__,___		$__,__,___		__%

COMPETITIVE LEAD TIME ASSESSMENT

End date of competitive lead time   Probability

1. _____, F19_ _–F19_ _   _ _%

2. _____, F19_ _–F19_ _   _ _

3. _____, F19_ _–F19_ _   _ _

324

On the following pages are title pages, section headings, and planning pages for your Market Penetration Plan. Use Exhibit 13-1 as a guide to the preceding planning pages to be included in each section of your plan.

MARKET PENETRATION PLAN

for

_____

F19_ _-F19_ _

I
ACTION DIRECTIVES

1. Venture charter
2. Objectives
3. Strategies to achieve objectives
4. Controls to monitor strategies

<u>1</u>

<u>VENTURE CHARTER</u>

1.1. Charter

1.2. Growth legend

1.3. Business-positioning statement

1.4. Selection criteria

1.5. Capabilities

328

2

OBJECTIVES

2.1. Financial objectives

2.2. Sales objectives

<u>2</u>

<u>OBJECTIVES</u>

	(Year 1) F19_ _–F19_ _			(Year 2) F19_ _–F19_ _		
	<u>Best</u> case	<u>Average</u> case	<u>Worst</u> case	<u>Best</u> case	<u>Average</u> case	<u>Worst</u> case
2.1. Financial objectives						
2.1.1. Return on investment (%)	--	--	--	--	--	--
2.1.2. Net profit contribution ($000)	-,---	-,---	-,---	-,---	-,---	-,---
2.2. Sales objectives						
2.2.1. Sales volume ($000)	---,---	---,---	---,---	---,---	---,---	---,---
2.2.2. Sales volume (#000)	---,---	---,---	---,---	---,---	---,---	---,---
2.2.3. Market share (%)	--	--	--	--	--	--

330

(Year 3) F19__-F19__			(Year 4) F19__-F19__			(Year 5) F19__-F19__		
Best case	Average case	Worst case	Best case	Average case	Worst case	Best case	Average case	Worst case
--	--	--	--	--	--	--	--	--
_,___	_,___	_,___	_,___	_,___	_,___	_,___	_,___	_,___
___,___	___,___	___,___	___,___	___,___	___,___	___,___	___,___	___,___
___,___	___,___	___,___	___,___	___,___	___,___	___,___	___,___	___,___
--	--	--	--	--	--	--	--	--

3

STRATEGIES TO ACHIEVE OBJECTIVES

3.1. Market penetration strategies

3.2. Business capability strategies

3.1

MARKET PENETRATION STRATEGIES

3.1.1. Product and service strategies

3.1.2. Promotion strategies

    3.1.2.1. Sales and physical distribution strategies

3.1.2.2. Advertising, sales promotion, and media distri-
          bution strategies

3.1.2.3. Publicity strategies

3.1.3. Pricing strategies

<u>3.2</u>

<u>BUSINESS CAPABILITY STRATEGIES</u>

3.2.1. Staff and organization strategies

3.2.2. Facilities strategies

3.2.3. Budget strategies

4

CONTROLS AND CONTINGENCIES

4.1. Appraisals

4.2. Controls

4.3. Contingency strategies

4.4. Revised objectives

<u>4.1</u>
<u>APPRAISALS</u>

4.2
CONTROLS

MONTHLY MONITOR

Month of _____, F19_ _-F19_ _

Planned monthly objectives	Actual performance	+/- Variances	Decision #

1. Profit on sales

   $ _ _,_ _ _,_ _ _ $ _ _,_ _ _,_ _ _   +/- $_ _,_ _ _,_ _ _   1 2 3 4 5 6

2. Sales volume ($)

   $_ _ _,_ _ _,_ _ _ $_ _ _,_ _ _,_ _ _   +/- $_ _,_ _ _,_ _ _   1 2 3 4 5 6

3. Sales volume (#)

   #_ _ _,_ _ _,_ _ _   #_ _ _,_ _ _,_ _ _   +/- #_ _,_ _ _,_ _ _   1 2 3 4 5 6

4. Market share (%)

   _ _%   _ _% +/- _ _%   1 2 3 4 5 6

Decision 1 is a green flag. Go full speed ahead.
Decisions 2 and 3 are yellow flags. Proceed with
caution. Decisions 4, 5, and 6 are red flags. Take
corrective action before proceeding further. If you make
Decision 5 or 6, you must create contingency strategies
on planning pages in the V4.3 series and revise your
objectives on Planning Page V4.4. See Exhibit 13-2 for
a full explanation.

MONTHLY MONITOR

Month of _____, F19_ _-F19_ _

Planned monthly objectives	Actual performance	+/- Variances	Decision #

1. Profit on sales

   $ _ _,_ _ _,_ _ _ $ _ _,_ _ _,_ _ _   +/- $_ _,_ _ _,_ _ _ 1 2 3 4 5 6

2. Sales volume ($)

   $_ _ _,_ _ _,_ _ _ $_ _ _,_ _ _,_ _ _   +/- $_ _,_ _ _,_ _ _ 1 2 3 4 5 6

3. Sales volume (#)

   #_ _ _,_ _ _,_ _ _   #_ _ _,_ _ _,_ _ _   +/- #_ _,_ _ _,_ _ _ 1 2 3 4 5 6

4. Market share (%)

   _ _%   _ _% +/- _ _%   1 2 3 4 5 6

Decision 1 is a green flag. Go full speed ahead.
Decisions 2 and 3 are yellow flags. Proceed with
caution. Decisions 4, 5, and 6 are red flags. Take
corrective action before proceeding further. If you make
Decision 5 or 6, you must create contingency strategies
on planning pages in the V4.3 series and revise your
objectives on Planning Page V4.4. See Exhibit 13-2 for
a full explanation.

MONTHLY MONITOR

Month of _____, F19__-F19__

Planned monthly objectives	Actual performance	+/- Variances	Decision #

1. Profit on sales

   $ __,___,___ $ __,___,___   +/-$__,___,___ 1 2 3 4 5 6

2. Sales volume ($)

   $___,___,___ $___,___,___   +/-$__,___,___ 1 2 3 4 5 6

3. Sales volume (#)

   #___,___,___   #___,___,___   +/-#__,___,___ 1 2 3 4 5 6

4. Market share (%)

   __%   __% +/- __%   1 2 3 4 5 6

Decision 1 is a green flag. Go full speed ahead. Decisions 2 and 3 are yellow flags. Proceed with caution. Decisions 4, 5, and 6 are red flags. Take corrective action before proceeding further. If you make Decision 5 or 6, you must create contingency strategies on planning pages in the V4.3 series and revise your objectives on Planning Page V4.4. See Exhibit 13-2 for a full explanation.

MONTHLY MONITOR

Month of _____, F19__-F19__

Planned monthly objectives	Actual performance	+/- Variances	Decision #

1. Profit on sales

$ __,___,___ $ __,___,___   +/- $__,___,___   1 2 3 4 5 6

2. Sales volume ($)

$___,___,___ $___,___,___   +/- $__,___,___   1 2 3 4 5 6

3. Sales volume (#)

#___,___,___   #___,___,___   +/- #__,___,___   1 2 3 4 5 6

4. Market share (%)

--%   --% +/- --%   1 2 3 4 5 6

Decision 1 is a green flag. Go full speed ahead.
Decisions 2 and 3 are yellow flags. Proceed with
caution. Decisions 4, 5, and 6 are red flags. Take
corrective action before proceeding further. If you make
Decision 5 or 6, you must create contingency strategies
on planning pages in the V4.3 series and revise your
objectives on Planning Page V4.4. See Exhibit 13-2 for
a full explanation.

MONTHLY MONITOR

Month of _____, F19_ _–F19_ _

Planned monthly objectives	Actual performance	+/– Variances	Decision #
1. Profit on sales			
$ _ _,_ _ _,_ _ _	$ _ _,_ _ _,_ _ _	+/– $_ _,_ _ _,_ _ _	1 2 3 4 5 6
2. Sales volume ($)			
$_ _ _,_ _ _,_ _ _	$_ _ _,_ _ _,_ _ _	+/– $_ _,_ _ _,_ _ _	1 2 3 4 5 6
3. Sales volume (#)			
#_ _ _,_ _ _,_ _ _	#_ _ _,_ _ _,_ _ _	+/– #_ _,_ _ _,_ _ _	1 2 3 4 5 6
4. Market share (%)			
_ _%	_ _%	+/– _ _%	1 2 3 4 5 6

Decision 1 is a green flag. Go full speed ahead.
Decisions 2 and 3 are yellow flags. Proceed with
caution. Decisions 4, 5, and 6 are red flags. Take
corrective action before proceeding further. If you make
Decision 5 or 6, you must create contingency strategies
on planning pages in the V4.3 series and revise your
objectives on Planning Page V4.4. See Exhibit 13–2 for
a full explanation.

MONTHLY MONITOR
Month of _____, F19_ _-F19_ _

Planned monthly objectives	Actual performance	+/- Variances	Decision #
1. Profit on sales			
$ _ _,_ _ _,_ _ _	$ _ _,_ _ _,_ _ _	+/-$_ _,_ _ _,_ _ _	1 2 3 4 5 6
2. Sales volume ($)			
$_ _,_ _ _,_ _ _	$_ _,_ _ _,_ _ _	+/-$_ _,_ _ _,_ _ _	1 2 3 4 5 6
3. Sales volume (#)			
#_ _,_ _ _,_ _ _	#_ _,_ _ _,_ _ _	+/-#_ _,_ _ _,_ _ _	1 2 3 4 5 6
4. Market share (%)			
_ _%	_ _%	+/- _ _%	1 2 3 4 5 6

Decision 1 is a green flag. Go full speed ahead. Decisions 2 and 3 are yellow flags. Proceed with caution. Decisions 4, 5, and 6 are red flags. Take corrective action before proceeding further. If you make Decision 5 or 6, you must create contingency strategies on planning pages in the V4.3 series and revise your objectives on Planning Page V4.4. See Exhibit 13-2 for a full explanation.

MONTHLY MONITOR

Month of _____, F19_ _–F19_ _

Planned monthly objectives	Actual performance	+/– Variances	Decision #
1. Profit on sales			
$ _ _,_ _ _,_ _ _	$ _ _,_ _ _,_ _ _	+/– $_ _,_ _ _,_ _ _	1 2 3 4 5 6
2. Sales volume ($)			
$_ _ _,_ _ _,_ _ _	$_ _ _,_ _ _,_ _ _	+/– $_ _,_ _ _,_ _ _	1 2 3 4 5 6
3. Sales volume (#)			
#_ _ _,_ _ _,_ _ _	#_ _ _,_ _ _,_ _ _	+/– #_ _,_ _ _,_ _ _	1 2 3 4 5 6
4. Market share (%)			
_ _%	_ _%	+/– _ _%	1 2 3 4 5 6

Decision 1 is a green flag. Go full speed ahead.
Decisions 2 and 3 are yellow flags. Proceed with
caution. Decisions 4, 5, and 6 are red flags. Take
corrective action before proceeding further. If you make
Decision 5 or 6, you must create contingency strategies
on planning pages in the V4.3 series and revise your
objectives on Planning Page V4.4. See Exhibit 13–2 for
a full explanation.

350

MONTHLY MONITOR
Month of _____, F19_ _ –F19_ _

Planned monthly objectives	Actual performance	+/– Variances	Decision #

1. Profit on sales

    $ __,___,___ $ __,___,___   +/– $__,___,___ 1 2 3 4 5 6

2. Sales volume ($)

    $__,___,___ $__,___,___   +/– $__,___,___ 1 2 3 4 5 6

3. Sales volume (#)

    #___,___,___   #___,___,___   +/– #__,___,___ 1 2 3 4 5 6

4. Market share (%)

    __%   __% +/– __%   1 2 3 4 5 6

Decision 1 is a green flag. Go full speed ahead. Decisions 2 and 3 are yellow flags. Proceed with caution. Decisions 4, 5, and 6 are red flags. Take corrective action before proceeding further. If you make Decision 5 or 6, you must create contingency strategies on planning pages in the V4.3 series and revise your objectives on Planning Page V4.4. See Exhibit 13–2 for a full explanation.

MONTHLY MONITOR

Month of _____, F19__-F19__

Planned monthly objectives	Actual performance	+/- Variances	Decision #
1. Profit on sales			
$ __,___,___	$ __,___,___	+/-$__,___,___	1 2 3 4 5 6
2. Sales volume ($)			
$___,___,___	$___,___,___	+/-$__,___,___	1 2 3 4 5 6
3. Sales volume (#)			
#___,___,___	#___,___,___	+/-#__,___,___	1 2 3 4 5 6
4. Market share (%)			
__%	__%	+/- __%	1 2 3 4 5 6

Decision 1 is a green flag. Go full speed ahead. Decisions 2 and 3 are yellow flags. Proceed with caution. Decisions 4, 5, and 6 are red flags. Take corrective action before proceeding further. If you make Decision 5 or 6, you must create contingency strategies on planning pages in the V4.3 series and revise your objectives on Planning Page V4.4. See Exhibit 13-2 for a full explanation.

MONTHLY MONITOR

Month of _____, F19__–F19__

Planned monthly objectives	Actual performance	+/– Variances	Decision #
1. Profit on sales			
$ __,___,___	$ __,___,___	+/– $__,___,___	1 2 3 4 5 6
2. Sales volume ($)			
$__,___,___	$__,___,___	+/– $__,___,___	1 2 3 4 5 6
3. Sales volume (#)			
#___,___,___	#___,___,___	+/– #__,___,___	1 2 3 4 5 6
4. Market share (%)			
__%	__%	+/– __%	1 2 3 4 5 6

Decision 1 is a green flag. Go full speed ahead.
Decisions 2 and 3 are yellow flags. Proceed with
caution. Decisions 4, 5, and 6 are red flags. Take
corrective action before proceeding further. If you make
Decision 5 or 6, you must create contingency strategies
on planning pages in the V4.3 series and revise your
objectives on Planning Page V4.4. See Exhibit 13–2 for
a full explanation.

MONTHLY MONITOR

Month of _____, F19__-F19__

Planned monthly objectives	Actual performance	+/- Variances	Decision #

1. Profit on sales

   $ __,___,___ $ __,___,___   +/-$__,___,___ 1 2 3 4 5 6

2. Sales volume ($)

   $___,___,___ $___,___,___   +/-$__,___,___ 1 2 3 4 5 6

3. Sales volume (#)

   #___,___,___   #___,___,___   +/-#__,___,___ 1 2 3 4 5 6

4. Market share (%)

   __%   __% +/- __%   1 2 3 4 5 6

Decision 1 is a green flag. Go full speed ahead. Decisions 2 and 3 are yellow flags. Proceed with caution. Decisions 4, 5, and 6 are red flags. Take corrective action before proceeding further. If you make Decision 5 or 6, you must create contingency strategies on planning pages in the V4.3 series and revise your objectives on Planning Page V4.4. See Exhibit 13-2 for a full explanation.

MONTHLY MONITOR

Month of _____, F19_ _-F19_ _

Planned monthly objectives	Actual performance	+/- Variances	Decision #
1. Profit on sales			
$ _ _,_ _ _,_ _ _	$ _ _,_ _ _,_ _ _	+/-$_ _,_ _ _,_ _ _	1 2 3 4 5 6
2. Sales volume ($)			
$_ _ _,_ _ _,_ _ _	$_ _ _,_ _ _,_ _ _	+/-$_ _,_ _ _,_ _ _	1 2 3 4 5 6
3. Sales volume (#)			
#_ _ _,_ _ _,_ _ _	#_ _ _,_ _ _,_ _ _	+/-#_ _,_ _ _,_ _ _	1 2 3 4 5 6
4. Market share (%)			
_ _%	_ _%	+/- _ _%	1 2 3 4 5 6

Decision 1 is a green flag. Go full speed ahead.
Decisions 2 and 3 are yellow flags. Proceed with
caution. Decisions 4, 5, and 6 are red flags. Take
corrective action before proceeding further. If you make
Decision 5 or 6, you must create contingency strategies
on planning pages in the V4.3 series and revise your
objectives on Planning Page V4.4. See Exhibit 13-2 for
a full explanation.

4.3

CONTINGENCY STRATEGIES

4.3.1

CONTINGENCY MARKET PENETRATION STRATEGIES

4.3.1.1. Product and service strategies

4.3.1.2. Promotion strategies

    4.3.1.2.1. Sales and physical distribution strategies

4.3.1.2.2. Advertising, sales promotion, and media
distribution strategies

4.3.1.2.3. Publicity strategies

4.3.1.3. Pricing strategies

<u>4.3.2</u>

<u>CONTINGENCY BUSINESS CAPABILITY STRATEGIES</u>

4.3.2.1. Staff and organization strategies

4.3.2.2. Facilities strategies

4.3.2.3. Budget strategies

4.4

REVISED OBJECTIVES

REVISION 1: OBJECTIVES

	(Year 1) F19_ _-F19_ _			(Year 2) F19_ _-F19_ _		
	Best case	Average case	Worst case	Best case	Average case	Worst case
2.1. Financial objectives						
2.1.1. Return on investment (%)	--	--	--	--	--	--
2.1.2. Net profit contribution ($000)	_,___	_,___	_,___	_,___	_,___	_,___
2.2. Sales objectives						
2.2.1. Sales volume ($000)	___,___	___,___	___,___	___,___	___,___	___,___
2.2.2. Sales volume (#000)	___,___	___,___	___,___	___,___	___,___	___,___
2.2.3. Market share (%)	--	--	--	--	--	--

(Year 3) F19__-F19__			(Year 4) F19__-F19__			(Year 5) F19__-F19__		
Best case	Average case	Worst case	Best case	Average case	Worst case	Best case	Average case	Worst case
--	--	--	--	--	--	--	--	--
_,___	_,___	_,___	_,___	_,___	_,___	_,___	_,___	_,___
___,___	___,___	___,___	___,___	___,___	___,___	___,___	___,___	___,___
___,___	___,___	___,___	___,___	___,___	___,___	___,___	___,___	___,___
--	--	--	--	--	--	--	--	--

REVISION 2: OBJECTIVES

	(Year 1) F19__-F19__			(Year 2) F19__-F19__		
	Best case	Average case	Worst case	Best case	Average case	Worst case
2.1. Financial objectives						
2.1.1. Return on investment (%)	--	--	--	--	--	--
2.1.2. Net profit contribution ($000)	_,---	_,---	_,---	_,---	_,---	_,---
2.2. Sales objectives						
2.2.1. Sales volume ($000)	---,---	---,---	---,---	---,---	---,---	---,---
2.2.2. Sales volume (#000)	---,---	---,---	---,---	---,---	---,---	---,---
2.2.3. Market share (%)	--	--	--	--	--	--

(Year 3) F19_ _-F19_ _			(Year 4) F19_ _-F19_ _			(Year 5) F19_ _-F19_ _		
Best case	Average case	Worst case	Best case	Average case	Worst case	Best case	Average case	Worst case
--	--	--	--	--	--	--	--	--
_,---	_,---	_,---	_,---	_,---	_,---	_,---	_,---	_,---
---,---	---,---	---,---	---,---	---,---	---,---	---,---	---,---	---,---
---,---	---,---	---,---	---,---	---,---	---,---	---,---	---,---	---,---
--	--	--	--	--	--	--	--	--

REVISION 3: OBJECTIVES

	(Year 1) F19__–F19__			(Year 2) F19__–F19__		
	Best case	Average case	Worst case	Best case	Average case	Worst case
2.1. Financial objectives						
2.1.1. Return on investment (%)	--	--	--	--	--	--
2.1.2. Net profit contribution ($000)	_,___	_,___	_,___	_,___	_,___	_,___
2.2. Sales objectives						
2.2.1. Sales volume ($000)	___,___	___,___	___,___	___,___	___,___	___,___
2.2.2. Sales volume (#000)	___,___	___,___	___,___	___,___	___,___	___,___
2.2.3. Market share (%)	--	--	--	--	--	--

	(Year 3) F19_ _-F19_ _			(Year 4) F19_ _-F19_ _			(Year 5) F19_ _-F19_ _	
Best case	Average case	Worst case	Best case	Average case	Worst case	Best case	Average case	Worst case
--	--	--	--	--	--	--	--	--
_,_ _ _	_,_ _ _	_,_ _ _	_,_ _ _	_,_ _ _	_,_ _ _	_,_ _ _	_,_ _ _	_,_ _ _
_ _ _,_ _ _	_ _ _,_ _ _	_ _ _,_ _ _	_ _ _,_ _ _	_ _ _,_ _ _	_ _ _,_ _ _	_ _ _,_ _ _	_ _ _,_ _ _	_ _ _,_ _ _
_ _ _,_ _ _	_ _ _,_ _ _	_ _ _,_ _ _	_ _ _,_ _ _	_ _ _,_ _ _	_ _ _,_ _ _	_ _ _,_ _ _	_ _ _,_ _ _	_ _ _,_ _ _
--	--	--	--	--	--	--	--	--

371

II

INFORMATION BASE

5. Situation survey

5

SITUATION SURVEY

5.1. Factual information base

5.2. Assumptive information base

5.1

FACTUAL INFORMATION BASE

5.1.1. Market opportunity profile

5.1.2. Technical capability profile

5.1.3. Competitive profile

5.1

FACTUAL INFORMATION BASE

5.1.1. Market opportunity profile

5.1.2. Technical capability profile

(modified by energy and materials availability)

5.1.3. Competitive profile

5.2

ASSUMPTIVE INFORMATION BASE

14

venture appraisal

Before a venture is signed off to enter commercial life, the most critical elements of the venture planning process should be subjected to final review. This will be the venture's last chance for appraisal before it goes public. Any further quality control will be imposed by the market: by potential customers who turn out to be noncustomers and by alleged noncompetitors who turn out to be competitors.

The three most important venture planning elements to appraise are the final estimates of the venture's *commercial potential*, the *market projections* on which they are based, and the venture's *assumptions about the unknowables* which underlie the market projections. From an appraisal of these key indicators of venture viability, the venture manager and top corporate management can gain the confidence they require to make market entry. "This is the venture's potential payoff," the manager must be able to say. "Are we all comfortable with it? Here are the sales projections on which it is based. And, finally, here are the assumptions which have governed our planning. If we are unable to challenge them or disagree with their implications, we must go ahead."

Commercial Potential Appraisal

Venture commercial potential summarizes for management what it is buying in return for its investment. There are three key criteria for appraisal. One is the venture's pro forma, projected for a minimum of five years. If market penetration is tortuous and break-even delayed well beyond the midpoint of a one-to-five year plan, or if the venture life cycle is predictably long, the pro forma may be extended to ten years. The pro forma will summarize the venture's year-by-year objectives and, from supplementary information, forecast the basic operating ratios, perhaps the cash-flow projections, and return on investment. Average-case projections, rather than best- or worst-case projections, should be used throughout since presumably they reflect the net effect on the venture of the assumptions which have been made about its unknowables.

> **Use Planning Page 63 to appraise your venture's commercial potential.**

COMMERCIAL POTENTIAL APPRAISAL

	Year 1 (F19___-F19___)	Year 2 (F19___-F19___)	Year 3 (F19___-F19___)	Year 4 (F19___-F19___)	Year 5 (F19___-F19___)
1. Objectives					
1.1. Return on investment (%)*					
1.2. Net profit (% and $000)**	% /$,	% /$,	% /$,	% /$,	% /$,
1.3. Dollar sales volume ($000)	$,	$,	$,	$,	$,
1.4. Unit sales volume (#000)	#,	#,	#,	#,	#,
1.5. % market share					
2. Operating ratios					
2.1. Gross margin*** (% and $000)	% /$,	% /$,	% /$,	% /$,	% /$,
2.2. Capital turnover per year	#	#	#	#	#

* Profit ÷ investment
** Gross profit ÷ sales
*** Sales ÷ cost of sales

381

Market Penetration Appraisal

Venture market penetration summarizes the anticipated annual sales growth of the business in relation to its remaining market opportunity after each year of commercial life. As sales progress, they may consume a greater share of the original opportunity. Or, to the contrary, opportunity may grow. Either event will affect year-by-year commercial potential. So will price, which can also be correlated with annual sales to show the three-way interrelationship between the expansion of sales, the contraction or expansion of market opportunity that it causes, and the elasticity of price over the commercial life cycle of the venture. Exhibit 14-1 illustrates a model of these elements which has been extended over a ten-year time frame to dramatize its correlations.

Appraisal of Assumptions about Unknowables

Venture assumptions are the foundation of the market projections and the commercial potential to be appraised. For this reason, they themselves must be assessed at the latest date possible before the venture is committed to market. At appraisal, each assumption should, in effect, be remade. The original level of confidence attributed to each assumption should be recalculated to see if any unknowable factor underlying venture objectives has taken on or lost some degree of certainty. A final probability should be assigned to each assumption and its most likely effect appraised on the venture's sales growth and ROI potential.

Use Planning Page 64 to appraise your venture's market penetration.

---

exhibit 14-1

market penetration appraisal

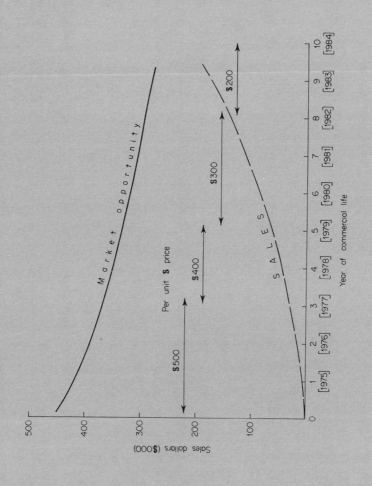

MARKET PENETRATION APPRAISAL

Sales volume ($000)

| 0 | 1 (F19__) | 2 (F19__) | 3 (F19__) | 4 (F19__) | 5 (F19__) |

Year of commercial life

> **Use Planning Page 65 to appraise your assumptions about venture unknowables.**

Up to the point of appraisal, the venture has been only a plannable proposition. At appraisal, it can become a defensible proposition. If it does, then it may meet the requirements of being a marketable proposition for a business.

APPRAISAL OF ASSUMPTIONS ABOUT UNKNOWABLES

Most probable effect on venture

Commercial potential   Market projections

Assumptions

% Level of
confidence

% ROI   Net profit   Sales   % Market share
             % and $ $ and #

15

venture caveat

Managers of ongoing businesses sometimes sign off their conversations with one another by saying, "Watch your margins." In the absence of an ongoing business to worry about as yet, venture managers might well say, "Watch your *assumptions*." Of all the skills a venture manager must have and of all the decisions that must be made and the hunches that must be played, none is more difficult or more crucial than determining what assumptions to hold about the unknowables in a venture's real world.

Assumptions are every venture's weakest link. Some managers try to hedge this weakness by casting multiple packages of assumptions as the basis for their strategies. Other managers rely on one assumption package and project multiple strategy sets from it on a contingent ABC basis, in which A stands for the most aggressive strategy that the assumption package will support, B for a basic strategy, and C for the most conservative, worst-case strategy. But no matter which hedge is used, a manager must eventually choose one option and put it into play in order to have a game plan for the venture as a genuine business.

Although every industry requires its own assumptive framework for venture planning, many assumptions have differed more in degree than in kind from industry to industry. In the next decade of venturing, this may no longer be true.

The familiar post-World War II assumption package has become irretrievably obsolete. Inflation can be expected to remain higher than the norms of ten years or more ago. This will continue to erode the value of the venture dollar and affect venture costs and prices, perhaps disadvantaging some ventures against established competitors and extending other venture payback timetables. Ventures in many industries can count on an increasing politicalization of constraint expressed as heightened government interest and involvement in venture planning and operating freedoms. Energy and raw materials, in addition to being more expensive, will impose additional restraints by their uncertain availability. The questions "Can we get it?" and "Can we afford it?" will be every bit as important for many ventures as "Can we sell it?"

Money for venture development will be tight, whether it is sought in capital or in equity markets. The cost of money expressed in long-term interest rates will make the provision of venture resources more expensive. In return, venture managers will be much more intensely under the gun to produce. Yet even the most astute managers may have to settle for a lower growth rate than the 8 percent minimum venture growth bogey that was tied to gross national product growth over the 1960s. Twice GNP may still be a valid criterion for new-enterprise selection. But the actual amount which that standard will come to represent will often be comparatively low.

These are all C-type, conservative assumptions. In the face of them, there are companies which may try to reach out for superior profits by divestitures, direct cost cutting, and doubling up of responsibilities for the management of scarce and expensive resources. But no business can achieve salvation by savings. The press for premium profits must go on. Conservative assumptions add to every venture's degree of difficulty but, at the same time, they make venturing even more necessary than difficult. Big winners will always be achievable and, true to form, will most likely be the rewards of managers who plan tight, run lean, and watch their assumptions.

index